Bishops, Councils, and Consensus in the Visigothic Kingdom, 589–633

Rachel L. Stocking

Ann Arbor

THE UNIVERSITY OF MICHIGAN PRESS

Copyright © by the University of Michigan 2000
All rights reserved
Published in the United States of America by
The University of Michigan Press
Manufactured in the United States of America
♾ Printed on acid-free paper

2003   2002   2001   2000   4   3   2   1

A CIP catalog record for this book is available from the British Library.

Library of Congress Cataloging-in-Publication Data

Stocking, Rachel L.
   Bishops, councils, and consensus in the Visigothic Kingdom,
589–633 / Rachel L. Stocking.
      p.   cm. — (History, languages, and cultures of the
Spanish and Portuguese worlds)
   Includes bibliographical references and index.
   ISBN 0-472-11133-7 (alk. paper)
   1. Spain—Church history.   2. Spain—History—Gothic period,
414–711.   3. Church and state—Spain—History—To 1500.
4. Catholic Church. Council of Toledo (3rd : 589)   5. Catholic
Church. Council of Toledo (4th : 633) 6. Visigoths—
Spain—History.   I. Title.   II. Series.
BR1024.S79   2000
274.6'02—dc21   99-50877

To my parents,
and to the best part of my life,
my son, Evan

Acknowledgments

Over the course of my education and the years it has taken me to produce this book, I have incurred numerous intellectual, economic, and emotional debts. The History Department at San Francisco State University offered professors upon whom I still model my classroom self, including Sally Scully, William Bonds, and Joseph Illick. I owe special thanks to Frank Kidner, whose attention and advice encouraged me to think of graduate school, Visigothic Studies, and an academic future as possibilities rather than sources of terror.

The History Department at Stanford University made graduate school possible, while Gavin Langmuir, Stephen Ferroulo, Amos Funkenstein, and Susan Treggiari made it meaningful by teaching me to see and "do" history with intellectual diligence and imagination. Philippe Buc was, and still is, enormously generous with his time, advice, and helpful and inspiring ideas. From Stanford to the present Sabine MacCormack's guidance has been essential: in navigating the alien worlds of both late antiquity and the modern university, in coping with the obstacles of single motherhood in an unforgiving environment, in researching and writing intelligible, creative, and responsible history, and in making the transition from student to professor and author. Her help and advice have been fundamental in conceiving and producing this book.

The History Department at Southern Illinois University at Carbondale has given me not only a job and travel money but also something quite unusual: a supportive, stimulating, and congenial working environment. Ted Weeks, Kay Carr, Robbie Lieberman, Mrinalini Sinha, Jim Allen, and Marji Morgan have helped me keep my head above water and have put up with a perhaps unreasonable level of ranting and complaints. Kay Carr also read parts of my manuscript, talked with me at length about ancient and modern consensus, and with characteristic generosity donated her time and computer expertise in making the map for this book. Jim Allen read the manuscript and gave me invaluable advice on the publishing process. I thank all my History colleagues for their pedagogical advice and the opportunity to teach and all my students for the inspiration and stimulation that their education has brought to my research and writing.

My gratitude also goes to J. N. Hillgarth for his comments on my dissertation, to Perry Pearson at University of Michigan Press for her ready attention, and to the press's referees for their careful readings and very useful suggestions on the manuscript.

My friends Debbie Lewites, Nina Feldman, and Bill Compton have never failed to give me the hospitality and conversation that made it imaginable to move so far away from home. I would never have been in a position to do so without Nancy Thompson's companionship and consolation in the world of early medieval studies as well as her many readings of my work and her help on translations. Susan Dever taught me Spanish and still teaches me how to teach, write, think, and exist as both a person and an academic.

In addition to substantial material support, my father, George Stocking, has been generous with his time and energy in reading many versions of this manuscript; his comments on the introduction were particularly helpful in framing the project. He has also provided me a model of meticulous history writing and uncompromising logic as well as a compelling picture of the many benefits offered by the life of the mind. Along with her understanding and affection, my mother, Mina Caulfield, has given me an alternative model of principled pedagogy and research as well as an equally compelling picture of a life committed to social change. I thank all the members of the Stocking and Davis families for teaching me to think critically, gather evidence, frame an argument, and, when necessary, shout the opposition into submission. Carol Stocking, Melissa Robinson, Becky Stocking, Susan Baltrushes, and Thomas Stocking have given me the toleration and love that make it possible to keep on trying. Finally, Evan Smith has been my main reason for living since he was born. His love, patience, inquisitiveness, criticism, and sense of humor will always inspire and sustain me.

Contents

Abbreviations

EW	*Epistolae Wisigothicae,* edited by Juan Gil, *Miscellanea Wisigothica* (Seville, 1972).
HG	Isidore of Seville, *Historia Gothorum, Vandalorum, Sueborum,* edited and translated by Cristóbal Rodríguez Alonso, *Las historias de los Godos, Vandalos, y Suevos de Isidore de Seville* (León, 1975).
John Bicl.	John of Biclar, *Chronicle,* edited by Theodor Mommsen, *MGH, Auctores Antiquissimi,* 11, *Chronica Minora,* 2 (Berlin, 1894).
La colección	*La colección canónica Hispana,* vol. 4, edited by Gonzalo Martínez Díez and Félix Rodríguez, *Monumenta Hispaniae Sacra,* Serie Canónica (Madrid, 1984).
LH	Gregory of Tours, *Libri Historiarum X,* edited by Bruno Krusch and Wilhelm Levison, *MGH, Scriptores rerum merovingicarum* I (Hannover, 1951).
LV	*Leges Visigothorum,* edited by Karl Zeumer, *MGH,* Legum Sectio I, *Legum Nationum Germanicarum,* vol. 1 (Hannover, 1902).
MGH	*Monumenta Germaniae Historica.*
MW	*Miscellanea Wisigothica,* edited by Juan Gil (Seville, 1972).
PL	*Patrologia Cursus Completus, Series Latina,* edited by J. P. Migne (Paris, 1844–64).
Settimane	*Settimane di studio del Centro italiano di studi sull'alto medioevo* (Spoleto, 1954ff.).
VPE	*Vitas patrum sanctorum emeritensium,* edited and translated by Joseph N. Garvin (Washington, D.C., 1946).
Vives	*Concilios hispano-romanos y visigodos,* edited and translated by José Vives (Barcelona, 1963).

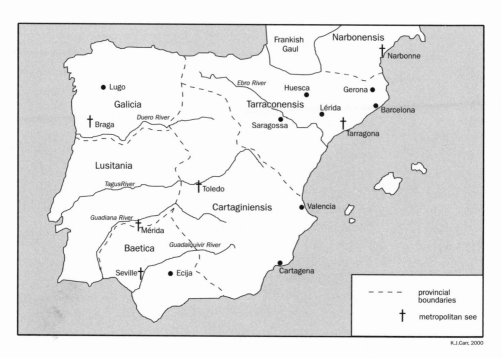

Map 1. Visigothic Iberia, ca. 633

Introduction

At a church council in 654 the Visigothic king Recceswinth (649–72) presented his kingdom's bishops and palace officials with a dilemma. Some years earlier the king's father, Chindaswinth (642–53), had forced all the kingdom's secular and clerical leaders, including Recceswinth, to take an oath to uphold a civil law against rebels and their supporters. The law had mandated particularly harsh punishments, including exile, confiscation of property, dismemberment, and death.[1] The oath takers had sworn never to pardon rebels or show mercy in inflicting these punishments. Upon Chindaswinth's death, however, a noble Visigoth, Froia, had raised a rebellion against the younger king, causing widespread death and destruction. Now faced with the religious obligation to carry out the sworn punishments, Recceswinth apparently wished to mend fences and reestablish unity by granting mercy to some of Froia's supporters. He asked the Eighth Council of Toledo to release himself and all those who had taken the oath—including the bishops and nobles in attendance—from its strictures against pardon. The bishops therefore had to decide between two important legal principles: the binding and holy authority of an oath taken in God's name or the peacemaking powers of Christian mercy requested by a divinely appointed king.

The question provoked a heated debate that threatened an irretrievable split. On the one hand, there were those who found a "profanation of the holy name" unacceptable;[2] on the other, there were those who thought "the prohibition of mercy" was "loathsome."[3] The implications of the choice were momentous. As the council records show, religious oaths were a fundamental mechanism in the kingdom's legal system. They gave divine authorization to treaties with foreign countries, to ties of patronage between individuals, to the testimony of witnesses in everyday dispute settlements, and to avowals of innocence in the absence of witnesses, for to commit perjury was to consign oneself to perdition. At the same time, oaths could be dangerously misused;

---

1. *LV* 2.1.8; 53–57. See E. A. Thompson, *The Goths in Spain* (Oxford, 1969), 191–92.

2. Tol. VIII, c. 2: "sancti nominis profanatio." Vives, 268.

3. Tol. VIII, c. 2: "ex prohibitione pietatis aderat quod taedebat." Vives, 268.

conditions could be added to them that might force people to perpetrate crimes as heinous as patricide or the rape of virgins who had taken religious vows of chastity.

Unable to reach consensus on this issue through their own debate, the council members instead agreed to stop the discussion and turn their "words and hearts, with crashing sobs and torrents of tears, to God, who is the fountain of piety."[4] Begging the Holy Spirit to "quiet the storms of our ignorance and lead us into the port of your will," they pled for the breath of divine inspiration that would save them from the "shipwrecks" of contention and "spread the sails" of their mutual decision.[5] The records detail the careful logic and extensive scriptural and patristic references that then allowed the assembly to understand the decision of the Holy Spirit and reach agreement. It was not acceptable for the position of either party to be overridden, and, therefore, neither side was wrong; "the justice of oath-taking and the peace of sworn mercy" did not contradict one another, so "mercy and truth met each other and justice and peace kissed."[6]

According to the council, the judicially indispensable authority of oath taking would not be undermined by the peace of mercy, for strictures against profanation did not apply to oaths that would "let forth rivers of vengeance" through the "sacrilege of evil deeds."[7] Inflicting dismemberment and death was a "detestable" and "impious cruelty" that would condemn its executors to eternal damnation.[8] The final compromise was simple: the oath takers were exempted from imposing the capital punishments they had sworn to uphold, but they were compelled to fulfill all other aspects of the oath, including the punishments of exile and dispossession of properties. Any future oaths against rebellion were to be kept vigilantly but were to continue to exclude capital punishment. The council went on to protect itself from any accusations that the decision constituted perjury or deviated from "the rule of holy faith."[9] With another outpouring of citations from ancient authorities, the bishops pointed out that God himself frequently had changed his mind for the sake of mercy.

Toledo VIII thus sought to resolve a number of contradictions and

---

4. Tol. VIII, c. 2: "quum fragoris singultuum et imbribus lacrymarum ad Deum, qui pietatis fons est, verba simul et corda convertimus." Vives, 269.

5. Tol. VIII, c. 2: "ducito nos in portum volumtatis tuae, sedatis fluctibus ignorantiae nostrae . . . obiantibus naufragiorum obicibus . . . dispositionis nostrae vela pandamus." Vives, 269.

6. Tol. VIII, c. 2: "iuramenti iustitiam aut iuramenti misericordiae pacem . . . 'misericordia et veritas obiaverunt sibi, iustitia et pax se complexae sunt.'" Quoting Psalm 84.11. Vives, 270.

7. Tol. VIII, c. 2: "emitteret rivulos ultionis . . . sacrilegia . . . provitatis." Vives, 271.

8. Tol. VIII, c. 2: "noxia . . . inpia crudelitate." Vives, 270.

9. Tol. VIII, c. 2: "sanctae fidei regulam." Vives, 274.

conflicting interests surrounding the exercise of divine justice and central authority in seventh-century Iberia. First of all, both Chindaswinth's efforts at forcefully repressing rebellion and Recceswinth's interest in sparing the condemned arose from an ongoing difficulty in maintaining ruling unity in the face of divergent local networks of power. The latter king sought to obtain through compromise the unity that the former king had failed to establish through coercion. Second, the divided opinions among the council's participants reflect a continuing tension between the exercise of collective, centralized, ecclesiastic authority and the interests of individual bishops and their local communities. The Holy Spirit's presence at the council depended upon episcopal harmony amid the antagonisms of partisan community leaders. Finally, Chindaswinth's reliance on coercive religious oaths and Recceswinth's request for the council's endorsement of obtaining peace through mercy indicate inadequate centralized enforcement of law and loyalty. This had led to the use of divine sanctions and scriptural rationalizations in secular efforts to maintain centralized order. Chindaswinth could not depend on powerful people to remain loyal without the threat of perdition, while Recceswinth could not contain vengeance without the approval of scriptural precedent and the Holy Spirit.

The efficacy of divine sanctions, however, was compromised by the lack of a common vision of the role of divine authority in worldly affairs. In mounting their rebellion, the rebels had demonstrated their lack of fear in the face of the threat of perdition for perjurers.[10] In addressing the consequences of this audacity, the council's participants were unable to invoke their collective holy authority unilaterally. Neither side would accept an outright loss through the council's decision, even if that loss were attributed to the Holy Spirit.[11] The council's enumeration of holy texts and its consciousness of the danger of reversing a previous policy reveal the limitations and pitfalls involved in relying upon theoretically immutable but frequently contradictory ancient legal principles to address turbulent contemporary circumstances.

The process by which Toledo VIII reached its compromise is an illustration of what had come to be an institutionalized ideal for Christian governance in the Visigothic kingdom: settling disputes and maintaining order through decisions reached by episcopal consensus at church councils, whose

---

10. For a discussion of "an indecently frivolous attitude towards oath-taking" among Germanic peoples in sixth-century Gaul, see Ian N. Wood, "Disputes in Late Fifth- and Sixth-Century Gaul: Some Problems," in *The Settlement of Disputes in Early Medieval Europe,* ed. Wendy Davies and Paul Fouracre (Cambridge, 1986), 16–17.

11. For general remarks on the early medieval tendency to attribute decisions to supernatural forces due to the "crushing" consequences of losing face, see Peter Brown, "Society and the Supernatural: A Medieval Change," in *Society and the Holy in Late Antiquity* (Berkeley, 1982), 327.

divine authority was sanctioned by the presence and inspiration of the Holy Spirit. In the case of Recceswinth's dilemma, the parameters of the decision were relatively narrow, involving a limited number of rebels among the kingdom's elite. By 654, however, Visigothic leaders had developed a much broader ideal of governance by conciliar consensus; church councils were envisioned as a means to impose obedience and unity upon all the inhabitants of the kingdom. The achievement of this broad ideal depended upon a practical, functioning consensus among all the communities of the kingdom: a general and uniform acceptance of a particular role for divine authority in worldly affairs. Throughout the seventh century kings and bishops struggled to make this ideal consensus real, thereby ensuring uniform obedience to secular and conciliar legislation. Their efforts were met with continuing diversity and disobedience—from local communities as well as from powerful people like Froia. Thus, the governance of the Visigothic kingdom came to be characterized by an ongoing tension between leaders' ideals for perfect Christian consensus and the notoriously imperfect practical consensus among themselves and among those they were attempting to govern. This book explores that tension, which generated a variety of contradictory attitudes and practices among kings and bishops—particularly between the years 589 and 633. The ideological and social processes played out during these years eventually led to the development of a coherent Visigothic vision of institutionalized religious, legal, and political consensus as the means to maintain Christian order. They did not, however, lead to the realization of that vision. Throughout the rest of the seventh century the kingdom continued to be plagued by rebellions, factionalism, and ineffectual demands for obedience to the legislation of both kings and councils.

Ideal and Practical Consensus

The legal and governmental paradoxes facing leaders in the Visigothic kingdom confronted powerful groups and individuals—bishops, nobles, and kings—in all of the Germanic kingdoms of early medieval Europe. During the fifth, sixth, and seventh centuries the administrative systems of the western Roman Empire fragmented into diverse pockets of local authority. In the preceding centuries under the Roman emperors, the effective exercise of central authority and administration had been partly dependent upon a set of assumptions shared by the empire's elites about the meaning and exercise of various mechanisms of social power and community leadership. These included longstanding and generally accepted meanings and practices tied to Roman citi-

zenship, legal culture, civic and personal patronage, education, and class privilege.[12]

Elite unity in the Roman Empire, however, had always been partly ficti-
tious. The horizontal cohesion of shared elite interests and values was in constant tension with the vertical loyalties of local relationships of power in culturally, geographically, and economically diverse communities. Long before
the final failure of central authority in the West, this tension was heightened
by political turmoil, military disturbances, economic changes, and cultural
transformations—particularly those associated with the rise of Christianity.[13]
In turn, increasing tension between elite solidarity and local interests engendered mutations and contradictions in peoples' ideas about power and its
exercise. The fictional principles of ruling unity began to soften and melt. As
the ornate edifice of late Roman government finally began to disintegrate in
the West during the fifth century, the shared elite assumptions that had supported it became ever more fluid and diverse while various groups struggled to
wield authority in changing and uncertain conditions.[14]

Nevertheless, during the course of the fifth, sixth, and seventh centuries
powerful people in western European communities were still, as a group, successors to Roman traditions and practices. As they reinvented concepts and
mechanisms of power in response to varying local circumstances, they still
worked with a common pool of loosely shared assumptions and practices.
These were based on comparable experiences and fluctuating mixtures of
Roman, Germanic, and provincial influences. Most areas of the former western Empire encountered, in one form or another, the same problems that confronted Iberian leaders: the tensions between elite solidarity and local interests, the inadequate central enforcement of law, the resulting dependence on
divine sanctions and scriptural authority, the lack of a shared vision of sacred
authority, and the contradictions and inflexibility of ancient precedents. Since
many of the problems facing rulers were quite similar, their various solutions,
innovations, and failures sometimes had much in common with one another.
The problems these leaders shared, however, were themselves contributors to
the continuing process of divergent transformation. The Iberian vision of consensus and society, therefore, is markedly different from paths taken in Gaul,
Italy, Britain, or North Africa.

12. For a discussion of such assumptions, with particular reference to the cities of the
"Greek East," see Peter Brown, *Power and Persuasion in Late Antiquity* (Madison, 1992), 3–70.

13. On the "fracturing" of elite unity in the East, see Brown, *Power and Persuasion,*
19–20.

14. On developments in the East, including the maintenance and christianization of a
shared urban political culture in relation to the imperial government, see Brown, *Power and
Persuasion,* 71–158.

The fact that these changes unfolded at uneven paces and with divergent consequences is reflected in the source materials available. An almost complete lack of sources, for instance, makes developments in Anglo-Saxon England during the fifth and sixth centuries notably obscure. Meanwhile, historians of Gaul during these centuries work with a comparative embarrassment of riches. Many of those Gallic sources, however, reflect a limited range of clerical interests and attitudes. The analysis of Christian communities in sixth-century Gaul, for example, is dependent upon the works of one prolific writer with a distinct, profoundly episcopal point of view: Gregory of Tours. North Africa has left us rich documentation of clerical culture and attitudes in the writings of Saint Augustine. With his death and the Vandal conquest in 430, however, the region fades from view. Iberian developments during these years are not much clearer.[15] Details only begin to emerge with the conversion of the Visigoths from Arianism to Catholicism in 589; again, these sources are overwhelmingly clerical. In brief, anyone attempting to reconstruct an overall picture of almost any aspect of historical change in the West during this period is working with a shattered mosaic, unevenly scattered and missing a majority of its most vital pieces; making generalizations about the period is a difficult and at times dubious enterprise.[16]

When viewing this fractured panorama as a whole, seeking some sort of adhesive element, one's attention is naturally drawn toward repeated colors and patterns. The most obvious of these are the various shades of Christian culture and differing configurations of sacred authority. As centralized governance in the West irrevocably splintered in the second half of the fifth century, community leaders who no longer enjoyed solidarity as privileged subjects of the Roman emperors continued to assume commonality and shared values through their self-identification as members of the universal church. They expressed that commonality in the vocabularies of traditional literate Christian and Roman culture and authority, which were increasingly monopolized and redefined by ecclesiastic leaders. Christian commonality in the diversifying West was also manifested in ways of daily community life: the rise of localized cults of the saints;[17] the sacralization of particular places, people, and power

---

15. On sources for fifth-century Iberia, see E. A. Thompson, *Romans and Barbarians. The Decline of the Western Empire* (Madison, 1982), 137. On sixth-century sources, see Thompson, *Goths,* 7 and 26.

16. On the difficulties of generalizing about early medieval legislation, see, e.g., Patrick Wormald, "*Lex Scripta* and *Verbum Regis:* Legislation and Germanic Kingship from Euric to Cnut," in *Early Medieval Kingship,* ed. P. H. Sawyer and Ian N. Wood (Leeds, 1977), 107.

17. The fundamental work is Peter Brown, *The Cult of the Saints: Its Rise and Function in Latin Christianity* (Chicago, 1981).

structures in small, "face-to-face" communities;[18] and what has been called a general "draining of the secular from society."[19] For historians seeking to create a coherent representation of this period, tracing the transformation of Christian culture and authority from the fourth to the seventh centuries has proven much more fruitful than earlier attempts to characterize the period using traditional economic, political, national, and racial categories.

During this period of transformation one important social and governmental element in the increasingly diverse pool of available ideals and practices was the ancient ideal of consensus. On the broadest scale of Christian ideals of consensus, the universality of the Christian mission for centuries had been considered proof of Christianity's message of salvation;[20] the second coming would occur when the entire world joined in Christian harmony. Christian teachers identified the normative force of Christian consensus in the notion that universal Christian agreement—among teachers of the past and the churches of the present—signified the unquestionable authenticity and authority of any given practice or teaching.[21] On a narrower level of authority, Christian leaders asserted that the consensus of bishops in attendance at church councils brought forth the Holy Spirit, based on the passage in the gospel of Matthew in which Christ said to his disciples "wherever two or three of you are gathered in my name, I will be among you."[22] This presence gave divine endorsement to the ancient precedents invoked at earlier councils, as well as to the new rules that a council might issue, and to the orthodox episcopate as a collectivity. Finally, Christian tradition associated the consensus of local communities with the election of individual bishops, which was meant to be carried out according to the "consensus of the people" in the diocese.[23]

Another traditional current of consensus during this period consisted of various Roman notions and practices that had attributed legitimating author-

18. See, e.g., Raymond Van Dam, *Leadership and Community in Late Antique Gaul* (Berkeley, 1985); and Van Dam, *Saints and Their Miracles in Late Antique Gaul* (Princeton, 1993); Peter Brown, "Relics and Social Status in the Age of Gregory of Tours," in *Society and the Holy in Late Antiquity* (Berkeley, 1982); Robert A. Markus, *The End of Ancient Christianity* (Cambridge, 1990), 139–55.

19. Markus, *End of Ancient Christianity*, 1–18.

20. Amos Funkenstein, "Anti-Jewish Propaganda: Pagan, Christian, and Modern," *Jerusalem Quarterly* 19 (1981): 62.

21. See, e.g., the fifth-century Gallic writer Vincent of Lérins, *Vincentii Lerinensis commonitoria*, 2.1–4, ed. Gerhard Rauschen (Bonn, 1906), quoted as the "classic definition" of the tradition by Karl Morrison, *Tradition and Authority in the Western Church* (Princeton, 1969), 4–5.

22. Matthew 18.20.

23. Brown, "Relics," 246; Dietrich Claude, "Der Bestellung der Bischöfe im merowingischen Reiche," *Zeitschrift der Savigny-Stiftung für Rechtsgeschichte, Kanonistiche Abteilung* 49 (1963).

ity to consensual displays of community harmony. The empire's subject communities demonstrated their own unity and support for the emperor through various imperial ceremonies (e.g., observances for the arrival, accession, and funeral of the emperor).[24] In the later Roman period and in the Byzantine Empire these ceremonies also expressed consensual recognition of the emperors' divine election.[25] During the fifth century ceremonies of consensus among Roman civic leaders marked the reception of imperial law.[26] The concept of the "consent of the people" was also central in traditional Roman definitions of law and justice.[27]

These various configurations of meaning saw continuing life throughout the period. Yet they were subject to redefinition under the exigencies of immediate circumstances. The very notion of a universal church, for instance, was often the subject of intellectual tinkering. Organizationally speaking, there was no such entity, and there had not been for centuries.[28] Furthermore, a full consensus of past Christian authorities was nearly impossible to establish and follow.[29] The establishment and exercise of episcopal consensus was also open to question. Christians based the divine authority of conciliar consensus on the passage in Matthew, but the actual process by which decisions were to be reached was ill defined and open to interpretation according to local expedience. The same was true of previous conciliar decisions, the ecclesiastic rules known as "canons."

The meaning of the consent of the people involved in the election of bishops was also vague. The composition of many Christian communities was diverse and frequently the subject of hostile argumentation, making the notion of "the people" unclear. The elections themselves were the objects of manipu-

---

24. Sabine MacCormack, *Art and Ceremony in Late Antiquity* (Berkeley, 1981).

25. MacCormack, *Art and Ceremony,* 272–73.

26. See, e.g., the acclamations of the Roman Senate on their reception of Theodosius II's message declaring his intention to codify the laws of the empire in the *Gesta Senatus Urbis Romae* (Minutes of the Senate of the City of Rome), discovered in 1820 and now usually printed as the introduction to the Theodosian Code of 438. See *The Theodosian Code and Novels,* trans. Clyde Pharr (New York, 1952), 3–7.

27. See, e.g., the *Institutes* of the emperor Justinian (d. 565), 1.1.2, in *Justinian's Institutes,* ed. P. Krueger, trans. Peter Birks and Grant McLeod (Ithaca, 1987), 39.

28. Morrison, *Tradition and Authority,* 27; Arnaldo Momigliano, "Ecclesiastical Historiography," in *The Classical Foundations of Modern Historiography* (Berkeley, 1990), 145.

29. Church leaders of the time acknowledged this difficulty. For instance, in his definition of the authenticating power of universal Christian agreement, Vincent of Lérins, *Commonitoria,* 2.3, 12, had to qualify its parameters: "We shall follow . . . consensus if in antiquity itself we keep following the definitions and opinions of all, or surely almost all, bishops and teachers" (consensionem . . . si in ipsa vetustate omnium vel certe paene omnium sacerdotum pariter et magistrorum definitiones sententiasque sectemur). Translated in Morrison, *Tradition and Authority,* 4–5.

lation depending on power struggles and factionalism in different cities.[30] Electoral manipulation was particularly probable when secular authorities interfered with episcopal appointments, a precedent set as early as the fourth century.[31] Similarly, Christian lawmakers may have had access to Roman legal materials that associated the idea of the consent of the people with the promulgation of law and administration of justice,[32] but the exact definition of the group known as the people was no clearer in Roman legal practice than it was in the election of bishops. The meaning of the concept must have become increasingly obscure as bishops and kings adapted late Roman vulgar law to the various nonterritorial legal traditions and practices of the ethnically diverse barbarian kingdoms.[33]

Ancient ideals of consensus as a mechanism of authority were also strained by the social realities of profound cultural and political change. For instance, despite their own insistence on universal Christian commonality, Christianized elites in most areas were at some point faced with the fact that they did not share their orthodox Christian values and assumptions with the heretical or pagan Germanic warriors who were their rulers.[34] Their concep-

---

30. Brown, "Relics," 246; Brown, *Power and Persuasion,* 100–101.

31. On episcopal elections in the late empire, see A. H. M. Jones, *The Later Roman Empire 284–602* (Baltimore, 1986), 915–20.

32. Most lawmaking Germanic kings relied, to differing degrees, on the knowledge of educated clerical legal advisors. See Wormald, "*Lex Scripta,*" 125–128. In the case of the Visigoths, the tie between royal lawmakers, clerical advisors, and late Roman law became a longstanding tradition. For instance, the "Breviary" of Alaric, also known as the *Lex Romana Visigothorum,* ed. Gustavus Haenel (Leipzig, 1889), was promulgated in 507 with the help of Gallo-Roman clerics and was drawn from the fifth-century Theodosian Code. See Jean Gaudemet, *Le Bréviaire d'Alaric et les Epitome,* Ius romanum medii aevi I (Milan, 1965).

33. Most Germanic law codes are believed to have been promulgated on the principle of "personality": their measures were meant to be applied on the basis of a person's ethnic identity—for instance, Frank, Visigoth, Burgundian, or Gallo- or Hispano-Roman—rather than on the basis of a territorially defined status as royal subject, or "citizen," of a particular kingdom. Consequently, one kingdom could have a variety of different law codes applying to the various ethnic identities of its inhabitants. The practical legal meaning, origins, and applications of the principle of personality, however, are debated topics—especially in the laws promulgated by Visigothic kings. On the principle of personality and its historiography in general, see Simeon Guterman, *The Principle of Personality of Law in the Germanic Kingdoms of Western Europe from the Fifth to the Eleventh Century* (New York, 1990). On Roman vulgar law, see Ernst Levy, *West Roman Vulgar Law. The Law of Property* (Philadelphia, 1951). On the influence of Roman and vulgar law in Germanic codes, see Levy, "Reflections on the First 'Reception' of Roman Law in the Germanic States," *American Historical Review* 48 (1942); and Levy, "Vulgarization of Roman Law in the Early Middle Ages," *Medievalia et Humanistica* 1 (1943). On the debates about personality and territoriality in the Visigothic law codes, see chap. 2, n. 70.

34. This was the case in Gaul until the conversion of Clovis, which occurred sometime around the beginning of the sixth century; in Africa until the reconquest by Byzantium in 533; in Italy under the Ostrogoths and then again under the Lombards; in Anglo-Saxon England until the seventh century; and in Iberia until 589.

tion of transcendent, universal unity was also subject to periodic theological tremors centered primarily in the East.[35] Finally, as ties between areas weakened, local bishops worked on consolidating their individual authority through community advocacy and local religious observances. This led to increasing regional variety in Christian identities and practices.[36] In other words, as elites in the West came to conceive of their own solidarity as Christian universality, tensions between that solidarity and local relationships contributed to regional diversities in Christianized conceptions and mechanisms of social power, community leadership, and consensus.[37]

Despite these continuing conditions of difference and diversity, however, there is one aspect of early medieval Christian culture that has allowed modern historians to bridge the gap between functional forms of early medieval social consensus and the ancient ideals that informed them. The continuity between late Roman imperial ceremonies and social relationships and early medieval practices associated with the cult of relics has proven particularly useful in the study of sixth-century Gaul. Local ceremonies on such occasions as the arrival of a saint's relics to a city, their authentication through miracles, and their placement in local basilicas can be interpreted as ritual expressions of community consensus parallel to those associated with the presence of emperors or their agents in the cities of the later Roman Empire.[38] The idea that rituals, sermons, art, and miracle stories associated with the cult of relics reflect the social dynamics and shared values of early medieval communities has opened a methodological window for many historians. Rituals of translation reflect community consensus not only in acceptance and reverence of the saint and his or her patronage but also in support of the holy authority claimed by the "impresario" of the saint's cult: the local bishop.[39] Ritual miracles of exorcism and healing can be understood as mechanisms for judging and reintegrating marginalized community members. Thus, they reflect both the community's values as well as the power bishops exercised through their mediation and interpretation of miracles.[40] The judicial overtones of many

---

35. The consequences of the Council of Constantinople in 553, for instance, were particularly troublesome to clerics in the West. See Judith Herrin, *The Formation of Christendom* (Princeton, 1987), 119–27.

36. Herrin, *Formation*, 106–19.

37. Peter Brown, *The Rise of Western Christendom: Triumph and Diversity AD 200–1000* (Oxford, 1996), 218, describes the increasing regionalism of Christianity in this period as the emergence of separate "micro-Christendoms," whose leaders "fastened with fierce loyalty on those features that seemed to reflect in microcosm, in their own land, the imagined, all-embracing macrocosm of a world-wide Christianity." For a discussion of the Visigothic "micro-Christendom," see 219–21.

38. Brown, "Relics," 247–49; and Brown, *Cult*, 97–105.

39. Brown, "Relics," 238–40; and Brown, *Cult*, 86–105.

40. Van Dam, *Saints*, 86–94.

miracles associated with relics may be seen as expressions of an episcopally led legal culture that accepted the authority of divine sanctions. As a source of supernatural—rather than human—judgment and punishment, miracles can be interpreted as a means of community peacemaking, compromise, and face-saving.[41] These analyses of early medieval relic cults make it possible for modern observers to identify means of maintaining order and cohesion that, although fundamentally different from those in our own society, do not lack internal logic or integrative capacities.[42] In so doing, historians can counter long-held images of early medieval society as culturally debased, chaotic, barbaric, and superstitious.

Caution should be exercised, however, when generalizing from these attributes of Gallic relic cults to the larger social function of early medieval consensus. Clearly, Christian elites in many areas during the early Middle Ages were concerned with mobilizing and reinterpreting traditional ideals of consensus to define their society and to reinforce its systems of authority. Yet the early medieval ideas and practices associated with those traditional ideals do not necessarily coincide with modern notions of consensus. Moreover, it is perhaps as difficult to pin down a general modern definition of social consensus as it is to identify an early medieval one. In relation to historical societies, social consensus generally connotes a network of shared values that explains and supports relationships and institutions such as systems of rank, authority, and decision making, thereby maintaining social cohesion and order.[43] While it is possible to detect indications of such a functional social consensus in some aspects of Gallic relic cults, the miracle stories, rituals, and sermons associated with those cults were at least as much instruments of instruction and normative expressions of ideals as they were descriptions of actual practices and relationships. The very fact that Christian leaders expended so much energy on orchestrating and publicizing community expressions of ideal consensus is an

---

41. Edward James, "*Beati Pacifici:* Bishops and the Law in Sixth-Century Gaul," in *Disputes and Settlements. Law and Human Relations in the West,* ed. John Bossy (Cambridge, 1983). See also Brown, "Society and the Supernatural." By removing decisions from human hands, mechanisms of divine judgment allowed compromise without one side seeming to have lost. According to James (46), agreeing with Brown, this served a need in early medieval society for a judicial mechanism that "avoided loss of face because it depended upon supernatural sanctions." This attribute of divine judgment was clearly an important factor in the Holy Spirit's decision at the Eighth Council of Toledo—neither side could be seen to have lost its case.

42. See, e.g., Brown's analysis of community consensus as a mode of community judgment and enforcement in trials by ordeal, in "Society and the Supernatural." Brown illustrates that these rituals of dispute settlement were not the irrational expressions of a superstitious society that they were once assumed to be.

43. For a discussion of the "macrosociological" meaning and function of consensus, primarily in modern societies, see Edward Shils, *Center and Periphery. Essays in Macrosociology* (Chicago, 1975), 164–88.

indication of how "fragile" functional consensus could be in the fractious communities of the early medieval West.[44]

A further complication involved in applying modern concepts to the early medieval evidence is that modern notions of consensus are at times by connotation posed against governmental mechanisms of coercion or forces of social conflict.[45] Although few people would consider them mutually exclusive,[46] in the most idealized modern models of consensual society, mechanisms of consensus can override the sources of contention and the necessity of coercion.[47] It is doubtful that anyone would deny the presence of conflict in any human society, especially not in the early medieval West. Still, in the effort to appreciate the social order of this unfamiliar culture in the distant past, it is tempting to conceive of early medieval consensus as separate from or opposite to the exercise of coercive authority in the enforcement of order and decision making.[48] The evidence from the Visigothic kingdom, however, discourages such an interpretation of early medieval consensus, ideal or practical. In that "barbarian" kingdom ideals of Christian consensus in a diverse and conflict-ridden society became fundamentally tied to the exercise of central authority. In the vision of the leaders of seventh-century Iberia consensus itself was meant to be coercive. This aspect of Visigothic religious and political culture is key to understanding the relationship between ideal and practical Christian consensus in the early Middle Ages.

The Conciliar Paradox

While the evidence from Gaul offers historians a relatively detailed view of local community dynamics, the evidence from Iberia is most reflective of the ideas and aspirations of bishops and kings who operated within the innermost circles of power. If one is looking for carefully constructed and clearly voiced early medieval ideals of Christian consensus, the material produced in Iberia

---

44. On the "very delicate and fissile" consensus surrounding sixth-century Gallic bishops, see Brown, "Relics," 246–47.

45. For general comments on consensus, coercion, and conflict, see Shils, *Center and Periphery*, x–xiii.

46. According to Shils, (*Center and Periphery,* 176), coercion "is a supplement to consensus, not a mutually exclusive alternative."

47. This modern idealization is perhaps most evident in the efforts by some progressive political groups to replace democratic decision-making processes with various forms of consensual decision making.

48. This separation, at least in an ideal form, is implied by James, "*Beati Pacifici,*" 46. Brown's suggestion of a twelfth-century "shift from consensus to authority" in "Society and the Supernatural," 324, implies an even more dramatic opposition.

between 589 and the Muslim invasion in 711 presents a veritable gold mine. Iberian society was characterized by religious, cultural, and political divisions from the early fifth century until the 580s. The conversion of the Visigoths from Arianism to Catholicism in that decade signaled the beginning of a close collaboration between ecclesiastic and royal authorities. For the next fifty years these men and their successors joined in developing the increasingly complex Visigothic vision of centralized Christian governance based on religious and political consensus.

This vision came to be expressed in a cultural movement led by Isidore of Seville that centered on the resurrection and redefinition of Roman, Byzantine, and patristic knowledge and ideals. The cultural renewal of the seventh-century Iberian church generated an outpouring of theological and educational tracts, chronicles, saints' *Lives,* letters, poems, and liturgy.[49] Isidore and his followers saw a commitment to organized clerical education and supervision as one of the means for establishing and maintaining Christian consensus in their kingdom. In their view a uniformly disciplined clergy would guard the kingdom-wide uniformity in liturgy and morality that they sought to create through ecclesiastic and secular legislation; religious uniformity would enforce a common consensus on the divine sanctions supporting laws and leaders. Thus, clerical education would ultimately ensure collective obedience, the orderly and lasting settlement of disputes, the mutual defense of the kingdom against its enemies, the honoring of recognized rank and authority in social relationships, and, in general, peace and justice throughout the kingdom. This would in turn guarantee God's favor and support for the kingdom as well as the salvation of its leaders and subjects.

The distribution of the Visigothic evidence makes the reconstruction of these ideals relatively straightforward. In their efforts to establish Christian consensus the leaders of seventh-century Iberia pursued an ongoing project of systematization. They produced elaborate compilations of liturgy, law, and legal formulas, which together with the literary output of kings and bishops constitute a cohesive and coherent monument to their own vision of ideal Christian society and governance. One of the primary goals of systematization was to create a body of theoretically immutable and universal precedents for imposing uniform religious practices and legal actions on diverse subject communities. The process of compilation removed the sources from their original contexts in a number of important ways, most obviously geographically and

---

49. The fundamental modern work on Isidore and his cultural project is Jacques Fontaine, *Isidore de Séville et la culture classique dans l'Espagne wisigothique* (Paris, 1959), 2 vols.

chronologically.[50] Consequently, the evidential monument to Visigothic ideals demands considerable caution when navigating the currents that flowed between the aspirations of leaders and the lives of their local communities. Moreover, the available materials are of an overwhelmingly pedantic and normative nature and are notably dependent upon ancient models and traditions. It is especially problematic to assume any direct relationship between these tradition-bound assertions of ideal consensus and specific local mechanisms of practical consensus. In constructing the monument to their own ideals, the authors of our sources have all but obliterated the immediate social genesis of their vision of consensus.

Analyses of the Gallic sources on relic cults and local community values may suggest some aspects of the social context for Visigothic visions. For instance, community displays of ceremonial consensus as demonstrations of shared values and support for local bishops are likely to have influenced Iberian bishops as they orchestrated their conciliar displays of episcopal consensus. Many of the immediate concerns behind the careful construction of Visigothic ideal consensus therefore were based in social relationships and conflicts similar to those that informed expressions of local consensus in Gallic communities. Likewise, the aims of the Visigothic program for legislated consensus probably mirrored those of the instructional and normative rituals, sermons, and miracle stories of sixth-century Gaul. Thus, the Visigothic efforts at consensus building, like those in Gaul, may in part reflect a fundamental fragility in functional forms of local community consensus. Furthermore, the conscientious Iberian efforts to impose elaborate ideals upon local communities were not utterly divorced from daily Iberian experience. The compilation of precedents and rules and the editing and publishing of pedagogical materials do reflect an active set of social policies, which leaders developed over a period of time in response to the immediate history and contemporary circumstances of their various communities.

---

50. Edited liturgical compilations, for instance, were reconfigured over generations extending into the Mozarabic period and therefore contain few hints as to the local provenance or date of any given piece. A modern edition of the Visigothic/Mozarabic *Liber Ordinem* is *Le Liber Ordinum en usage dans l'église wisigothique et mozarabe d'Espagne du cinquième au onzième siècle,* ed. Marius Férotin, *Monumenta Ecclesiae Liturgica,* vol. 5 (Paris, 1904). Legal codifications are by nature reflections of the aspirations of central powers, and it is difficult to attach individual laws to the immediate circumstances of their promulgation. The Visigothic codes are extensive and have been extensively analyzed, with many of the laws dated and attributable to particular kings, but the process of codification entailed the deletion or alteration of unknown numbers of previous laws, resulting in static collections that primarily reflect the intentions of the few individuals involved at the intermittent moments when the codes were created. Narrative sources offer some windows onto datable events and specific communities surrounding the promulgation of laws, the enactment of rituals, and so forth, but those sources are rare, and the windows themselves are often glazed by the pervasive power of idealized Christian consensus.

The relationship between Visigothic ideals and local community life is particularly well documented in one product of the seventh-century compilers: the collected acts of the Iberian church councils. Between 516 and 694 Iberian bishops met in councils at least thirty-four times. Most of the records of these councils were included in a seventh-century canonical collection now known as the *Hispana*. As a compilation, the *Hispana* represents a carefully crafted corpus of canonical tradition reflecting the social ideals of its editors: clerics in the cities of Seville and Toledo during the latter two-thirds of the seventh century.[51] The records of individual councils, however, offer glimpses—which sometimes widen into more comprehensive vistas—of specific moments at particular places when leaders attempted to regulate their communities through consensual decision making. While the conciliar scribes recorded these ceremonious tribunals in the transcendental language of ideal Christian consensus, the actions taken at councils were firmly grounded in the mundane business of applying previous precedents, settling disputes, and punishing offenders.[52] As the episode surrounding Recceswinth's dilemma shows, these moments of intersection between ritual expressions of episcopal consensus and the life and disputes of kingdoms and communities bring into sharp focus many of the judicial contradictions of early medieval governance.

As the seventh-century compilers indexed and edited the records, they preserved them in chronological order, dated them, and named them according to their locations. The sequence of councils was distributed (albeit unevenly) over a lengthy period of time and throughout the Iberian Peninsula. The extant records include those for the series of thirteen "general" councils— gatherings of bishops from the entire kingdom—that began with the celebration of the Visigoths' conversion to Catholicism in 589.[53] With one exception, these councils were held in the "royal" city of Toledo, which during the course

---

51. The *Hispana,* which included Gallic and North African conciliar records as well as pontifical epistles, was assembled in three different recensions during the course of the seventh century. The original recension, now known as the *Isidoriana,* is not extant, but it has been reconstructed, dated to around 633, and traced to a Sevillan origin. See Gonzalo Martínez Díez, *La colección canónica Hispana,* I, *Estudio, Monumenta Hispaniae Sacra,* Serie Canónica (Madrid, 1966), 306–25. The two later recensions were the *Juliana,* c. 681, and the *Vulgata,* c. 694 (see 323–25). The compilers of these recensions retained most of the material from the *Isidoriana,* adding the records of subsequent Iberian councils from the later seventh century. See also Martínez Díez, "Concilios españoles anteriores a Trento," in *Repertorio de Historia de las Ciencias Eclesiasticas en España,* vol. 5, *Siglos I–XVI* (Salamanca, 1976), 306–7.

52. Given the decontextualizing nature of legal codifications, conciliar records are particularly important in providing evidence, however opaque, of the specific circumstances involved in these processes. There are no secular court records extant from the Visigothic period.

53. The "general" councils of the Visigothic Church were as follows: the Third (589), Fourth (633), Fifth (636), Sixth (638), Seventh (646), Eighth (653), Tenth (656), Twelfth (681), Thirteenth (683), Fifteenth (688), Sixteenth (693), and Seventeenth (694) Councils of Toledo and the Second Council of Saragossa (691).

of the seventh century also came to be recognized as kingdom's preeminent diocese.[54] There are also records extant for nine "provincial" councils—meetings of the bishops of a single province—held before 589[55] and fourteen provincial councils held between that year and the end of the kingdom.[56] Of course, one must keep in mind the pitfalls involved in the analysis of conciliar records. Most important, there is no guarantee that the extant records include all the councils held in any given period.[57] In theory any number of provincial councils could have been held but their records lost or otherwise adulterated, thus compromising conclusions based on the frequency or infrequency of conciliar activity.[58] Yet the extant Iberian *acta* contain numerous references to an ongoing lack of conciliar activity and to clerical ignorance of past measures, indicating that the canonical requirement for regular provincial councils often went unheeded. Provincial councils were therefore unusual events; it is probable that more often than not they were carefully recorded and preserved.[59] When analyzed in sequence, the records that do survive provide a rare and relatively complete picture of conflict and variation in the changing relationship between Christian ideals of consensus and the problems confronting social

---

54. On the process by which Toledo reached this status, see chap. 3, n. 105; chap. 4, n. 13; chap. 5, n. 107; and concl., n. 20.

55. The sixth-century provincial councils held between the loss of the Aquitanian kingdom in 507 and the Visigothic conversion to Catholicism were the following: the Councils of Tarragona (516) and Gerona (517); the Second Council of Toledo (527); the Councils of Barcelona I (540), Lérida (546), and Valencia (546); and the First (561) and Second (572) Councils of Braga.

56. Of these fourteen, six were held in the decade after 589: the Council of Narbonne (589); the First Council of Seville (590); the Second Council of Saragossa (592); the Council of Huesca (598); the Second Council of Barcelona (599); and a council in Toledo in 597, which was something of an anomaly—although its agenda was strictly provincial, its attendees included some bishops from other provinces. See chap. 3, n. 104. Two of the fourteen provincial council records come from the period between 600 and 633: the Council of Egara (614) and the Second Council of Seville (619). The *Hispana* also contains the records of a council held in Toledo in 610 under the king Gundemar; the authenticity of these records is questioned. See chap. 4, n. 13. The final five provincial councils in the *Hispana* were as follows: the Ninth (655), Eleventh (675), and Fourteenth (684) Councils of Toledo; the Council of Mérida (666); and the Third Council of Braga (675).

57. For instance, there are some indications that a final Council of Toledo was held in 703, although the *Hispana* does not contain its records. See Gonzalo Martínez Díez, "Los Concilios de Toledo," *Anales Toledanos* 3 (Toledo, 1971), 123. It also appears that the records of the Third Council of Seville, a provincial council held c. 624, were intentionally supressed. See chap. 4, n. 79. The records of the Council of Huesca, held in 598, were not written down until 614. Moreover, the editors of the *Hispana* excluded five of the six provincial councils held in the 590s; these records survive in one manuscript only. See chap. 3, n. 78.

58. For more details on this issue, see chap. 4, n. 79; and concl., n. 26.

59. It is particularly unlikely that there were any unrecorded general councils held prior to the final recension of the *Hispana* in 694. General councils were held on occasions of major political or theological import, they were carefully numbered by the editors, and they form the backbone of the collection.

authorities as they attempted to govern the communities of the early medieval West.

In early medieval society people attempting to administer justice and settle disputes faced a fundamental paradox in the exercise of social power. The weakness of central coercive authority meant that the enforcement of the decisions of any judicial tribunal depended on a community's shared recognition of the tribunal's authority.[60] Yet ongoing contention between different sources of authority made such recognition unreliable, thus increasing the importance of access to coercive force in order to enforce decisions and punishments. A community's Christian consensus could, in theory, generate a shared recognition of a tribunal's authority and thus resolve the paradox. This was particularly important in terms of people's acceptance of the divine sanctions attached to such legal instruments as oaths, excommunication, and penance. For these instruments to work everyone had to agree that God participated in human judicial affairs and meted out eternal punishment for actions defined by human authorities as crimes. Such a consensus could obviate the necessity of coercion and thus resolve the paradox.

Yet gaining a general agreement on these concepts would not resolve the issue of the location of holy authority. Over time, as orthodox Christians worked to develop a strong consensus on the idea of divine judgment in human affairs, various leaders also struggled to foster further consensus on the association of divine authority with many different traditional sources of community power and order, such as the local status of a particular noble family, royal lawmaking, or local customs.[61] Christian leaders not only fought to achieve community consensus on the authenticity of divine judgment and holy authority but also contended with one another over which individuals, tribunals, and sources of law had access to it, and so to its powers of enforcement through divine sanction. Thus, church councils were one of many judicial mechanisms struggling to achieve consensual recognition as vehicles of holy authority.

A shared recognition of holy authority that might resolve the paradox of early medieval community justice was also impeded by the changing composition of many communities and regions. The general concept of divine participation in human judicial affairs was but one of a number of currents in the pool of ideas and practices of governance and social ordering. Different com-

---

60. See Chris Wickham, "Land Disputes and Their Social Framework in Lombard-Carolingian Italy, 700–900," in *Settlement of Disputes*, 123.

61. On royal lawmaking and divine law, see Wormald, "*Lex Scripta*," 130–32. On competition in Gaul over the location of holy authority, see Van Dam, *Leadership*, 203–220, and Patrick Geary, *Before France and Germany. The Creation and Transformation of the Merovingian World* (Oxford, 1988), 167–78.

munities and groups valued other traditional mechanisms and concepts, including those associated with secular law (Roman, Germanic, and provincial), patronage or kinship obligations, and local customs and systems of social ranking.[62] Competition from non-Christian sources of community justice and authority would be particularly strong at times or in places where orthodox Christianity was overtly rejected by some subjects or compromised by suspicions about the residual Judaism, heresy, or "rusticitas" of others.[63] There would be little reason for a community to entrust the enforcement of its judicial decisions to sanctions that some of its own members were believed to hold in contempt.

The complexities of the struggle to locate holy authority in human governmental instruments are well illustrated in the confusion surrounding Chindaswinth's loyalty oath. The oath originally was imposed as a means to support a royal law, which by itself apparently did not command unequivocal obedience. The oath takers therefore swore in God's name that they would inflict the punishments contained in the law. The divine sanctions for violating oaths were meant to reinforce the royal sanctions for violating the law, thus preventing rebellions. For this oath to serve its intended purpose, the oath takers had to share a series of connected beliefs: that God participates in human judicial affairs, that violating oaths would bring God's judgment upon the perjurer, and that Chindaswinth's royal oath would automatically gain that divine sanction. This clearly was not the case; Froia and his followers challenged both royal and divine judgment by breaking their oaths and rebelling, and Toledo VIII, despite its hedging, ultimately endorsed the idea that sworn oaths did not automatically carry divine sanctions. In this case Chindaswinth had failed to establish a lasting consensus on the tie between divine sanctions and royal law. In 654, on the other hand, it does appear that consensus existed, at least for the moment among those at Toledo VIII, on the location of holy authority and access to divine judgment in councils of the Catholic Church.

---

62. On the various earthly elements of early medieval judicial practices, see Wood, "Disputes"; Chris Wickham, et al., conclusion to *Settlement of Disputes;* and J. M. Wallace-Hadrill, "The Bloodfeud of the Franks," in *The Long-Haired Kings and Other Studies in Frankish History* (Toronto, 1982).

63. In Brown's analysis of the late antique church leaders' struggles to replace the "tainted" power of non-Christian or unauthorized sources of authority with the "clean" power of saints and their relics (*Cult,* 86–127), the term *rusticitas* (119) signifies the opposite of "reverentia," or reverence for the power of saints and the urban aristocratic value system that accepted them as new, invisible community patrons. While Brown's discussion focuses on "a conflict of models of healing" (120), he describes an awareness among sixth-century leaders of "pockets of 'raw rusticity' " (122) that seems likely also to have had implications for the struggle to establish the concept of divine sanctions as an accepted legal principle. On the judicial problems engendered by suspicions about ex-Arians and ex-Jews in the Visigothic kingdom, see chaps. 3 and 4, respectively.

In some senses locating the power of divine judgment in the decisions made by episcopal consensus at church councils was a natural extension of the holy authority claimed by local bishops in individual communities. Not surprisingly, the evidence from Gaul shows that local bishops there were the most active proponents of the notion of divine judgment among Christian communities.[64] Christian clerics, moreover, as the inheritors of Roman literate culture in general, had access not only to centuries of ecclesiastic legal precedent but also to the procedures, principles, and precedents of Roman law. In efforts to infuse secular judicial processes with holy authority, rulers had for centuries included bishops in various aspects of legal procedure. The emperor Constantine had extended broad legal jurisdictions to episcopal courts, and, although the scope was narrowed over the succeeding years, bishops continued to administer justice in lay cases and sometimes in concert with secular authorities.[65] Under Germanic kings they often brought their knowledge to bear as advisors to royal lawmakers.[66] Thus, in many areas of the West, as local bishops sought to assert their own holy authority in community governance, they could draw on a nexus of traditional and emergent ideas about episcopal authority. These included the general notion of divine judgment, the association of episcopal office with that notion, long-term traditions of episcopal judicial authority in many legal arenas, as well as the bishops' carefully fostered personal association with saints, relics, and their often judicially flavored miracles. Joined together in church councils, bishops could strengthen their claims for episcopal access to divine judgment and sanctions through scriptural legitimation for collective episcopal authority and through other Christian and Roman traditions of authoritative consensus.

With the notion that local episcopal power was somehow a cumulative phenomenon, however, one returns to the realm of ideal consensus. In practice, achieving episcopal consensus was problematic, making conciliar justice perhaps less likely than other judicial mechanisms to gain a general recognition of its status as a vehicle of holy authority. At the same time, councils were more dependent upon that recognition than other tribunals or individuals, for they could not independently threaten coercive force to encourage obedience, as royal and noble authorities might. In order to gain recognition and enforce decisions without relying on the threat of earthly coercion, councils needed to call upon the local influence that individual bishops wielded in their own communities. If a powerful local bishop commanded his own flock's obedience to the collective authority of bishops in groups, then councils might begin to see

---

64. James, "*Beati Pacifici*," 32–33.

65. James, "*Beati Pacifici*," 29–31; Wood, "Disputes," 18; Jones, *Later Roman Empire*, 91, 362, and 480; Brown, *Power and Persuasion*, n. 100.

66. Wormald, "*Lex Scripta*," 125–27.

their decisions enforced and their holy power recognized. Yet the influence of local bishops arose in large part out of their integral involvement in the conflictual networks of power in individual communities.[67] Episcopal solidarity, like other forms of elite solidarity, was subject to the pressure of local concerns and loyalties. Episcopal office was often the focus for the ambitions and machinations of powerful people seeking to further their own interests and the interests of their particular communities.[68] Bishops, therefore, could not necessarily be depended on to agree with one another or to promote the authority of councils when conciliar decisions conflicted with local interests. In societies in which some of the most basic orthodox Christian values—including divine participation in human judicial matters—were not fully accepted, the lack of independent coercive force and the dependence upon the consensus and active support of often contentious local bishops fundamentally compromised the efficacy of church councils as judicial tribunals.

These factors may explain the fact that in most areas during the early Middle Ages the authority of church councils was not called upon regularly or consistently. Their judicial role, their procedures, and the authority of conciliar precedents were defined variously, often according to the immediate circumstances in particular times and places. For instance, church councils occasionally met at the behest of secular authorities seeking to marshal conciliar holy authority for their own purposes. Under these circumstances councils generally welcomed the support of secular powers, for the implicit threat of coercive authority that came with royal support might enable them to extend their jurisdiction to lay communities. For the most part, however, local church councils confined their competence to clerics and their ecclesiastic communities—from isolated rural priests to monks and their monasteries to the complex urban hierarchies surrounding bishops in their sees.[69]

---

67. See Ian N. Wood, "The Ecclesiastical Politics of Merovingian Clermont," in *Ideal and Reality in Frankish and Anglo-Saxon Society: Studies Presented to J. M. Wallace-Hadrill,* ed. Patrick Wormald, Donald Bullough, and Roger Collins (Oxford, 1983).

68. See chap. 4; and Rachel Stocking, "Martianus, Aventius, and Isidore: Provincial Councils in Seventh-Century Spain," *Early Medieval Europe* 6, no. 2 (1997).

69. On church councils from the third to the fifth centuries, see Jean Gaudemet, *L'Église dans l'Empire Romain IVe–Ve siècles* (Paris, 1989), 451–66. On Iberian councils prior to 711, see José Orlandis and Domingo Ramos-Lissón, *Historia de los concilios de la España romana y visigoda* (Pamplona, 1986). On Merovingian conciliar activity, see J. M. Wallace-Hadrill, *The Frankish Church* (Oxford, 1983), 94–109; and Odette Pontal, *Die Synoden im Merowingerreich Konziliengeschichte* (Paderborn, 1986), French version, *Histoire des conciles mérovingiens* (Paris, 1989). On conciliar terminology and capacity, see Brigitte Basdevant-Gaudemet, "Les évêques, les papes et les princes dans la vie conciliare en France du IVe au XIIe siècle," *Revue historique de droit français et étranger* 69 (1991): 2. For bibliography, see Jean Gaudemet, *Les sources du droit de l'Église en Occident du IIe au VIIe siècle* (Paris, 1985), and "Regards sur l'histoire du droit canonique antérieurement au Décret de Gratien," *Studia et Documenta Historiae et Iuris* 51 (Rome, 1985), reprinted in *Droit de l'Église et vie sociale au Moyen Âge* (London, 1989).

Ideally, clerics could be depended upon to recognize the power of divine judgment, episcopal consensus, and the precedents of ecclesiastic legislation; thus, conciliar decisions could be enforced among them. In practice, however, even this limited jurisdiction proved difficult for councils to govern. Clerical communities could be just as conflictual and diverse as lay communities. Consequently, as bishops met and struggled to enforce their collective decisions and canonical precedents, these tribunals were often the forums not only for dispute settlements between clerics but also for the insistent ceremonial reiteration and legislated redefinition of conciliar holy authority. These ceremonial displays and solemn acts of legislation were in many ways self-referential; the act of holding a council was in part meant to remind the participants and their subordinates of the divine power embodied in canonical tradition. It is at these moments, when bishops reiterated and redefined their collective authority in response to specific disputes and the dynamics of social power, that conciliar records offer their most revealing insights into early medieval ideals and community practices of consensus and governance. Beginning in 589, such moments occurred in the Visigothic kingdom with relative frequency.

Drawing heavily on the records of church councils, this book traces the development of the Visigothic vision of a kingdom centrally organized and regulated by Christian consensus. The story unfolds from its long-term roots in Christian conciliar traditions and sixth-century Iberian society, through the circumstances surrounding its initial articulation in 589 and its further elaboration over the subsequent forty years, past the first concerted effort at its implementation at the Fourth Council of Toledo in 633, to its increasingly evident failure in the last half of the seventh century. Chapter 1 explores the sixth-century context for the initial stages of this process by looking at conciliar traditions and episcopal authority in the religiously divided Visigothic kingdom prior to 589. In that year the Third Council of Toledo formalized the Visigoths' conversion from Arianism to Catholicism, along with the resulting alliance between *regnum* and *sacerdotium* that was meant to be the foundation for the kingdom's governance henceforth. Chapter 2 analyzes the varying ideals and practices embedded in Toledo III's formulation of this alliance, which was meant to be implemented through the regular and orderly exercise of conciliar authority.

Over the next forty years Iberian bishops struggled among themselves, with the royal office, and with their own communities as they confronted and tried to overcome the limitations that the changeability and contradictions of early medieval culture and society placed on conciliar authority. Chapters 3 and 4 describe how successive generations of bishops and kings variously defined the parameters of conciliar jurisdiction, its relationship to secular authority, and conciliar procedure and rituals of consensus. One of the central dynamics in this process of definition and redefinition was the paradoxical nature of early medieval justice in its conciliar incarnation. The enforcement of conciliar decisions depended upon a kingdom-wide consensual acceptance of collective episcopal holy authority and its access to divine sanctions. This consensus did not exist in a society characterized by religious diversity and conflict among clerics, within individual lay communities, and in the kingdom as a whole. As Christian leaders debated the means to establish and maintain the consensus needed for effective enforcement, they experimented with various configurations of legislation, education, and coercion. These included secular laws, forced conversion, clerical supervision, cultural renewal, liturgical uniformity, and the development of models and rules for holding councils. During this period of debates and experimentation the kingdom's elites remained divided, and the kingdom's communities remained contentious. Eventually, the various measures proved inadequate to the task of realizing in practice the complex construct of ideal Christian consensus.

In the face of continuing conflict on many fronts, including a royal usurpation in 630, the Christian leaders of the kingdom gathered in 633 at Toledo IV, the subject of chapter 5. Toledo IV once again declared mutual support between king and bishops and the necessity of Christian consensus for political survival. The council's participants vigorously asserted their agreement on a carefully defined framework for elite solidarity that placed particular responsibilities on the king, the entire episcopate, and the Visigothic nobility. The council's legislation addressed the problems created by forced conversion, by the failure to honor oaths and obey conciliar legislation, by widespread clerical incompetence and corruption, by the abuse and neglect of conciliar judicial procedures, and by the political factionalism behind the political crisis of 630. These rules established as a central principle of government the maintenance of absolute Christian uniformity. They instituted a complex system of supervision, education, and election for maintaining clerical probity and authority. They also reiterated the overriding authority of divine sanctions in punishing crime and ensuring a dependable judicial system. And they delineated detailed instructions for the administration of conciliar justice, extending the jurisdiction of church councils into every clerical and lay community in the kingdom. According to Toledo IV, the scandals and contention of the past would now be eliminated by mobilizing elite solidarity and conciliar authority to create and maintain absolute Christian consensus. Consensus among Christian leaders would thus ensure the establishment of the general consensus necessary to enforce Christian governance. In this sense, in the Visigothic construction of the ideal, Christian consensus was meant to be coercive.

Visigothic Difference

The path taken by Christian leaders in Iberia, with their fascination for legislation, centralization, systematization, and repressive uniformity diverges
sharply from those taken in other areas, particularly Merovingian Gaul.[70] This
divergence, combined with the Visigothic kingdom's conquest by the Muslims
and the Iberian Peninsula's subsequent incorporation into the Islamic world,
has contributed to a tendency among some modern historians to place the
Visigothic kingdom, as well as Islamic Iberia, outside the mainstreams of early
medieval history.[71] In something of a defensive posture, many Iberian special-
ists have adopted a viewpoint that gives particular attention to the political
and cultural achievements of the Visigothic kingdom and its church during the
period of the Catholic monarchy.[72] Adopting this viewpoint, however, sometimes involves an acceptance of, and even an emphasis on, the kingdom's fundamental distinction from the rest of western Europe.[73]

On the one hand, the distinctiveness of the Visigothic ideals and practices
should not be minimized in an attempt to incorporate them into generalizations about early medieval society. One of the most important characteristics
of western Europe during this period was its diversity. Visigothic difference,
moreover, is an important tool in understanding other periods of Iberian history. For instance, the Visigothic leaders' particular configuration of ideas
about holy authority and consensus has its roots in the truly "dark" ages of
Iberian history—the fifth century and the first two-thirds of the sixth. Thus,
the distinctive nature of the seventh-century Visigothic vision may help shed
light on the divergent developments in Iberia during the earlier period. On the
other hand, while Visigothic difference can help illustrate the diversity of early
medieval western Europe, and can be useful in explaining various aspects of
Iberian history, it should not be overemphasized. The diversity of western
European society during this period was also characteristic of the Iberian
Peninsula. A monolithic image of the distinctive Visigothic forms of ideology
and governance, although perhaps true to the intentions of seventh-century
systematizers, does not adequately reflect the diverse communities from which

---

70. James, "*Beati Pacifici*," 45.

71. Roger Collins, *Early Medieval Spain. Unity in Diversity 400–1000* (New York, 1983),
ix. This isolating tendency may help to explain the lack of new work on the Visigothic period
bemoaned by Collins in the preface to the second edition of his survey, published in 1995 (xi).

72. See, e.g., Fontaine, *Isidore de Séville*. For a comprehensive bibliography of works
dealing with the kingdom, see Alberto Ferreiro, *The Visigoths in Gaul and Spain, AD 418–711:
A Bibliography* (Leiden, 1988).

73. This emphasis is particularly noticeable among some Spanish ecclesiastic historians.
See, e.g., Gonzalo Martínez Díez, "Nota sobre la colección 'Hispana,' " in Vives, xii–xv.

those forms arose. It was their diversity, their conflicting distributions of power and loyalties, and the consequent flux and contradiction in ideas and practices of authority that these communities had in common with other areas of the West. As the Christian leaders of Iberia struggled to define authority and methods of control in response to this diversity, conflict, and contradiction, it is not surprising that they, like leaders in other regions, gave particular significance to idealized forms and rituals of Christian consensus.

Nor should it be surprising that in their vision, which drew on Christian and Roman traditions that were also available to other western European leaders, Christian consensus came to be seen a means of coercive force. Whether dressed in the language of universal Christian harmony, modern communitarian political ideals, or the egalitarian social arrangements of idealized "traditional" communities, consensus is, in part, a normative construct. Even among people whose interests and values do in general coincide, the development and enforcement of community consensus on any debated issue involves identifying and silencing dissenters—whether through gossip, group ostracism, or forceful exclusion from the community. In the diverse, hierarchical communities of the early medieval West, symbolic rituals of consensus probably were expressions of shared values and a mutual acceptance of a system of divine sanctions. But they were also orchestrated events supporting the authority of specific people and formalizing the exclusion of dissenters. In these communities, with their multiple competing sources of authority and marked fluidity in governmental culture, ideals and rituals of consensus expressed the normative aspirations of some leaders—particularly orthodox Christian bishops—as much as they reflected the forces of social cohesion. To be sure, the aspirations of many of these leaders included maintaining peace and order through compromise and mercy. Yet their aspirations also included the careful regulation of their communities and kingdoms and the maintenance of their own power and patronage in the face of competing value systems and sources of authority. For these men the shared values that Christian consensus signified included maintaining the strict hierarchies of Christian authority.

In the Visigothic kingdom the confluence of a particular set of political, cultural, and religious developments eventually led secular and ecclesiastic leaders to tie their interpretation of Christian consensus to aspirations for centralized authority. The process through which this tie came to be made, like the communities in which it took place, was characterized by diversity, conflict, and contradiction. It led to the particularly forthright, overtly coercive vision of consensual governance that was first articulated at Toledo IV. While this vision was indeed unusual in the early medieval West, many of the social conditions from which it arose and the traditions informing its development were not. Visigothic difference in the area of ideal Christian consensus may be a matter of degree, rather than kind.

Ultimately, understanding the degree to which Visigothic ideals were coercive may help to illuminate the initial success of the Muslims and thus the beginnings of the profound divergence of Islamic Iberia from the rest of the West. With Toledo IV's assertion of elite solidarity and its program for centrally defined and locally enforced consensus, the traces of elite dialogue and redefinitions in the meaning and practice of holy power all but disappear from the sources. Yet, as Recceswinth's dilemma and the debate at Toledo VIII show, many of the forces standing in the way of centralized governance and the enforcement of conciliar justice continued to prevail over Christian leaders' efforts at maintaining order. The sequence of Visigothic church councils from 633 through 694 also shows that noble factionalism, episcopal contention, clerical incompetence, religious diversity, royal weakness, and the inability to enforce legislation continued as characteristics of Iberian society. Although general councils continued to meet, they did so irregularly. The failure of Toledo IV's effort at institutionalizing conciliar governance is most evident in the nearly complete absence of records for provincial councils for the remainder of the kingdom's existence.

The council in 633, however, did lay the basis for the continuing efforts at establishing elite unity, clerical discipline, and coercive consensus that also characterized the subsequent years of Visigothic rule. In secular law codes, conciliar legislation, and literary works, using the ornate vocabulary of Roman and Christian tradition, Iberian leaders repeatedly asserted the necessity of liturgical uniformity, centralized control, enforced loyalty, and Christian consensus for the survival of the kingdom. These efforts to make ideal consensus a functional reality appear to have exacerbated divisions and conflicts among the communities of the kingdom. As one surveys the increasingly repressive legislation from this period, the inability of community leaders to enforce it grows increasingly evident. Despite multiple laws designed to eliminate Judaism, Jewish communities continued to receive support from local Christians and continued to thrive long past the end of the Visigothic kingdom. Despite repeated threats of eternal damnation for rebellion and perjury—not to mention vigorous secular sanctions—nobles, clerics, and their local communities continued to violate oaths of loyalty, foment civil war, and refuse to honor royal military summonses. While the rigidity of these laws and their lack of enforcement may not constitute a direct cause, they contribute to an explanation for the kingdom's obvious lack of mutual defense when the Muslims arrived in 711.

CHAPTER ONE

Holy Authority and the Holy Spirit in Sixth-Century Iberia

In the year following his ascension to the Visigothic throne, the new king, Reccared (586–601), converted from Arian to Catholic Christianity. Two years later, in 589, Reccared, his wife, Baddo, and a group of formerly Arian nobles and clerics attended the Third Council of Toledo. Here, amid the first gathering of Catholic bishops from all the Iberian provinces ever held under a Visigothic monarch,[1] the king and his followers confirmed their conversion. In their turn the Catholic bishops received the confession with acclamations for the king. The records of the council are charged with an awareness of the moment's importance. The leading bishop of the day, Leander of Seville, gave voice to that awareness in a closing homily:

> Its novelty itself shows that this celebration is the most solemn of all celebrations, since just as the conversion of so many people is an unusual event, so the joy of the church is out of the ordinary. . . . The cause of our previous tribulation is the reason for our current joy. We groaned while we were oppressed, while we were reproached; but our groans have caused those who were our burden through their faithlessness now to become our crown through their conversion.[2]

Leander went on to explain that the peace achieved through the conversion of the Goths not only ended the history of suffering in the persecuted church but

---

1. The bishops at Toledo III did not include those from the territories still held in the South by the Byzantines. See n. 10 of this chapter.

2. Leander of Seville, *Homelia in laude ecclesiae ob conversionem gentis,* in Felix Rodríguez' edition of Toledo III's records, "El Concilio III de Toledo," in *Concilio III de Toledo. XIV Centenario, 589–1989* (Toledo, 1991), 35: "Festiuitatem hanc omnium esse sollemniorem festiuitatum nouitas ipsa significat, quoniam sicut noua est conuersio tantarum plebium causa, ita et nouiora sunt solito ecclesia gaudia . . . . Ergo materia gaudii nostri tribulationis praeteritae occasio fuit. Gemebamus dum grauaremur, dum exprobraremur; sed gemitus illi id egerunt, ut ii qui per infidelitatem nobis erant sarcina, fierent nostra per suam conuersionem corona."

also served as proof that the whole world would be united within that church and thus be saved.[3]

A contemporary chronicler, John of Biclar, described the meaning of the council in different but equally momentous terms: he compared it to the Council of Nicaea and Reccared to Constantine. For John, Toledo III constituted so profound a turning point in history that he linked it to the end of wars between the Byzantines and Persians and to the Persian emperor's conversion to Catholicism.[4] The peace of the church had descended upon the entire world; 589 marks the final year of his chronicle.

When Leander, Reccared, Baddo, the Gothic nobles and clerics, and the Hispano-Roman bishops gathered in St. Leocadia's basilica, they sought to express an ideal consensus that operated on a number of interlocking levels. Perhaps most obvious to the modern observer, and definitely the level that resonates most strongly in modern analyses of the meaning of Toledo III, is the common accord they asserted between *regnum* and *sacerdotium*: an alliance in governing that would transcend the preceding years of religious division among the kingdom's leaders. What gave this alliance its holy authority, however, was a much longer-standing traditional source of sacred power: the common concord of Christian leaders assembled in the name of Jesus Christ, which was believed to bring forth the attendance of the Holy Spirit.[5] By gathering in a council, the Iberian bishops expressed harmony among themselves and between themselves and their God. What enabled each bishop to participate in this episcopal accord, and thus enabled the council to act collectively as a vessel of holy authority, was the status a bishop could claim as the curator of his local community's Christian consensus. Finally, episcopal harmony represented for these men not only the concord within each individual community but also the consensus and the joint Christian obedience of all the communities of the kingdom.

The council's organizers, led by Leander,[6] and probably including a team of clerical royal advisors, marshaled a wide array of Christian and Roman traditions as they orchestrated an impressive ceremonial display for this complex consensual package. Simply by holding a council, the Iberian prelates evoked not only the authority of the Holy Spirit but also that of all the church councils of preceding centuries. They defined the authority of this broad tradition more narrowly by specific and repeated references to the great councils of the fourth and fifth centuries—the councils of Nicaea, Constantinople, Ephesus,

---

3. For an analysis of Leander's homily, see Jacques Fontaine, "La homilía de San Leandro ante el Concilio III de Toledo: temática y forma," in *Concilio III de Toledo.*

4. John Bicl., *anno VII Mauricii,* 1, 219.

5. See intro., n. 22.

6. John Bicl., *anno VII Mauricii,* 1, 219.

and Chalcedon. As "ecumenical" councils, these gatherings had spoken for all Christian communities in the Roman Empire; likewise, Toledo III spoke for all Christian communities in the Visigothic kingdom. The great councils had defined Catholic orthodoxy to end doctrinal divisions in the Empire; Toledo III asserted the same orthodoxy to end the "plague" of Gothic Arianism. Convened and presided over by Roman emperors, the fourth- and fifth-century councils had recognized and celebrated imperial religious leadership and participation in conciliar consensus; convened by the king of the Visigoths, Toledo III was centered on a ceremonial acknowledgment of royal religious leadership and participation.

The council's participants enacted these conscientious parallels to the great councils in a series of carefully announced and recorded proceedings that invoked the authority of both Christian ritual and imperial legal ceremony: a three-day fast, the public signing of confessions and oral abjurations by the converting Arians, a communal recitation of anathemas against the rejected faith, and mass acclamations for both king and God. The local community consensus behind each bishop at the council and the kingdom-wide Christian obedience that they collectively claimed was articulated through the traditional activity of councils, kings, and emperors: legislation. Reccared acknowledged the bishops' community leadership when he called for them to enact their decisions; the bishops responded with rules for governing their Christian followers. The king, in turn, issued a secular law in confirmation of the council intended to apply to his entire body of subjects. Through these acts of legislation the leaders of Iberia asserted the individual and collective obedience of every person and community in the kingdom.

Even though the visual impact of this celebration is lost to us, the skillful orchestration and narration of its ritual message renders such an apparently seamless image of harmonious Christian society that one is almost compelled to share in the bishops' boundless optimism. John of Biclar may have been wrong about peace in the East and the Persian conversion, but it is difficult to argue with his presentation of the council as a turning point. The resounding claims of governmental, religious, and political unity made in 589 were repeated in a series of church councils held during the remaining 122 years of Visigothic rule. While the participants in Toledo called upon previous great councils of the church as models for their own actions, Toledo III itself served as a precedent for seventh-century leaders giving ceremonial expression to their governing consensus, which in time came to be equated with centralized rule over the entire peninsula from the royal city, Toledo.[7] During the "Reconquista" the Catholic unification of the peninsula was envisioned in images derived from this Visigothic tradition. Indeed, the power of images of Visigothic unification

---

7. See chap. 3, n. 105.

has survived until the present in Spain: in 1989 scholars and clerics gathere
Toledo to observe the fourteenth centenary of Toledo III amid an outpouring
of newspaper articles and papal messages celebrating the moment in 589 when
"Spain was born."[8] Historians still regard Toledo III as a turning point in the
Visigothic kingdom. Yet, while this characterization is undoubtedly accurate,
the nature of the turn taken is not immediately obvious.

Fragmentation and disharmony became central facts of community life
on the Iberian Peninsula with the collapse of Roman rule in the early fifth century, which left local communities without centralized leadership. The reloca-
tion of the Visigothic kingship to the peninsula after Alaric's defeat in 507 did
not bring an end to the virtual independence of many areas. The instability
and factionalism among the Visigothic nobility during the first two-thirds of
the sixth century have since become legendary,[9] and the monarchy's efforts at
territorial consolidation were generally ineffectual. The weakening of the
Visigothic kingship after 507 eventually led to a major rebellion in Cordoba in
550 and a revolt by the noble Athanagild (551–68) in the same year. In his
effort to usurp the throne Athanagild appealed for help to the Byzantines, who
invaded in 552, and held a province in the South until 624.[10] Athanagild's
usurpation was successful, but after his death in 568 the kingdom saw a five-
month interregnum.[11] In 569 Reccared's Arian father, Leovigild (569–86), was
associated on the throne by his brother Liuva (569–72) and began a series of
campaigns to bring independent cities under Visigothic control.[12] While
Leovigild was quite successful militarily,[13] his centralizing efforts met local
resistance, which, combined with religious divisions, contributed to a rebellion
against the king led by his son Hermenegild in the early 580s.[14]

Even by 589, despite the new king's conversion, many of the conditions

---

8. From the headline to an interview with Cardinal M. González Martin, "España nació
en el III Concilio de Toledo," in the collection of commemorative material printed with the
proceedings of the centenary celebration in *Concilio III de Toledo*, 192.

9. See *LH*, 3.30, 126.

10. On the Byzantine province, see E. A. Thompson, *The Goths in Spain* (Oxford, 1969),
320–34.

11. Thompson, *Goths*, 18.

12. Leovigild was brought to the throne as a coruler by his brother Liuva (568–73), who
governed Narbonensis and possibly Tarraconensis, leaving the rest of the kingdom to Leovigild. On Liuva's death Leovigild became sole ruler.

13. John Bicl., *anno III Justini–anno III Mauricii*, 212–17.

14. Roger Collins, "Mérida and Toledo: 550–585," in *Visigothic Spain. New Approaches*,
ed. Edward James (Oxford, 1980) 215–18; and Collins, *Early Medieval Spain. Unity in Diversity 400–1000* (New York, 1983), 46–48. For other views of the rebellion, see Thompson, *Goths*,
64–87; Jocelyn N. Hillgarth, "Coins and Chronicles: Propaganda in Sixth-Century Spain and
the Byzantine Background," *Historia* 15 (1966), reprinted in *Visigothic Spain, Byzantium and
the Irish* (London, 1985); José Orlandis, *El poder real y la sucesión al trono en la monarquía
Visigoda* (Madrid, 1962), 3–12; Jacques Fontaine, "Conversion et culture chez les Wisigoths d'Espagne," *Settimane* 14 (Spoleto, 1966), reprinted in *Culture et spiritualité en Espagne du IVe au*

behind the preceding years of instability remained. Most important, it is unlikely that the independent traditions of local authorities would have evaporated in the few years since Leovigild's conquests and Hermenegild's rebellion.[15] Reccared's position as a hereditary successor compounded this longstanding obstacle to centralization. During the fifth century Visigothic kings had been, in theory, elected from the ranks of a royal family: the "Balthi." The political instability of the period after the fall of the Aquitainian kingdom, however, had brought increasing uncertainty to the question of Visigothic royal succession. Liuva and Leovigild had attempted to established a new "royal family" by associating their chosen heirs on the throne before their deaths. As a novelty in sixth-century practice, however, this offered a potential focus for what had become a tradition of noble discontent.[16] Another point of possible factionalism lay in the king's conversion. While most Arian leaders appear to have been brought over to Catholicism between 587 and 589,[17] some Arian bishops gained noble support in rebellions against the king during that period.[18] Furthermore, the territorial cohesion of the kingdom was hypothetical at best; not only did the Byzantines occupy their province in the

---

VIIe siécle (London, 1986); Luis A. García Moreno, "La coyuntura política del III Concilio de Toledo. Una historia larga y tortuosa," in *Concilio III de Toledo,* 274–79; and Walter Goffart, "Byzantine Policy in the West under Tiberius II and Maurice: The Pretenders Hermenegild and Gundovald (579–585)," *Traditio* 13 (1957).

15. On tensions between "centre and periphery" prior to Toledo III, see Collins, "Mérida and Toledo."

16. The Visigothic principles of succession are a source of some historiographical confusion. After the death of Amalaric (511–31), the last of the "Balthi," sixth-century Visigothic kings were either chosen by the nobility or seized the throne by violence. The new royal dynasty established by Liuva and Leovigild met a new round of noble opposition at the death of Reccared, introducing a new period of elective and/or usurped kingship. Generally, Visigothic hereditary successions tended to arouse noble antipathy at least when the new king was young and militarily inexperienced. Church leaders took an increasingly vocal role in promoting orderly methods of elective succession beginning with Toledo IV and reaching its most articulate expression during the career of Julian of Toledo. On the Balthi, see Herwig Wolfram, *History of the Goths* (Berkeley, 1988), 202–4. On the question of succession in general, see Orlandis, *El poder real,* 57–100, and Collins, *Early Medieval Spain,* 111–15. On the role of the church, see José Orlandis, "La Iglesia visigoda y los problemas de la sucesión al trono en el siglo VII," *Settimane* 7, reprinted in *El poder real.* On the role of Julian of Toledo, see Roger Collins, "Julian of Toledo and the Royal Succession in Late Seventh-Century Spain," in *Early Medieval Kingship,* ed. P. H. Sawyer and Ian N. Wood (Leeds, 1977).

17. Roger Collins, "¿Donde estaban los arrianos en el año 589?" in *Concilio III de Toledo.*

18. John Bicl. (*anno VI Mauricii–anno VII Mauricii,* 218) and the seventh-century author of the *VPE* (5.10.1–12.4, 233–47) recount a total of four rebellions between 587 and 590: three before Toledo III and one after, all of which, according to these authors, had a religious component, being at the same time aimed at deposing the king.

south, but the Basque territories in the northern mountains remained uncon-quered. The Franks also constituted an external menace.[19]

If the canons of Toledo III are any indication, local Catholic leaders also faced significant difficulties in maintaining order. The bishops in 589 legislated against, among other things, idolatry, infanticide, the forced marriage of women who had taken vows of chastity, the abuse of vows of penitence, and the harassment of clerics by royal agents.[20] Moreover, the long-term presence of an alternative Christian faith created conflicts among the clergy of some communities that did not disappear immediately.[21]

Given the forces standing in the way of peace, harmony, and centralized control, it is not surprising that evidence for fundamental change in leaders' attitudes and actions in the decades following the council is ambiguous. Rhetorical support for elements of the monarchy's centralizing ambitions did come from clerics like John of Biclar, Leander, and even Gregory the Great.[22] Yet in centralized rule, local governance, and ongoing cooperation between the episcopate and the royal office—the practical core of the alliance of 589—there is little testimony to any dedicated implementation of the council's man-dates or to any ongoing enthusiasm for its call for kingdom-wide unity in sup-port of the monarchy.

In order to understand the social meaning of Toledo III and its nature as a turning point in Iberian history, one must look beyond the rhetoric, cere-mony, and multilayered image of consensus projected by the council's records and by commentators like John of Biclar. For instance, one might wonder how the people outside the walls of St. Leocadia's basilica—the various rank-and-file Christians upon whom kingdom-wide consensus ultimately depended—received and perceived the good news of unification and harmony. One can imagine processions of bishops in Toledo and homilies in local churches throughout the kingdom. The only known public event in Toledo soon after the council, however, was probably less than comforting to those who wit-nessed it: Reccared, having uncovered a usurpation conspiracy led by the *dux*

---

19. In 589, the Frankish king Guntramn sent an army into the Gothic province of Narbo-nensis to support one of the rebellions against Reccared. John Bicl., *anno VII Mauricii*, 218; and *VPE*, 5.12.1–5, 247.

20. Tol. III, c. 10, 11, 16, 17, and 21. Rodríguez, 30–31.

21. Prior to Toledo III, the former Arians and Catholics apparently worked out an agree-ment allowing ex-Arian bishops to remain in their offices. See chap. 2, n. 14. The distribution of Arian church property was addressed by Tol. III, c. 9 (Rodríguez, 30), and questions con-cerning ex-Arian priests, relics, and churches were on the agenda at the Second Council of Saragossa in 592. See chap. 3, n. 67.

22. John Bicl., *anno VIII Mauricii*, 219; Leander, *Homelia* (Rodríguez, 38); Gregory the Great, *Epistola* 9.228, *MGH, Epistolarum* II, ed. Paulos Ewald and Ludo Hartmann (Berlin, 1894).

of the province, had the leader scalped, cut off his hands, and then paraded him through the streets as an example to the people of the city.[23]

It may be that Toledans were pleased to see the king acting so decisively against political disruption. John of Biclar included this episode as his last entry—almost a footnote to the council, which itself stands as the culmination of his chronicle. Perhaps for him the incident was simply a salutary sign of Reccared's strength and resolve. Yet it is difficult not to take the story, coming immediately after John's careful description of the council, as a further explanation of the council's message. Whatever his intentions, John's description of Reccared's example to the people of Toledo lays bare another meaning of the consensus celebrated by the bishops, king, and Gothic nobility. In choosing the Christian conciliar tradition as the vehicle for the celebration of their alliance, the episcopate and monarchy in the Visigothic kingdom adopted a forum that traditionally had served a dual purpose in Christian governance: church councils were not only arenas for the ritual display of consensus but also legal tribunals for settling disputes and establishing precedents for the maintenance of order.

The settlement of disputes and maintaining order generally entail some means of enforcement. When Reccared displayed his mutilated opponent to the people of Toledo, he illustrated that practical reality in particularly harsh, and exclusively secular, terms. In the eyes of the men meeting in Toledo the essential dispute they were settling was doctrinal, between the Arianism of the Goths and their king and the Catholicism of the Hispano-Romans and their episcopate. On the surface enforcement of this settlement was straightforward—there was no compromise, no middle road. The conversion of the king signified the conversion of all his nobles; Gothic opposition to the conversion, the council, the alliance with the Catholics, or the king's leadership violated the terms of the settlement. Any Arian reaction amongst the Gothic nobility against Reccared's conversion, which the episode of usurpation probably represents, was short-lived and apparently did not constitute a real threat to the new alliance.[24] Vigorous royal justice, meted out publicly, did the trick.

The men at Toledo III, however, believed that the settlement of their doctrinal dispute redressed divisions throughout their society. Consensus between the king, the Gothic nobility, and the episcopate made possible not only world peace but also the future governance of the kingdom based on principles of conciliar consensus and dispute settlement. Gothic factionalism and residual heresy were not the only obstacles standing in the way of this future. Although Reccared's display of the coercive side of Christian consensus to the people of Toledo was made at the expense of a Gothic *dux,* its message was aimed at an

23. John Bicl., *anno VII Mauricii,* 218.
24. Collins, *Early Medieval Spain,* 57; Thompson, *Goths,* 104.

audience consisting of a variegated urban population with demands on their loyalty and obedience coming from a multitude of directions that did not necessarily have anything to do with doctrine. The bishops attending the council came from similarly diverse communities and would face equally complex networks of loyalty, obedience, and conflicting interests when they returned home to implement their consensus and settle disputes. Nor would the local interests of individual bishops and their communities necessarily coincide with those of other communities or with those of the king's central authority. Each interlocking layer in the seamless image of consensus so carefully woven out of tradition and optimism at Toledo III was subject to pressures arising from those communities and from the peninsula's 150-year prior history of fragmentation and conflict. Each layer of consensus needed a corresponding means of enforcement, or the whole construct might burst at its theoretically nonexistent seams.

Countering these pressures on a symbolic level, the participants at the council found full agreement in their adoption of conciliar ceremony and the principle that doctrinal unanimity was the necessary basis for social harmony. Those aspects of the inherited Christian conciliar tradition were magisterially demonstrated by Leander and his associates. Yet the practical realities of exactly how the king or the bishops as a group or any individual bishop in any given community was to go about enforcing the settlement celebrated in Toledo—thus establishing and maintaining kingdom-wide consensus—was another question entirely. Consensual dispute settlement might ideally involve the compromise, cooperation, and community-based, noncoercive enforcement that appeal so strongly to some modern political imaginations. It is highly doubtful, however, that the men meeting in Toledo in 589, or any late antique or early medieval council participants for that matter, had such a picture of communitarian bliss in their minds as they pondered the meaning of conciliar authority in the various and collective futures of their communities and kingdom. They could hardly have been blind to the volatility of those communities and the conflicting interests and relationships of power that would militate against such a fine function for their consensus. Still, not even Reccared could cut off the hands of every dissenter. In practical terms the traditional conciliar legislative activity that symbolized the individual and collective obedience of all Christians in the kingdom also represented for the men at Toledo III a mutually agreeable means for exercising their newly shared holy authority and realizing the broadest meanings of consensus in their local communities without the use of coercive force.

Given the complexity of their conception of social consensus, the various divisive forces facing these men as they legislated, and the breadth of the authority they claimed, one might expect that their legislation would be equally complex, various, and broad. It was not. Toledo III issued only twenty-three rules, which are as a group characterized by a hesitant and narrow vision of the meaning and practice of local governance. To be sure, the legislation called upon the vastness of traditional written conciliar authority for support[25] and created a means for ascertaining the orthodoxy of every Christian in the kingdom and thus their participation in the kingdom's religious consensus.[26] The acts also included a call for yearly provincial councils to establish ongoing local conciliar governance.[27] The other rules issued, however, treat the idea of cooperation between *regnum* and *sacerdotium* very gingerly, leaving important arenas of potential conflict in local community governance ill defined and open to interpretation. The dissonance between the hesitance and narrowness of the legislation, and the grandiose ceremony and rhetoric of consensus inscribed in the council's records is one among many indications that the settlement of the doctrinal dispute between the Gothic and Hispano-Roman leaders of the kingdom was not as definitive as Leander, Reccared, John, and others might have wished. In fact, a close reading of the council's records reveals that the men meeting in Toledo held differing opinions on several central aspects of their consensus. They disagreed on the immediate significance of the settlement of their doctrinal differences, on the roles of the king and of the universal church in the events leading up to that settlement, and on the meaning of their alliance in the future governing of their kingdom.

What allowed these men to disagree on such fundamental issues while at the same time asserting their complicated vision of consensus was their choice of the Catholic conciliar tradition as the framework for expressing and implementing their putative unanimity. This tradition was much more flexible than is at first apparent in Toledo III's evocation of the holy authority associated with the eastern councils of the fourth and fifth centuries. By referring to those ecumenical councils, the men in Toledo could draw implicit parallels between empire-wide and kingdom-wide consensus and between Roman emperors and Reccared. At the same time, however, church leaders in sixth-century Iberia also had available to them a much more fluid set of precedents for local conciliar governance, which for many years had been open to interpretation and responsive to local expedience. This combination of authority and flexibility made the conciliar tradition, in theory at least, adaptable to the varying and potentially conflictual interests of the men at the council and thus an almost ideal vehicle for the expression of Toledo III's vision of kingdom-wide and local Christian consensus.

In practice, however, conciliar authority had been exercised only inter-

---

25. Tol. III, c. 1. Rodríguez, 29.
26. Tol. III, c. 2. Rodríguez, 29.
27. Tol. III, c. 18. Rodríguez, 31–32.

mittently in sixth-century Iberia prior to 589. During that period the sporadic nature of conciliar activity influenced the exercise of holy authority in local communities in important, and sometimes contradictory, ways. In the early 580s the issues were further complicated by increasing doctrinal hostilities and conflicts between Arian and Catholic bishops and congregations. By 589 the attitudes and experiences of local bishops in regards to conciliar theology and practice were far more complex than is immediately evident in the triumphant references to the transcendent authority of Catholic conciliar tradition that permeate the records and ceremony of Toledo III. In order to understand a fuller range of the practical and conceptual difficulties facing Iberian consensus builders in 589, as well as some of the more immediate forces that informed their choice of the conciliar framework for their alliance, it is useful to look briefly at the nature of local conciliar governance in sixth-century Iberia and at the changing ideas and circumstances in the individual authority of local bishops in the decade before Toledo III.

Sixth-Century Conciliar Tradition

The councils of the Catholic Church derived their institutional origin from the "Apostolic Synod" of Jerusalem (c. 52 C.E.).[28] The decisions of this assembly, which appear in Acts XV, 23–29, reflect the apostles' conviction that the Holy Spirit was present in their council and their belief that this presence gave divine authority to their judgment. In a letter to the Christians in Antioch they prefaced their decisions with the announcement that "it has seemed good to the Holy Spirit and to us to lay no further burden upon you than these necessary things."

Through the first centuries of Christianity's development the presence of the Holy Spirit at assemblies of church leaders remained a central element in the conciliar tradition. It provided the key vehicle for assertions of divine guidance in the promulgation of conciliar acts. It was through the transmission of this legislation that Iberian leaders received their most intimate knowledge of what it was that "the holy fathers, filled with the spirit of God, [had] sanctioned" in the distant past.[29] From the fifth century on, various editors gath-

---

28. Charles J. Hefele, *A History of the Councils of the Church*, vol. 1 (1895; reprint, New York, 1972), 1.

29. Tol. III, c. 1: "quod sancti patres spiritu Dei pleni sanxerunt." Rodríguez, 29. Collections of the canons of earlier councils constituted a primary source of authority for western church leaders, especially after the mid-fifth century. For general background on canonical collections, see Gerard Fransen, *Les collections canoniques* (Brepols, 1975); on their relationship to ideas about authority and tradition, especially in the fifth and sixth centuries, see Karl Morrison, *Tradition and Authority in the Western Church* (Princeton, 1969), 85–87.

ered canons into collections, creating a cumulative authority out of individual acts that came to be seen as nearly equal to that of Holy Scripture. For sixth-century Iberian leaders this authority included not only the acts of the great councils but also the decisions of previous provincial councils from their own territory as well as from some eastern provinces, Gaul, and North Africa.

Conciliar governance, however, had never been institutionalized anywhere in the West as an ongoing, regular means of dispute settlement or of maintaining religious consensus. In fact, perhaps the most consistent element in the church's conciliar tradition during this period was its lack of clear definition, particularly in regards to provincial councils. In theory, during the years of the Roman Empire, general, or ecumenical, councils assembled the bishops of the entire church and were held only on extraordinary occasions of great doctrinal import. Early canons called for provincial episcopates to hold regular provincial councils under the leadership of the metropolitan bishops to deal with local issues and clerical discipline.[30] The fall of the empire in the West, however, blurred this distinction, creating an intermediate level of councils: gatherings of the bishops of an entire kingdom or, as in the case of Merovingian Gaul, more than one kingdom.[31] Kingdom-wide councils were never held regularly, and provincial councils were particularly erratic and infrequent. Their form and function in most of early medieval western Europe were, as far as the few records show, open to various interpretations according to time, place, and relations with royal or local secular authorities.[32]

The content of conciliar decisions, or the meaning of any individual canon, was also traditionally open to interpretation. For many years the canonical status of the acts of the great councils—their acceptance as possessing universally agreed-upon divine authorization—had been open to a certain amount of interpretation, particularly by the pope but also by individual bishops and, under certain circumstances, by secular powers.[33] Controversies over the doctrinal decisions of ecumenical councils were well-known in Iberia dur-

---

30. Nicaea (325), c. 5; Antioch (341), c. 15 and 20; Carthage IV (398), c. 25, 28, and 29; Chalcedon (451), c. 19. For a brief discussion on the origins of provincial councils, see Odette Pontal, *Clercs et laïcs au Moyen Âge d'après les statuts synodaux* (Paris, 1990), 9–13.

31. For records of Merovingian councils, see *Les canons des conciles mérovingiens (VIe–VIIe siècle)*, ed. Jean Gaudemet and Brigitte Basdevant, 2 vols., Sources Chrétiennes 353 (Paris, 1989). See intro., n. 69.

32. See Pontal, *Clercs et laïcs*, 13–15; Basdevant, "Les évêques," 2.

33. See Morrison, *Tradition and Authority*, 77. From the fourth century, he says, church tradition in general was faced with "new patterns of authority"—especially in temporal government and hierarchic order. The lack of a rationalization for how these different elements should function produced different solutions, one of which he labels "universality in particularism" and describes in these words: "It held, in effect, that each bishop was the final judge of true faith and practice in his see. He could decide whether, for his church, decrees of specific councils were 'oecumenical' (i.e., orthodox) or heretical." On the conflict between papal discretion and tradition in general, see 77–110.

ing the sixth century.[34] Canons originating in provincial councils were less likely to provoke widely publicized controversies. While many of these councils were concerned with local heresies,[35] more often they were concerned with questions of clerical discipline, liturgical uniformity, the maintenance of lay obedience, and episcopal prerogatives in the daily governance of local churches. While it is difficult to document individual interpretations of the canonicity of these more local and practical decisions, a look at the Iberian provincial conciliar records for the sixth century prior to 589 shows that many clerics from parish priests to the episcopate were either ignorant of or disobedient to any number of these "institutes of the ancient canons."

While some areas of the West during some periods, such as North Africa before the Vandal invasion and Gaul after Clovis's conversion, saw relatively intensive conciliar activity, this was not the case in sixth-century Iberia prior to 589. We have the records of only nine provincial councils during that period: one in Narbonensis, prior to the Visigoths' loss of their Gallic kingdom; four in Tarraconensis; two in Cartaginiensis; and two in the Suevic kingdom of Galicia.[36] It is quite likely that these councils do not represent the entirety of sixth-century Iberian conciliar activity, yet it is still possible to draw some conclusions from the records that survive on the nature of a "living" Iberian conciliar tradition—that is, how local decisions were interpreted in local communities and how the actual practice of provincial councils might have affected the exercise of local ecclesiastic authority and thus the ideas of the men at Toledo III.

The records that do exist are rather vague about the purpose of the gatherings they describe. Most make no mention of the circumstances surrounding their convocation nor of any general theory or rules on conciliar governance

---

34. During the sixth century in the West the doctrinal decisions of the four great ecumenical councils (Nicaea, Constantinople, Ephesus, and Chalcedon) assumed a position of unassailable authority. However, the unquestionable canonicity of the Council of Chalcedon only became solidified following more than a century of controversy over the christological doctrine authorized there. This doctrinal struggle was played out mainly in the East, but the interference of the emperor Justinian had repercussions in the western churches, and the acceptance of Chalcedon as definitive eventually involved the implicit rejection of a fifth ecumenical council: the Council of Constantinople, held in 553. For a narrative account of this debate and its consequences in the West, see Herrin, *The Formation of Western Christendom* (Princeton, 1987), 106–25. For knowledge of this dispute in the Visigothic kingdom, see Hillgarth, "Coins and Chronicles," 487.

35. See, e.g., on the Donatist heresy in North Africa, the Fifth through Fifteenth Councils of Carthage, held during the first decade of the fifth century (summarized in Hefele, *History of the Councils*, 425–44); the Sixteenth Council of Carthage of 418 (a pluriprovincial council, including some prelates from Spain), dealing with Pelagianism (Hefele, 458–62); the Council of Saragossa in 380, the Council of Bordeaux in 383, and the Council of Toledo held in 397, against Priscillianism (Hefele, 292, 383, and 419).

36. See intro., n. 55.

or procedure.[37] The predominant themes in all these records are like those of other early medieval provincial councils: first, the discipline of lower clergy in their relations with women, liturgical duties, church property rights, stipends, ordination, and obedience to bishops; and, second, the prerogatives and duties of bishops in such areas as decisions about excommunication and reconciliation, dividing property, receiving gifts, disciplining lower clerics, respecting the rights of abbots and other bishops (particularly metropolitan bishops), and supervising parochial churches. While the issues involved and the ultimate approaches to these matters differed widely, many of the decisions are specific enough to indicate that they were made in response to particular incidents or disputes. Thus, it is clear that these intermittent provincial councils served in part as tribunals for settling specific clerical disputes arising out of the distribution of powers, rights, and duties within the church's hierarchy, particularly in episcopal control over lower clergy.

Numerous references to the "ancient canons," or even to specific previous councils, make it clear that the bishops at most of these councils had access to at least some decisions of the past as they settled the disputes of the present.[38] One wonders, however, how often this cumulative authority was actually consulted in the day-to-day life of ecclesiastic communities as particular squabbles and incidents of insubordination arose. A series of canons from three councils, all dealing with the same problem, indicates that existing canonical legislation was not even capable of ordering an event inevitably repeated in all dioceses: the death of the bishop. Apparently, a bishop's demise could open a window of opportunity for lower clerics and the dead man's relatives to loot the episcopal palace.

The problem first appears in the sixth-century records at the Council of Tarragona, held in 517. Here the procedures laid out were relatively simple: when a bishop died intestate, after his burial the local priests and deacons were to make an inventory of all the items in the house, "from the smallest to the largest," so that anyone who had taken anything would be found out and forced to make restitution "as if it were a matter of theft."[39] About thirty years later, however, this rule, or others like it, did not prevent some of the lower clergy in an unidentified diocese in the same province from "savagely invading the episcopal residence and seizing" everything they could find.[40] In 546 the

---

37. The only explicit description of the competence of church councils occurs in the last of this series, Braga II. See n. 62 of this chapter.

38. See, e.g., Tarragona, preamble and c. 2; Gerona, c. 7; Tol. II, c. 3; Lérida, c. 16. *La colección*, 271, 273, 288, 350, and 307.

39. Tarragona, c. 12: "a minimo usque ad maximum . . . ita tamen si quis exinde uel praesumpsisse uel occulte fuerit tulisse conuictus, secundum furti tenorem restituat uniuersa." *La colección*, 279.

40. Lérida, c. 16: "immaniter quae in domo pontificali reperiuntur inuadant et abradant." *La colección*, 307.

Council of Lérida issued a much more detailed set of guidelines for dealing with the problem. The bishops at this council noted that the "ancient authority of the canons [had] not kept completely silent in regards to this affair."[41] The fear of discipline and the provisions of the previous canons, however, had not contained the avarice of the looters involved, making it necessary to define more detailed guidelines. Now, according to the canon, on the death of a bishop, "or in his last moments,"[42] the cleric in charge of the house was to choose one or two "honored persons" to help him protect the goods until the new bishop arrived, in the meantime distributing the customary "sustenance" to the clergy in residence.[43] The new prelate would then distribute the goods as his predecessor had wished.

Soon after this council it seems that a bishop died in another province, this time with particularly dire consequences. This death had apparently provided the opportunity for the lower clergy and the relatives of the deceased to descend on the episcopal estate and take books, ornaments, tableware, crops, and animals, leaving the new bishop to "painfully enter into the possession of an empty ecclesiastic residence."[44] In 549, again citing canonical precedent,[45] the Council of Valencia issued three canons on the subject.[46] The bishops laid out procedures even more complex than those outlined at Lérida, in order to "put an end to the pillage and plunder of avaricious clerics"[47] and to ensure that the dead bishops' relatives should wait until the metropolitan bishop distinguished between the hereditary and ecclesiastic goods on the estate before seizing anything as family property. The bishop closest to the dead man's diocese was to rush to the scene, take an inventory, and present it to the metropolitan, who would then choose an interim custodian until the next bishop could be ordained. All claims by relatives were to be brought before the metropolitan. Anyone who disdained the "authority of the canons" and disobeyed these provisions was to be threatened by both the metropolitan and the other provincial bishops until they restored what they had taken.[48]

Obviously, the clerics involved in the cases at Lérida and Valencia had not consulted the "authority of ancient canons" when it became clear that their bishop was about to die, and it seems doubtful that doing so would have

---

41. Lérida, c. 16: "de re huiuscemodi . . . prisca auctoritas canonum nequaquam siluerit." *La colección,* 306–07.

42. Lérida, c. 16: "in supremis agente." *La colección,* 307.

43. Lérida, c. 16: "cum . . . uno uel duobus fidelissimis . . . debeat . . . clericis consueta alimonia administrare." *La colección,* 308.

44. Valencia, c. 2: "ad uacuum ecclesiae domum futurus pontifex non sine dolore succedat." *La colección,* 316–17.

45. The Council of Riez (439), c. 5 and 6.

46. Valencia, c. 2, 3, and 4. *La colección,* 316–19.

47. Valencia, c. 2: "ne quid . . . inhiantium clericorum subuersioni uel direptioni iam liceat." *La colección,* 316.

48. Valencia, c. 2: "canonum auctoritate." *La colección,* 315.

prevented the incidents. The incremental elaboration of procedures in this sequence of canons reveals a complex array of conflicting interests, rights, and emotions that the bare bones of canonical precedent could not adequately contain. For instance, while the canons decry the avarice of the plunderers, it is also clear that the death of a bishop could deprive lower clerics of their sustenance; hence, the provisions in these decisions to make sure that any custodian in charge of the episcopal estate made sure to provide the lower clergy with their customary stipends. A lack of clear distinctions between hereditary and ecclesiastic property when a bishop died intestate might encourage a bishop's family to seize church goods illegally, but, at the same time, their legitimate rights had to be ascertained and respected by a suitably powerful authority—at Valencia, the metropolitan.

Resentment and disputes among the clerical members of the dead man's household eventually seem to have made it necessary for outside supervisors to be brought in. Tarragona left the management of the estate to unidentified and presumably local "priests and deacons."[49] At Lérida the bishops provided that in the future the cleric left in charge would choose "honored" helpers until the newly ordained bishop arrived, who would then be informed about which clerics had "responded faithfully to the orders of his antecessor."[50] One can almost feel the hostilities of the immediate case in the canon's final provision that anyone who had taken anything from the bishop's residence before the promulgation of the rule was to be excommunicated, because it wasn't fair that those who had refrained from looting should then be "tormented" with the contempt of those who had "only busied themselves with their own gain."[51] Valencia decided that the matter should be put immediately into the hands of a series of outside supervisors under the oversight of the metropolitan. Yet outsiders were not necessarily disinterested, and the volatility of the situation could extend to the funeral itself, where provincial bishops gathered. Valencia also issued provisions concerning the ordering of those affairs—which included carrying out the dead bishop's wishes—because the bishops coming to the funerals would take offense if they were left waiting too long for their fellow prelates to arrive.[52]

It cannot be known if these decisions resolved the specific conflicts they addressed. Both Lérida and Valencia invoked retroactive punishments for people who had committed the crime of looting in the past—presumably in refer-

---

49. Tarragona, c. 12: "presbyteris et diaconibus." *La colección*, 279.
50. Lérida, c. 16: "decessoris sui fideliter paruisse." *La colección*, 308.
51. Lérida, c. 16: "Quia durum est ut ii quos constat in seruitio Domini . . . illorum, qui suarum rerum incubatores uel utilitatibus seruientes atque uacantes fuisse noscuntur, despectibus aliquatenus crucientur." *La colección*, 309.
52. Valencia, c. 4. *La colección*, 318–19.

ence to the immediate cases at hand. Whether or not those punishments were effectively enforced, it is clear that the bishops at these councils were at least as interested in establishing procedures that would prevent future incidents of abuse as they were in settling the disputes of the past. It was this concern that led to the increasingly detailed instructions. Yet the canons at Lérida and Valencia both acknowledged the fact that canonical authority was frequently disdained and neglected—another recurring theme in conciliar legislation. As the bishops decided these and other cases, they were carefully outlining procedures and setting precedents that were not likely to be followed in the future.

Without a periodic ceremonial and spiritual reiteration of the larger meanings behind provincial conciliar governance—that is, the authority of episcopal consensus, the Holy Spirit, and the cumulative wisdom of the canonical compilations—the councils' role in the maintenance of order in the churches must have been overwhelmingly focused upon specific applications in immediate local ecclesiastic conflicts. Their decisions would be carefully preserved by the parties involved in individual disputes—for instance, the successors, relatives, and episcopal colleagues of dead bishops—who were interested in maintaining the rights assigned to them. The rules and procedures established at one council might also be consulted by later councils as they decided new cases. Thus, the conciliar tradition would have enjoyed an ongoing but almost purely practical, localized, and backward-looking continuity in the archives of the people associated with past cases and in the infrequent moments when councils grappled with new disputes. In order for conciliar precedents to have achieved a forward-looking, preventive capacity, whereby their authority would actually prevent disruptions and contain the conflicting loyalties and interests in local clerical communities, they would have had to have been backed up by an effective apparatus of education and supervision, along with the frequent ceremonial affirmation of those communities' Christian consensus through the regular convocation of councils. These supports for conciliar authority were clearly lacking in sixth-century Iberia.

Even if the number of unrecorded councils during this period were greater than the number of recorded ones, it is clear that interruptions in continuity was one of the central and most consistent characteristics of the provincial conciliar tradition in all areas. Only two provinces, Tarraconensis and Galicia, provide records of councils held in close succession during this period.[53] At the same time, the few extant records show that continuity did exist in the profession of an ongoing belief in the efficacy of conciliar authority. The records that remain reassert that authority unquestioningly. The knowledge that a tran-

---

53. In Tarraconensis, such a sequence occurred twice during this period, with Tarragona (516) and Gerona (517) and with Barcelona I (540) and Lérida (546). In Galicia, the first two councils of Braga were held eleven years apart, in 561 and 572.

scendent source of collective episcopal authority existed in the conciliar tradition seems to have lurked in the backs of bishops' minds, ready to reassert itself at sporadic moments in widely varying geographical areas.[54] The very intermittence of those moments, however, meant that most of those bishops lacked any previous personal experience of conciliar ceremony or decision making, leading to noticeable variety in the content, tone, and elaboration of the different records.

Although the predominant theme in all the councils was clerical discipline and episcopal prerogative, the participants at these councils seem to have seen their moments on the conciliar stage quite differently. For instance, one council, Lérida, stands out for its unusual concern with lay behavior. Three councils took up issues of heresy, while others register no concern with the matter, despite the fact that most of these councils took place under heretical kings.[55] Some councils served as the platforms for lengthy speeches by apparently overbearing prelates. For instance, at the Second Council of Toledo, in 527, the provincial metropolitan, a certain Montanus, used the opportunity for a lengthy diatribe against a group of priests at the gathering, whom he accused of willful insubordination against their bishops, violating the interests of the king, and heresy.[56] The elaborate records of this council, which also contain a letter from Montanus to a bishop in another province (implying that the recipient was fostering heresy),[57] contrast sharply with other much more businesslike records.

Perhaps the most unusual records from this period are those from Galicia: the First and Second Councils of Braga, held in 561 and 572.[58] In the years

---

54. Sometimes, these moments coincided with the presence of, or at the order of, a cooperative secular authority. In such cases, the bishops pointed out that fact. See, e.g., Tol. II, c. 5 (*La colección,* 354); Braga I, prologue, and Braga II, prologue (Vives, 65 and 78). Lérida and Valencia merely note the regnal year of the king (in both cases, Theodoric, also known as Theudis [531–48]). *La colección,* 299 and 314.

55. Of these nine councils, only Braga I and II were held under Catholic kings. Priscillianism was on the agenda at Toledo II and Braga I; an unnamed heresy, most likely Arianism, was addressed at Lérida.

56. *La colección,* 356–63.

57. *La colección,* 363–66.

58. Of all the regions of the Iberian peninsula in the sixth century, the Galician church showed the clearest tendencies toward provincially based ecclesiastic unification. The province also possessed perhaps the most distinct regional politico-cultural identity at that time. Historically, Galicia had been set off from the rest of the peninsula; Roman influence had been much lighter there than in the south and east, and the Suevic kingdom had encouraged a distinct political identity. The province had also been the one most heavily influenced by the Priscillianist heresy, which arose in the later fourth century. On the origin and repression of Priscillianism in the later fourth and fifth centuries, see Henry Chadwick, *Priscillian of Avila: the Occult and the Charismatic in the Early Church* (Oxford, 1976); and Raymond Van Dam, *Leadership and Community in Late Antique Gaul* (Berkeley, 1985), 88–114. A sensitivity to this particular brand of heterodoxy remained strong in the area until the later sixth century.

around 550, under unclear circumstances, the Suevic kings of Galicia converted from Arianism to Catholicism.[59] Convened by the newly converted kings, these councils also coincide with the episcopacy of Martin of Braga. The writings of this Pannonian immigrant have survived to our own time; in his own era he was well-known enough to appear in the works of Gregory of Tours.[60] The detailed description of the procedures in these councils indicate something of a renaissance in conciliar theory in Galicia during the 560s and 570s. Under the auspices of their newly orthodox kingship the Galician episcopate eagerly accepted the instructions of an educated eastern prelate. Yet the records also indicate how much instruction they needed in order to overcome decades of conciliar inactivity.

Both councils included lengthy ceremonial readings of canonical collections, along with other materials deemed appropriate for the business at hand.[61] At each council the presiding bishop gave speeches describing the purpose of councils and the principles by which the bishops should reach their decisions. For instance, Martin of Braga, in a speech opening the council held in 572, instructed the bishops in detail on the difference between general councils, which he said were held for the "unity of correct faith," and provincial councils, which were meant "to put an end to contentions or to correct the negligence of some people."[62] He went on to call for the bishops to use the "testimony" of Scripture and of ancient canons to inform their "common consensus" so that they might correct with "rational judgment" anything that "through ignorance or negligence is found reprehensible in us."[63] Both councils emphatically underlined the authority of canonical precedent. The last canon issued in 561 affirmed all "the precepts of the ancient canons," calling

59. See E. A. Thompson, "Conversion of the Spanish Suevi to Catholicism," in *Visigothic Spain. New Approaches;* and Fontaine, "Conversion et culture," 95–96.

60. Gregory of Tours, *de virtutibus Martini,* 1.2, ed. Bruno Krusch, *MGH, Scriptores rerum merovingicarum* I (1885); and *LH,* 5.37, 243. See Thompson, "Conversion of the Suevi," 83–84.

61. In 561 the current metropolitan, Lucretius, opened the council with a speech against the Priscillianist heresy, which included the reading of a rule of faith generated in the fifth century by Pope Leo I (440–61). The bishops then issued seventeen anathemas against Priscillianism. Vives, 67–69. In 572 the canons of the previous Bragan council were read out before the council, "so that their utility will be more easily recalled to memory" (ut possit evidentius in memoriam revocari). Vives, 79. At this council Martin of Braga also had read aloud the instructions to priests by the "prince of apostles" (princeps apostolorum)—1 Peter 5.1–4—as an inspiration for the bishops to take measures to guide their own behavior. Vives, 80. The council went on to issue ten canons dealing mainly with the duties of bishops. Vives, 83–85.

62. Braga II, preamble: "pro unitate rectae fidei . . . pro resecandis contemtionibus vel emendandis aliquorum negligentiis colligerunt." Vives, 79.

63. Braga II, preamble: "per ignorantiam aut per negligentiam reprehensibile invenitur in nobis recurrentes ad testimonia sanctarum scribturarum vel antiquorum canonum instituta adhibite conmuni consensu omnia quae displicuerint rationabili iudicio corrigamus." Vives, 79.

for the ousting from office of any cleric who should transgress them.[64] In 572 Martin selected for inclusion in the records eighty-four canons from eastern councils. Martin translated, simplified, and organized for quick reference these canons, which covered a wide variety of both clerical and lay issues.[65]

The Galician councils illustrate a number of the obstacles to ongoing conciliar practice and the application of canonical precedent generally in sixth-century Iberia. The heavy emphasis these councils placed on the ceremonial reading of conciliar records, the conscientious instructions on precedent and practice, the elaborate explanations of the duties and responsibilities of councils, and the care Martin gave to making the "obscurities" of his eastern canons accessible to the Galician bishops constitute careful lessons on conciliar authority. The bishops of Galicia were not familiar with the decisions of previous councils. They did not know the traditional purposes of general or provincial councils. They needed instruction on how to reach their decisions, and their canonical collections—at least those from the east—were badly translated, disorganized, and filled with scribal errors. The simple fact that the bishops in 572 needed to have the decisions of the council of 561 read out loud to refresh their memories indicates that even those recent decisions had not become a part of their regular diocesan duties. Martin presumably intended that his instructions should establish an expanded competence for conciliar practice in Galicia, one that would reach beyond the settlement of immediate disputes into the realm of ongoing episcopal consensus and the consultation of precedents in order to prevent disruption. It is doubtful, however, that his efforts overcame the obstacles they faced. There are records of only two councils in Galicia during his episcopacy[66] and of only one more council in the province between 572 and the end of the Visigothic kingdom: the Third Council of Braga in 675.

Thus, the sixth-century Iberian provincial conciliar tradition was characterized by a combination of authority, interruption, and local specificity. This combination allowed considerable leeway for variety in interpretations of the competence and meaning of councils at the infrequent moments when bishops actually met. Whatever circumstances made it possible for these meetings to occur probably included a period of ascendence in the moral or material authority of the provincial episcopate—as was the case in Galicia under its Catholic kings and Martin's leadership—making it possible to enforce the settlements of specific disputes. When given the opportunity and some hope of effective enforcement, local bishops would gather and invoke the authority of

---

64. Braga I, c. 22: "praecepta antiquorum canonum." Vives, 76.

65. Vives, 86–106.

66. Thompson ("Conversion of the Suevi," 90–91) argues that another Galician council was held in Lugo in 569, for which the records do not survive.

their conciliar consensus in an expedient response to local circumstances. Yet the infrequency of the meetings and the lack of personal experience on the part of most bishops made it impossible to maintain the decisions of previous councils as an independent and ongoing source of holy authority applicable to or enforceable in the day-to-day life of local communities. For individual bishops faced with the conflicting interests of their lower clergy and lay constituencies, the potentially transcendent authority of the church's entire conciliar tradition remained for the most part confined, but not forgotten, in frequently inaccessible compilations of canonical precedent.

Masona, Sunna, and the Holy Spirit

It is almost certain that none of the prelates present in Toledo in 589 had participated in any previous councils. The records of the last provincial council before that date, Braga II in 572, have no signatures in common with those from Toledo III.[67] Aside from the councils in Galicia, there appear to have been no councils held in the kingdom since 549.[68] These men brought with them to Toledo an awareness of the potential for increased authority and community concord at hand, but at the same time they probably knew that councils had to this point been an imperfect and not very reliable tool in local ecclesiastic governance. They were undoubtedly receptive to the ideals of consensual, collective episcopal authority—particularly in as much as it would bolster their power to order their communities through the application of canonical precedents. In their personal experience, however, holy authority—including the power to settle disputes and administer divine justice—had been a predominantly individual affair.

While willing to be educated on the meaning of Christian consensus, collective episcopal authority, and the new alliance, the Catholic bishops of the kingdom came to the council as individuals involved in a long-standing dispute, each with his own specific grievances based in the experiences of his

---

67. Nor are Martin or the councils in Braga mentioned in the records of Toledo III or by John of Biclar. Thompson ("Conversion of the Suevi," 89) remarks upon these omissions as "surprising." Alberto Ferreiro ("The Omission of St. Martin of Braga in John of Biclaro's *Chronica* and the Third Council of Toledo," *Los Visigodos, historia y civilización*, Antigüedad y Christianismo 3, [Murcia, 1986]) argues that these omissions are to be expected, given the agendas of both John and Toledo III, which were focused on the unification of the Iberian peninsula. In any case, Martin of Braga and these Bragan councils do not seem to have transmitted any conciliar knowledge to the bishops in the subsequent decades. Martin of Braga does not reappear in the Iberian sources until Isidore of Seville's *de viris illustribus*, 22, *El "de viris illustribus" de Isidoro de Sevilla*, ed. Carmen Codoñer Merino (Salamanca, 1964), 145–46. This work was written between 615 and 618.

68. Thompson, *Goths*, 35–36.

community and each expecting a beneficial settlement. The records of Toledo III make a general reference to the disruptive role of Arian "patronage" in individual churches "throughout the Spains."[69] Although the passage gives little detail on the exact nature of these problems, one can assume that the presence of Arian communities enjoying the support of an Arian kingship had periodically challenged, and thus molded, the individual holy authority of some local Catholic bishops. These bishops' status as disputants and their expectations about their judicial roles in defining a full settlement with the Arians constitute a context for understanding the disagreements at Toledo III that is as important as the bishops' conceptions of conciliar, or collective, episcopal justice.

Unfortunately, the Iberian sources for the sixth century make it difficult to generalize about such issues. There is only one detailed narrative source available for the activities of a sixth-century Iberian bishop: the *Vitas patrum sanctorum emeritensium*,[70] an anonymous work that focuses on Masona of Mérida, the metropolitan of Lusitania from c. 570 to c. 600.[71] The author, probably a deacon in Mérida during the mid-seventh century,[72] described the experiences of a number of bishops and monks in sixth- and seventh-century Mérida. According to his preface, the author's purpose was to prove the truth of the miracles related in Gregory the Great's *Dialogues* by showing that similar events had occurred in Mérida in "our own times."[73] For all intents and purposes the work is hagiographical and as such contains a series of highly stylized characters and interchanges that play on contemporary expectations for the behavior of stereotypical saints and sinners. The author, however, drew heavily on oral tradition, and his descriptions of Masona's activities reflect the highly charged atmosphere of the decade prior to Toledo III.[74] The account illustrates the potential for tension and contradiction in individual bishops' judicial roles and ideas about dispute settlement before the Goths' conversion to Catholicism.

---

69. Tol. III, c. 1: "per Hispaniarum ecclesias . . . omnis excessus haeresis foueretur patrocinio." Rodríguez, 29. See chap. 2, at n. 61.

70. *The Lives of the Fathers of Merida* (*VPE*). Another critical edition is that of Antonio Maya Sánchez, published under the title *Vitas Sanctorum Patrum Emeretensium*, Corpus Christianorum, Series Latina CXVI (Turnhout, 1992). Except where noted, I use Garvin's English translations. The *VPE* is also translated into English by A. T. Fear, *Lives of the Visigothic Fathers* (Liverpool, 1997).

71. On the dates for Masona's episcopacy, see Garvin, commentary, *VPE*, 426–29.

72. On the debates over the dating and authorship of the *VPE*, see Garvin, introduction, *VPE*, 1–6; and Fear, introduction, *Lives of the Visigothic Fathers*, xxx–xxxi.

73. *VPE*, "Praefatio" 3: "hodiernis temporibus," 137.

74. The *VPE* has been mined extensively and very successfully by modern historians, not only for details of the conflicts between the various characters but also for more general aspects of the social structure and relationships in sixth-century Mérida. See, e.g., Thompson, *Goths*, 78–80; Collins, "Mérida and Toledo"; and Collins, *Early Medieval Spain*, 51–54.

At some point around 580 the Arian king Leovigild began a struggle with Masona, a Catholic Goth, over the privileges of the Arian community in Mérida.[75] According to the *Vitas,* in the course of this drawn-out confrontation Leovigild appointed a new bishop for the Arian community in Mérida, an aggressive man by the name of Sunna. After seizing a number of Catholic churches, along with their privileges, Sunna turned his sights on the basilica of Mérida's patron saint Eulalia. When the Catholic community, led by their bishop, refused to give up the property, Sunna submitted written accusations against Masona to the king and suggested that Leovigild seize the basilica by royal decree. Rejecting this advice, the king instead issued a decree that called for a hearing of the dispute before a group of judges, the majority of whom, according to the *Vitas,* were "patrons" of the Arian "party."[76] Despite this disadvantage, Masona agreed to the hearing, and he and Sunna made their respective cases before the panel, which then decided in favor of the Catholic community.

Apparently, in dealing with this altercation Leovigild was striving for some semblance of judicial impartiality. He was not officially a participant in the dispute, but he seems to have felt obligated by expectations of objectivity to turn the case over to a group of judges for resolution. Perhaps his ties to Sunna made it impossible for him to assume the role of a disinterested judge in such a volatile community dispute.[77] Moreover, the king chose his judges with at least a gesture toward equity. While the *Vitas* complains that the members of the tribunal were predominantly "patrons" of the Arians, it does not assert that these men actually were Arians, and, since the work makes it clear that they constituted a majority, one can assume that the panel also included a minority of pro-Catholics. The Catholic community shared Leovigild's concern with impartiality. While the *Vitas* accuses the judges of partisanship, calling them "perverse mediators,"[78] its emphasis on their bias indicates a sentiment that the king was violating accepted principles of impartial justice, making Masona's victory all the more praiseworthy.

Masona may indeed deserve praise for overcoming a stacked panel, but it does seem that Leovigild went out of his way to satisfy all the participants' expectations of fairness. The situation was complex: because Masona and

---

75. The dating of these episodes is vague. The only clearly dated event in Leovigild's efforts to promote Arianism, of which the struggle with Masona was a part, is the king's Arian council in 580. See Collins, *Early Medieval Spain,* 50; and n. 117 of this chapter.

76. *VPE,* 5.5.13: "fautores Arrianae partis," 205.

77. Collins (*Early Medieval Spain,* 51–52) cites this episode as illustrating the "practical workings of the restrictions of the [Visigothic] law on the arbitrary use of royal authority," as well as defining "the limits of royal power over local autonomy" in the kingdom.

78. *VPE,* 5.5.17: "mediatores perversi." Garvin (207) translates this as "perverse partisans."

Sunna represented competing religious communities, what was essentially an ecclesiastic dispute had to be decided by a secular court.[79] Apparently recognizing that in these circumstances finding an acceptably impartial adjudicator was impossible, the king balanced the pro-Arian majority of judges with a decidedly pro-Catholic venue: he called for the hearing to be held in Masona's residence.[80] Finally, he ensured that the case would be decided if not by impartial adjudicators then by appealing to perhaps the only available judicial principles shared by all involved: he ordered that both disputants "fortify and back up whatever claims each one made by arguments drawn from the books of Holy Scripture."[81] Masona's command of this legal idiom was apparently overwhelming. Sunna's "scabrous"[82] speeches were no match for the Catholic bishop's oratory, and, despite their bias, the judges were won over.

While all the parties seem to have expected judicial fairness and impartiality, no one, including the popular Catholic bishop, could serve as a mutually accepted mediator or force for compromise. Both bishops acted as advocates for their respective communities. Each man came to the hearing with large crowds of vocal supporters, prepared to carry on a "mighty verbal struggle" with the other.[83] The judges may have been convinced by Masona's scriptural arguments, but they were probably equally influenced by the presence of his impassioned congregation, who after winning the decision paraded noisily through the streets to claim their saint's basilica.[84]

If one accepts the *Vitas* as representing the views of these Catholics, it is apparent that they attributed their advocate's victory to two aspects of his individual holy authority. First of all, unlike the hysterical Sunna, Masona knew how to act. Before the hearing began, while the disrespectfully late Arian bishop kept the Catholics waiting for his arrival, Masona reassured the faithful with his "joyful countenance" and confident exhortations.[85] After Sunna, "puffed up with arrogant pride,"[86] made a splashy entrance in the company of the tainted judges and a throng of Arian supporters, Masona displayed "his

79. The jurisdictional lines between ecclesiastic and secular justice were often blurred during this period. On Gaul, see Edward James, "*Beati Pacifici*: Bishops and the Law in Sixth-Century Gaul," in *Disputes and Settlements. Law and Human Relations in the West*, ed. John Bossy (Cambridge, 1983), 30–31.

80. *VPE*, 5.5.9, 205.

81. *VPE*, 5.5.9: "de sanctarum scripturarum voluminibus quaeque ab eis essent dicta prolatis testimoniis adstruerent vel roborarent," 205.

82. *VPE*, 5.5.14: "scabra," 207.

83. *VPE*, 5.5.15: "verborum ingens . . . certamen," 207.

84. *VPE*, 5.5.22, 209.

85. *VPE*, 5.5.12: "vultus sui iocunditate," 205. Episcopal tardiness seems to have been a particularly provocative affront. See the measures taken to prevent late arrivals at episcopal funerals at Valencia, n. 52 of this chapter.

86. *VPE*, 5.5.13: "turgidusque fastu superbiae," 205.

usual dignity and good judgment, pointedly remaining silent with his eyes fixed upon heaven."[87] Foolishly jumping into the breach, Sunna opened the debate with "strident, harsh," and "insolent" words, allowing Masona to display his contrasting patience, gentility, and sweetness when he in turn "brilliantly set forth the whole truth."[88] Sunna was eventually silenced by this "learned exposition"[89] and, as a final signal of his gracelessness, blushed. At this point the judges, likewise blushing "in consternation of mind and deep admiration, praised him [i.e., Masona] whom a little before they had tried to overcome."[90] Although in no way giving up his partisanship and advocacy, Masona was able to demonstrate his own holy authority and the objective truth of his case through his rather ostentatious display of Christian dignity, or *reverentia*.[91] Sunna's lack of divine endorsement was blatant in his grotesque display of human emotions and bad manners.

Second, since Masona still had access to the contested basilica, he could call on the power of Eulalia, the saint buried beneath the altar. It was at her tomb that he prepared himself for the struggle. By fasting and weeping there for three days before the hearing, the bishop had augmented his customary learnedness, making himself the vehicle for the Holy Spirit, against whom there could be no argument.[92] Masona's astonishingly eloquent argumentation at the hearing was, quite simply, the word of God.[93] Everyone involved recognized this obvious fact: since "fleshly power could in no way resist the wisdom of God and the Holy Spirit who spoke through the mouth of His servant,"[94] justice prevailed. In the absence of any suitable human adjudicator for this dispute, Masona—the ideal advocate—made possible the participation of the only acceptable judge in the matter: God. His ability to do so was rooted in his status as the source of holy authority within his community, displayed for all concerned through his *reverentia* and through his relationship with Eulalia.

These two characteristics of episcopal holy authority are well-known features of early medieval Christian culture, as is the community advocacy

---

87. *VPE*, 5.5.14: "ut erat summae gravitatis summaeque prudentiae, diu multimque oculis coelo intentis silentium tenuit," 207.

88. *VPE*, 5.5.14–15: "Sunna episcopus prius loqui exorsus est coepitque nefanda oris strepentia, aspera, scabra, et obscoena summo cum fragore producere verba. Cui cum vir Dei patienter leniter suaviterque responderet et omnem veritatem insigniter demonstraret," 207.

89. *VPE*, 5.5.18: "doctrinae loquelam," 207.

90. *VPE*, 5.5.18: "mente consternati atque in stupore nimio conversi cum multa admiratione quem expugnare paulo ante voluerant collaudabant," 207.

91. On the early medieval concept of "reverentia," see intro., n. 63.

92. *VPE*, 5.5.10–11, 205.

93. The words of the Holy Spirit would normally be equated with the word of God only by Catholics. On this verbal victory as a doctrinal victory over the Arians, see n. 128 of this chapter.

94. *VPE*, 5.5.16: "nulla ratione potuit moles carnea sapientiae Dei sanctoque Spiritui qui per os servuli sui Masonae episcopi loquebatur resistere," 207.

demonstrated by both Masona and Sunna.[95] The author of the *Vitas* does his best to present the conflict as a stereotypical confrontation between the bishop and evil representatives of heresy and secular power, thus emphasizing Masona's expected episcopal qualities: he appears as the ideal peaceful, dignified man of God, supported by his saint and fostering community well-being.[96] Yet the outlines of the event behind the stereotypical characters set Masona's episcopal qualities and his relationship with the saint apart from other such early medieval bishops and saints. For instance, Eulalia's perceived role in the affair is unusual. According to the *Vitas,* this "aloof" saint took little active part in administering divine justice.[97] While Eulalia made possible a miraculous resolution of the conflict by way of Masona's three-day vigil before her tomb, her involvement was indirect when compared to other early medieval saints, who were known to reach out from their tombs to protect criminals,[98] to cause gallows to collapse to prevent executions,[99] and personally to protect refugees from royal justice seeking sanctuary in their churches.[100] God's direct involvement in judicial decisions, a concept carefully fostered and publicized by Gallic bishops during the sixth century,[101] was obviously the key to Masona's victory. In this case, however, the miracle announcing that involvement was remarkably subdued[102] and was focused on the bishop and his *reverentia,* rather than on the actions of the saint.

Moreover, in this episode Masona did not act as a mediator, peacemaker, or consensus builder, other ideal episcopal judicial roles of the era.[103] Although the issue was settled by everyone's recognition of Masona's divine endorsement, there is no indication that the momentary shared acceptance of God's judgment brought community peace or consensus or that it was viewed as a means toward that end. At the moment of Masona's victory the Catholics

95. For archtypical early medieval bishop/advocates, see, e.g., Constantius of Lyons, *Vita Germanii,* ed. and trans. René Borius, Sources Chrétiennes 112 (Paris, 1965); and the *Vita S. Caesarii Arelatensis a discipulis scripta* I, ed. Germain Morin, *S. Caesarii Arelatensis Opera Omnia,* III (Maredsours, 1942).

96. These themes are developed at great length in other parts of the *VPE*'s descriptions of Masona and his further conflicts with Leovigild. On Masona's special relationship with St. Eulalia, see *VPE,* 5.8.1–4, 223–25. On his many civic benefactions and beneficient leadership in Mérida, see *VPE,* 5.2.9, 191–97.

97. On the general absence of "homely" miracles on the part of this saint, see Collins, "Merida and Toledo," 197.

98. Gregory of Tours, *Liber in gloria confessorum* 61, ed. Bruno Krusch, *MGH, Scriptores rerum merovingicarum* 1 (1885); Van Dam, *Leadership and Community,* 272.

99. *LH,* 6.8, 278. See James, "*Beati Pacifici,*" 34.

100. *LH,* 4.18, 151. See James, "*Beati Pacifici,*" 37.

101. James, "*Beati Pacifici,*" 31.

102. On the strangely nonmiraculous nature of the *VPE,* despite its announced purpose of publicizing miracles, see Collins, "Merida and Toledo," 193.

103. See, e.g., James, "*Beati Pacifici.*"

shouted praise to God in the faces of their overwhelmed enemies, and their parade through the streets of Mérida appears as an expression of their own unity in defiant victory over the Arians of the city. In fact, Masona's administration of divine justice ultimately served to inflame the situation further. Thwarted in this instance, the Arians continued their campaign against the Catholic community, eventually forcing the bishop into exile and replacing him with a particularly vicious (although Catholic) man who brought disaster to the city.[104]

These aspects of Masona's authority and their differences from Gallic representations of episcopal holy power are obviously based in the volatile circumstances surrounding this particular incident. Yet those circumstances are key to understanding the attitudes and ideas of the men attending Toledo III. Sixth-century Gallic ideas about holy power, the judicial role of bishops and saints, and God's involvement in the administration of justice developed at least partly in response to the shared orthodoxy of episcopal and secular judicial authorities in Merovingian Gaul. To be sure, doctrinal agreement among bishops and secular leaders in the Merovingian kingdoms did not eliminate differences of opinion, struggles over access to divine justice, and hostile confrontations. Yet the basic principles behind a mutual recognition of holy authority had been set by Clovis's conversion to Catholicism. Under the Arian kings these principles had been in question throughout the sixth century. Under Leovigild they had become increasingly muddied. Although Masona's assertion of individual holy authority and divine judicial endorsement was framed within the specific local circumstances in Mérida, Leovigild's claims for central authority and his active attempts to legitimate and express that authority in religious terms had implications for the authority of Catholic bishops in local communities throughout his kingdom.

Leovigild's religious and centralizing activities are well-known. Modern scholars give the Arian king, who ruled alone from 572 to 586, credit for instigating a trend toward political consolidation and territorial unification. Leovigild's extensive and generally successful military activities brought a halt to the period of fragmentation in the Visigothic kingdom that had begun with the loss of the Aquitanian kingdom in 507.[105] According to his contemporary John of Biclar, Leovigild "wonderfully restored to its former boundaries" the area under the authority of the Goths, "which by that time had been dimin-

104. *VPE*, 5.6.29, 219.

105. For detailed discussions of Leovigild's conquests and political achievements, see Thompson, *Goths*, 57–92; Luis A. García Moreno, *Historia de España Visigoda* (Madrid, 1989), 113–31; and P. D. King, *Law and Society in the Visigothic Kingdom* (Cambridge, 1972), 11–15.

ished by the rebellions of various men."[106] John goes on to report numerous expeditions and victories by Leovigild—against Basques, Byzantines, rebellious Hispano-Romans, and Franks—culminating in the defeat and incorporation of the Suevic kingdom in Galicia in 585.[107] Leovigild's military success was accompanied by a number of measures to extend and strengthen royal power by affecting Byzantine imperial accouterments and activities.[108] According to Isidore of Seville, he was the first among Visigothic kings to sport royal clothing and to sit on a throne;[109] he was the first to enrich the royal fisc and treasure;[110] and he reformed the Visigoths' law code.[111] John of Biclar reports that he founded the city of Reccopolis, named—in Greek fashion—after his son.[112] Leovigild also went against current Visigothic succession practice by associating his two sons with him on the throne[113] and reformed the coinage, minting coins "wholly independent" of Byzantium.[114]

These activities represent important inroads against the political autonomy of local community leaders.[115] What provoked criticism from contemporary observers, however, were Leovigild's religious endeavors; many of the

106. John Bicl., *anno III Iustini:* "Leovegildus . . . provinciam Gothorum, quae iam pro rebellione diversorum fuerat diminuta, mirabiliter ad pristinos revocat terminos," 212. I use the English translation of Kenneth Wolf, *Conquerors and Chroniclers of Early Medieval Spain* (Liverpool, 1990), 64.

107. John Bicl., *anno V Iustini,* 212. Wolf, 65–70.

108. King, *Law and Society,* 12–15. For a detailed discussion of the evidence for and use of Byzantine influences on the Visigothic kingship, see Jocelyn N. Hillgarth, "Historiography in Visigothic Spain," *Settimane* 17 (Spoleto, 1970) reprinted in *Visigothic Spain, Byzantium and the Irish* (London, 1985).

109. *HG,* 51, 259. This passage has caused some modern debates. Sidonius Apollinaris (*Epistulae,* 1.2.4, ed. and trans. W. B. Anderson [Cambridge, 1965]), a fifth-century bishop who lived under Visigothic rule in their Aquitanian kingdom, reported that the king at that time, Theodoric II (453–466) sat on a throne and displayed other such visual symbols of royal power. Michael McCormick (*Eternal Victory. Triumphal Rulership in Late Antiquity, Byzantium and the Early Medieval West* [Cambridge, 1986], 299–300), suggests that Isidore's statement refers to Leovigild as being the first Visigothic king to adopt such behavior in dealing with the Gothic nobility; Theodoric had acted in this way only before his Roman subjects.

110. *HG,* 51, 259.

111. *HG,* 51, 259.

112. John Bicl., *anno II Tiberii,* 215. This type of city creation, dating back to the ancient Greeks, was a traditional expression of the extension of political and cultural power. In the Byzantine Empire, this tradition, along with the custom of naming cities to commemorate their founders, continued through the sixth century: Justinian was commemorated in the names of at least fifteen new cities. See A. H. M. Jones, *The Later Roman Empire 284–602* (Baltimore, 1986), 719. For a seventh-century Iberian interpretation of this tradition, see Isidore of Seville's description of the Mediterranean urban world, *Etymologiarum sive originum libri XX,* 2 vols., ed. William M. Lindsay (Oxford, 1911), 15.1, *"de civitatibus,"* which lists cities and their founders dating back to Cain's establishment of a city he named Enoch, after his son.

113. John Bicl., *anno III Iustini,* 212. See n. 16 of this chapter.

114. Thompson, *Goths,* 57.

115. Collins, "Mérida and Toledo," 215–17.

tensions caused by the king's centralizing efforts were played out and explained as conflict between Arians and Catholics. For instance, Leovigild's son Hermenegild rose in rebellion against his father in around 579. During the course of the struggle the rebel converted to Catholicism and garnered the active support of Catholic leaders in a number of cities in the south—notably, Leander of Seville.[116] Possibly in response to the heightening of doctrinal tensions that the rebellion provoked, Leovigild made significant innovations and reforms in Arian Christianity. In 580 he called the first known council of the Visigothic Arian church, which met in Toledo. According to John of Biclar, the king's intention was to "change the ancient heresy with a new error." Leovigild announced that "those coming from the Roman religion to our catholic faith" (i.e., Arianism) no longer needed to be rebaptized. Rather, they needed only to undergo the laying on of hands, to receive communion, and to give glory "to the Father, through the Son, in the Holy Spirit"—the traditional Arian formulation.[117]

During the same period the king further modified the content of his faith, according to the Gallic chronicler Gregory of Tours, who repeated a report heard from Frankish ambassadors returning from the peninsula:

> Those Catholics who still exist in Spain keep their faith unimpaired. The king has a new trick by which he is doing his utmost to destroy it. In his cunning way he pretends to pray at the tombs of the martyrs and in the churches of our religion. Then he says: "I accept without question that Christ is the Son of God and equal to the Father. What I cannot believe is that the Holy Spirit is God, for that is written in none of the Scriptures."[118]

---

116. The dating and significance of this revolt and of Hermenegild's conversion are debated. In 579 Leovigild had married this son to a Catholic Frankish princess and had made him the ruler of part of the kingdom—presumably the southern province of Baetica. Although the sequence of events is unclear, after taking up his rule and rising in rebellion Hermenegild converted to Catholicism. Once the rebellion had begun, Leander went to Constantinople in an effort to raise Byzantine support for Hermenegild; however, despite the support of many of the important and relatively wealthy cities of the South, the rebellion eventually failed. In 585 Hermenegild was murdered in exile, thereby making him eligible for martyrship, a status promoted by Pope Gregory I, who (*Dialogues*, 3.31, ed. Adalbert de Vogüé, Sources Chrétiennes 251, v. 2 [Paris, 1978]) explicitly blamed his death on Leovigild and described the subsequent miracles. Gregory of Tours (*LH*, V.38, 243–45) offers another contemporary version of the story. For modern works on this subject, see n. 14 of this chapter.

117. John Bicl., *anno IV Tiberii*: "Leovegildus rex in urbem Toletanam synodum episcoporum sectae Arrianae congregat et antiquam haeresem novello errore emendat, dicens de Romana religione a nostra catholica fide venientes non debere baptizari, sed tantummodo per manus impositionem et communionis praeceptione pollui," 216. Wolf, 72.

118. *LH*, 6.18: "Christiani, qui nunc apud Hispanias conmorantur, catholicam fidem integre servant. Sed rex novo nunc ingenio eam nititur exturbare, dum dolose et ad sepulchra martirum et in eclesiis religionis nostrae orare confingit. Dicit enim: 'manifeste cognovi, esse

In other words, Leovigild made a major concession to Catholic dogma concerning the equality of the persons of the Trinity.[119] Leovigild's exact intent in these actions is the subject of modern debates.[120] Whatever his motivations, one can see from Gregory's report that Leovigild publicized his doctrinal innovations in his own activities as king; the Arians also published a document on the subject during this period.[121] It is unclear how many Catholics were convinced by the Arian concessions,[122] but the removal of the necessity of rebaptism was an important incentive.[123] According to John of Biclar, after the council in 580 "many of our own inclined toward the Arian doctrine out of self-interest rather than a change of heart."[124]

In any case, Catholic bishops clearly saw these innovations as a threat, and Leander of Seville and Severus of Saragossa mounted a doctrinal "counteroffensive" by publishing anti-Arian treatises.[125] Yet Leovigild's concessions to Catholicism had important implications in areas other than pure theology. By heightening leaders' awareness of doctrinal differences, Leovigild's active involvement in religious matters also would have heightened the tensions involved in governing both ecclesiastic and secular communities. In the midst of an active polemical interchange the reinvigorated royal support for the Arians, and a civil war with religious overtones, Catholic bishops would have seen any individual conversion to Arianism not only as the loss of the apostate's soul but also as a threat to their communities and to their own positions of leadership, including their judicial authority. As Arian communities gained

---

Christum filium Dei aequalem Patri; sed Spiritum sanctum, Deum penitus esse non credo, eo quod in nullis legatur codicibus Deus esse,' " 287; trans. Lewis Thorpe, *History of the Franks* (Middlesex, 1974), 349. Leovigild's new formulation was, according to Thompson (*Goths*, 85), the same as that espoused by the "Macedonians," or semi-Arians, during the Roman Arian controversy in the fourth century.

119. The exact circumstances of this change in doctrine are unclear. Collins (*Early Medieval Spain,* 50) attributes it to the Arian council in 580, although John of Biclar does not mention it in his report. The date of Gregory's report is 582. It seems possible, however, that in that year Leovigild was articulating and publicizing an action previously taken by the council.

120. Thompson (*Goths,* 108) argues that Leovigild's general aims included an effort to maintain separation between Gothic Arians and Hispano-Roman Catholics. Others read his efforts at religious direction as part of his overall plans for creating a religiously and ethnically united Arian kingdom, thereby foreshadowing his son Reccared's Catholic unification strategy. See, e.g., King, *Law and Society,* 12–15; and Hillgarth, "Coins and Chronicles," 498.

121. For Toledo III's condemnation of this "libellum detestabilem," see the sixteenth anti-Arian anathema in the records of Toledo III. Rodríguez, 25. See also Thompson, *Goths,* 84.

122. Isidore (*de viris illustribus,* 30, 151) noted the acceptance of Arianism by one bishop, Vincent of Saragossa. Collins (*Early Medieval Spain,* 51) suggests that the Arians' "intellectual offensive" in the 580s may have led to a "disturbing number of defections" by Catholics.

123. Collins, *Early Medieval Spain,* 51.

124. John Bicl., *anno IV Tiberii:* "plurimi nostrorum cupiditate potius quam impulsione in Arrianum dogma declinant," 216. Wolf, 72.

125. Isidore, *de viris illustribus,* 28 and 40, 149 and 151. See Collins, *Early Medieval Spain,* 51. Neither of these works survives.

royal support and converts, the divine authority wielded by Catholic bishops in dealing with conflicts in their cities faced increasing judicial competition and uncertainty, particularly in disputes between Arians and Catholics. How would a bishop act as a mediator, a force for compromise, if one side did not recognize his impartiality and divine endorsement? How would a community constitute any acceptable panel of judges in such a dispute? What terrestrial judicial authority could claim to administer the judgment of God?

Within this context of increasing judicial uncertainty and conflict, the Arians' acceptance of the equality of the Father and Son within the Trinity, not to mention their convoking and publicizing a council of their church, had particularly important significance for the judicial authority of Catholic bishops. As is evident in Leovigild's explanation of his acceptance of the equality of Father and Son, that concession to Catholic doctrine was accompanied by an explicit reiteration of the Arians' rejection of any scriptural basis for the Holy Spirit's identity as God. While Leovigild's position on the Holy Spirit was not new, given the religious climate, with its mounting hostilities and increased awareness of doctrinal difference, one can assume that Leovigild's actions served to emphasize the importance of that aspect of Arian doctrine. Whether Leovigild intended it or not, the rejection of the Holy Spirit's identity with God undermined the basis of Catholic conciliar authority. The councils of the Catholic Church claimed to speak with the voice of the Holy Spirit—that is, God; the claim was scripturally based on the words of Jesus to his disciples in the Gospel of Matthew. No one can know what divine authority the Arian council claimed or how they explained it, but, by holding the council, Leovigild would have appeared to the Catholics to be introducing and advocating an alternative, Arian source of collective episcopal authority.

Of course, conciliar authority was not a central aspect of episcopal power in sixth-century Iberia. The reconfiguration of Arian Trinitarian doctrine would have constituted a primarily theoretical threat in local bishops' conceptions of their collective authority. The case of Masona, however, shows that individual Catholic bishops could speak with the voice of God—that is, the Holy Spirit. According to the *Vitas*, after Masona had prepared himself for the hearing with Sunna by fasting for three days before Eulalia's tomb, all the "faithful" of Mérida knew that Jesus was coming to aid the bishop in his debate. The narrative makes clear the identity of the Holy Spirit with Jesus by quoting Christ's words to his disciples in the Gospel of Mark: "Be not thoughtful beforehand what you shall speak, but whatever shall be said to you in that hour, speak that, for it is not you that speak, but the Holy Spirit."[126] In describing the Catholics' victory, the *Vitas* reiterated the point when it attrib-

---

126. *VPE,* 5.5.11: "nulli fidelium ambiguum videretur illum in eius pergere adiutorium qui dixit: 'Nolite praecogitare qui loquamini; sed quod dictum fuerit vobis in illa hora illud loquimini: non enim vos estis loquentes sed Spiritus sanctus,' " quoting Mark 13.11, 205.

uted the judges' decision to "the wisdom of God and the Holy Spirit who spoke through the mouth of His servant, Bishop Masona."[127] For the Catholics of Mérida, Masona's victory over Sunna was both judicial and doctrinal. Not only did their advocate retain possession of their most important basilica, but he forced the Arians to recognize the identity of the Holy Spirit with God, thus confirming his individual access to divine judgment and his resulting supreme holy authority within the community.[128]

While the confrontation between Arians and Catholics in Mérida may have been particularly hostile, and while the overtly judicial context within which this incident was played out may have been unusual, one can imagine that similar difficulties occurred in other Iberian communities in the years before 589, raising similar uncertainties about the divine authority of local bishops. Despite the unique specifics of Masona's case, the episode and the circumstances surrounding it do suggest some conclusions concerning the ideas about episcopal authority, divine justice, and Christian consensus that the bishops brought with them to Toledo in 589. First of all, although their episcopal ideals included such common characteristics as peacemaking, mediation, and consensus building, the heightened tensions of the last decade of Leovigild's reign had served to emphasize the importance of other aspects of individual episcopal authority: the role of bishops as aggressive advocates for particular factions within divided communities. Second, challenged by Leovigild's doctrinal innovations, these bishops' conceptions of the source of impartial divine judgment had become focused particularly on the role of the Holy Spirit, to whom they believed they might gain individual access through their personal dignity and saintly support. Finally, if Masona of Mérida is any indication, the meaning of Christian consensus involved a local community's shared recognition of these men's status as vehicles for impartial divine judgment. In disputes between Arians and Catholics, their community advocacy might initially stand in the way of their acceptance as sources of impartial judgment. Yet in the Catholics' view the recognition of a bishop's access to the Holy Spirit could bring doctrinal consensus on the equality of the Trinity and thus community consensus on the settlement of a dispute.

Thus, these men's conceptions of their individual judicial authority had

---

127. See n. 94 of this chapter.

128. It could be argued that since the *VPE* was written in the seventh century, this interpretation of Masona's victory does not necessarily reflect the ideas of Catholics in the 580s. The author's assertion of the identity of Jesus, God, and the Holy Spirit, however, is emphatic enough to reflect an urgent anti-Arian sentiment. While Catholics in the author's generation were obviously conscious of their kingdom's Arian past, it seems unlikely that the question would still provoke the urgency of this particular claim more than fifty years later. I see no reason to reject the idea that in this case, as in many others, the author is reporting an interpretation of the events that was current in the 580s.

been molded particularly by the tensions of the last decade of Leovigild's reign. While one cannot know exactly how other conflicts between Arians and Catholics in communities outside of Mérida were played out during this period, it seems safe to assume that they did occur. In the wake of such disputes and hostilities, many of the Catholic bishops at Toledo III came as advocates or disputants rather than as judges. Consequently, one of the primary tasks of the council was to transform these advocates, each with his own specific grievances based in the experiences of individual local communities, from parties to a dispute into parties allied to their long-time opponents. Doctrinal agreement, the basis of the alliance, had been achieved prior to Toledo III through the conversion of Reccared and the leading Gothic nobles and bishops.[129] The dispute, however, could not be fully settled, and the transformation of the Iberian bishops from profoundly partisan community leaders to a collective source of transcendent justice could not be completed until the individual grievances had been addressed. Furthermore, Toledo III had to mediate between the establishment of that collective source of kingdom-wide justice and consensus and the individual authority and local community consensus that these men tied to their personal roles as vehicles for the voice of God and the Holy Spirit. The holy authority of individual bishops, so important in the governance and administration of ecclesiastic justice in local communities, did not necessarily conflict with a shared recognition of collective access to the Holy Spirit. Still, one can imagine instances in which an individual bishop's settlement of a local dispute might serve local interests but conflict with province-wide or kingdom-wide concerns and principles.

These tasks would be further complicated by the fact that most of the participants at Toledo III were presumably as much in need of a conciliar refresher course as the bishops of Galicia had been under Martin. Consequently, much of the rhetoric and display at Toledo III must have served a didactic purpose—not only for the Catholic bishops but also for the converting Arian prelates and Gothic nobility. The kingdom-wide consensus and centralized ecclesiastic and secular authority embodied in their "general" church council, modeled on the ecumenical councils of the Roman Empire, constituted the core of the lesson taught. At the same time, the local Catholic bishops' understandings of conciliar governance were focused on the local episcopal authority that had been confined for generations in the flexible, and thus variously understood, traditions of conciliar dispute settlement, canonical

---

129. In one of his speeches at Toledo III, Reccared reminded the bishops that he had converted to Catholicism "not many days" ("non multos . . . dies") after the death of his father—three years before the council. Rodríguez, 19. The Gothic notables and bishops also pointed out in their confession that they too had rejected their Arian faith prior to the ceremony in 589. Rodríguez, 24.

precedent, and provincial episcopal consensus. The central lesson of the council did not automatically run counter to the expectations of the bishops; indeed, in many ways they were mutually dependent. Kingdom-wide consensus needed local enforcement, and local conciliar practice had traditionally profited from, if not depended upon, some form of central recognition and support. On the other hand, the convergence of these conceptions of the meaning of conciliar authority was not automatic either.

In 589 the men meeting in Toledo brought with them expectations and priorities that were at least as complex, multilayered, and potentially contradictory as the social vision the council's organizers sought to express and to put into local practice. It is not surprising that Toledo III's records reveal disagreements and ambiguities beneath their rhetoric and ceremony of harmony, peace, and unity. The lack of sources for the period prior to 589 has necessitated in this chapter a conjectural discussion of the episcopal experiences and attitudes that fed into those disagreements. Suggesting some of the social and doctrinal bases for those attitudes, however, is essential for an analysis of their expression in Toledo III's records and for understanding why these differing views on the ultimate meaning and location of holy authority forced Iberian leaders in 589 to leave many of the day-to-day workings, as well as the overall governmental function, of conciliar authority ill-defined, and thus open to subsequent local variations in interpretation. Ultimately, despite their repeated assertions of unity and harmony, the men at Toledo III failed to achieve fundamental agreement on the meaning and enforcement of Christian consensus in their kingdom.

CHAPTER TWO

Consensus and Conflict at the Third Council of Toledo

No one can now know exactly why Iberian leaders chose to celebrate their alliance between *regnum* and *sacerdotium* with the elaborate ritual and rhetoric of a kingdom-wide council in 589. Given the fluidity of conciliar practice in the West during this period—not to mention the fluctuating relations between kings and bishops in general—it was not as natural a choice as one might think. As far as conciliar records show, Toledo III was in some ways an unprecedented occasion in the Western kingdoms. Although Germanic kings had converted from Arianism to Catholicism earlier, either they did not see the utility of formalizing their conversion and asserting their authority by calling and participating in a general church council, or the opportunity was not made available to them by Catholic leaders.[1] Leander of Seville and John of Biclar both made a point of the unusual nature of Toledo III.[2] While their rhetoric coincides with the general self-aggrandizing tenor of the event, the consciousness of innovation it reveals suggests the deliberation involved in orchestrating such a momentous occasion.

Of course, some sources of inspiration for Toledo III are readily apparent. Leander had been to Constantinople earlier in the decade and may have returned with a particular awareness of the symbolic power of grandiose conciliar ritual and rhetoric.[3] At the same time, the role played by Reccared at the council probably reflects the increasing use of Byzantine imperial images that

---

1. The Suevi rulers of the kingdom of Galicia converted from Arianism ca. 560, under unclear circumstances. E. A. Thompson ("The Conversion of the Suevi to Catholicism," in *Visigothic Spain. New Approaches,* ed. Edward James [Oxford, 1980], 91) argues the Galician council he proposes was held in 569 met for the purpose of "confirming the faith." See chap. 1, n. 66. The Burgundian king, Sigismund (516–24), also converted to Catholicism but did so while still subordinate to his Arian father, Gundobad.

2. Leander opened his homily by noting the newness of the event; see chap. 1, n. 2. John, in comparing Toledo III to the Council of Nicaea of 325, remarked that the Iberian council was even more momentous than Constantine's council; see chap. 1, n. 5.

3. Gregory I, *Moralia in Iob, epistula ad leandrum,* vol. I, ed. Robert Gillet (Paris, 1952), 113. On the Byzantine influences apparent in Toledo III's ceremonies, see Jocelyn N. Hillgarth, "El Concilio III de Toledo y Bizancio," in *Concilio III de Toledo. XIV Centenario, 589–1989* (Toledo, 1991), 301–2.

had become a central aspect of Visigothic royal activities during the reign of his father, Leovigild.[4] It is also possible that the Hispano-Roman church leaders conceived of their council in opposition to the Byzantines' aspirations for religiopolitical leadership in the western Mediterranean. Not only did the Eastern Empire possess a province on Iberian soil at the time, but resistance to the decisions of the Second Council of Constantinople held in 553 was widespread in the West.[5] By holding their own "general" council in their newly united orthodox kingdom, Leander and his associates may have been asserting their own ascendancy as a source of both territorial and religious authority equal to their doctrinally questionable eastern competitors.[6]

Yet to ascribe the inspiration behind Toledo III's convocation primarily to Byzantine influence and to the Iberian leaders' aspirations for centralized Christian authority does not do justice to the immediate context informing these leaders' choice to base their alliance on conciliar traditions. The intermittency of sixth-century conciliar activity in Iberia makes an unbroken continuum of indigenous conciliar development from the early part of the century forward to 589 a questionable proposition.[7] Events during the last years of Leovigild's reign, however, had brought into sharper focus questions surrounding the exercise of collective and individual holy authority, particularly in regards to councils and the Holy Spirit, making a conciliar expression of consensus particularly appropriate and perhaps even necessary. Moreover, Iberian church leaders revered the long-standing authority of church councils but had little or no experience with actual conciliar practice. Their inexperience enabled them to innovate in conciliar form and content. By calling and organizing this council, Leander, Reccared, and their associates laid hold of a powerful but malleable tool that could, ideally, contain and guide to a predetermined resolution the conflicts and contradictions that had surfaced in local communities.

Some of those conflicts already had been addressed in the two years prior to the council. A large part of its agenda was therefore the formalization and publication of previous agreements.[8] According to Gregory of Tours, after his succession to the throne in 586 Reccared held a series of meetings with various

---

4. See chap. 1, n. 108.

5. See intro., n. 35; and chap. 1, n. 34.

6. On the effects of the Byzantine conquests and their Iberian province on the conversion of the Visigoths and Toledo III, see Hillgarth, "Concilio III de Toledo y Bizancio."

7. See J. Orlandis and D. Ramos-Lissón, *Historia de los Concilios de la España romana y visigoda* (Pamplona, 1986), 101–2; and Carmen García Rodríguez, *El Culto de los Santos en la España Romana y Visigoda* (Madrid, 1966), 381–83.

8. According to Collins ("¿Donde estaban los arrianos en el año 589?" in *Concilio III de Toledo*, 211), in terms of the Visigoths' conversion Toledo III was "solamente . . . una ceremonia formal."

bishops—in effect, a series of informal church councils.[9] The first was a meeting of Arian prelates, at which he decried the schism in his kingdom and called for a debate between the bishops of both faiths in order to resolve it. At the second meeting the debate was held; Gregory says that, in addition to the usual doctrinal haggling, the king pointed out to the Arians that no healing miracle had ever been performed by an Arian bishop. Gregory does not report a clear victory in this debate but relates that Reccared subsequently called a meeting of Catholic bishops only, at which he "questioned them closely" and learned that he should confess the Catholic Trinity, "equal and omnipotent, to be the true God."[10] Finally fully convinced, Reccared "put an end to the dispute and submitted to the Catholic faith," probably in February 587.[11] Gregory's version of the conversion, not surprisingly, focuses particularly on the problem of miracles.[12] One can assume, however, that these meetings involved some more mundane considerations, such as the disposition of previously Arian properties and bishops. Probably in the same year he converted, Reccared turned over all the Arian basilicas, property, and privileges to the Catholics.[13] During the same period the parties came to an agreement on the status of former Arian bishops: they were to maintain their offices, even in cities where there was also a Catholic bishop—leaving a number of cities in the potentially problematic position of having two bishops.[14]

Apparently, some of the details of these settlements were not acceptable to all Gothic nobles and bishops. Reccared faced a military rebellion and two conspiracies headed by apostate Arian converts in the years between his conversion and Toledo III.[15] Indeed, Reccared was only able to muster the attendance of eight Arian bishops at the council in 589, and he was threatened by another conspiracy shortly afterward.[16] The new king had also become involved in a series of complex marriage negotiations with the Franks, which led to the Frankish king Guntramn's invasion of Septimania in 589 in support

9. *LH*, 9.15, 429. John Bicl., *anno V Mauricii*, 218, mentions only the meeting of Arian bishops. See Collins, "¿Donde estaban," 211.

10. *LH*, 9.15: "quibus perscrutatis . . . in una aequalitate atque omnipotentia hanc Trinitatem verum Deum fateri," 429. Thorpe, 498.

11. *LH*, 9.15: "postposita altercatione, se catholicae lege subdidit," 429. Thorpe, 498. See also Collins, "¿Donde estaban," 211.

12. *LH*, 9.15, 429. Gregory reports that Reccared expressed his concern that Arian bishops could not perform miracles at two of these meetings.

13. Collins, "¿Donde estaban," 212; E. A. Thompson, *The Goths in Spain* (Oxford, 1969), 95.

14. Collins, "¿Donde estaban," 214.

15. See chap. 1, n. 18. Collins ("¿Donde estaban," 213–14) suggests that the Arian bishops involved were all metropolitans and that the agreement on dual bishops in a city did not allow for the coexistence of two metropolitans in a province, provoking these former Arian metropolitans to join with the nobles in rebellion.

16. See chap. 1, n. 23.

of the rebellious Arians there. Although this invasion was turned back decisively and although historians agree that the Arian reaction was short-lived and not a true threat to Reccared's position, this may not have been so apparent in 589.[17] Whatever the sentiments of the Arians and former Arians at the time, the chance for a timely public affirmation of support from the Catholic episcopate—and through them the support of divine judgment—undoubtedly made calling a general council particularly attractive to the king, who had already begun to establish the precedent of conciliar consultation between *regnum* and *sacerdotium* during the course of his conversion.

In many ways, then, these men's choice of the conciliar forum was truly inspired. Drawing on the most authoritative of traditions, they molded ancient symbols and ideals, originally generated under vastly different circumstances, to address a complex set of immediate social, ideological, political, and religious needs. In so doing, they expressed what was probably, at least on the uppermost levels of their social hierarchy, a genuine consensus on a key source of power and authority in their society: the Holy Spirit and the collective episcopal voice through which it had spoken in the past and would continue to speak into the future. Conciliar traditions provided an authoritative but flexible framework for the aspirations and claims of both secular and ecclesiastic leaders in 589, allowing them to assert the kingdom-wide consensus that they believed would give them the power to contain and resolve the conflicts and divergent interests of their various communities.

Still, although the choice to formalize and implement the new alliance upon that framework arose out of the immediate conditions of Iberian society in the 580s, the very pliability that made the choice appropriate was itself based partly in the disuse and ill definition that had characterized Iberian conciliar practice for most of the sixth century. In that period many of the necessary supports for the ongoing recognition and exercise of conciliar authority— education, supervision, and the regular convocation of councils—had been lacking, even on the provincial level. For the ideal Christian consensus of church councils to have gained lasting and practical authority within the communities of Iberia—particularly in the arena of dispute settlement—it would have had to have been recognized and reiterated and shown to be effective much more frequently than had been the case. In this sense conciliar authority, as well as the consensus upon which it was theoretically based, was fundamentally foreign to Iberian society in 589.

The fact that the organizers of Toledo III so strenuously emphasized the traditional authority of the Roman ecumenical councils, with their resounding claims for central control over the universal community of Christians, made

---

17. See chap. 1, n. 19.

the claims for transcendent authority and obedience emanating from Toledo even more foreign. Catholic conciliar ceremonies and rhetoric might lend weight and legitimacy to claims of consensus and central authority, but they could not create the social or political basis for their realization. Lacking the basis for establishing a functional consensus in their kingdom, the leaders of Visigothic Spain relied instead upon rhetoric and demands for uniform obedience. They did so in order to call forth the harmony necessary for the attendance of the Holy Spirit at their council and for a favorable divine judgment on the authority of their newly united government. Their choice to locate their kingdom's transcendent holy authority in conciliar traditions and governance, modeled on the great ecumenical councils of the distant past and based on the ritual display of absolute Christian consensus, left little room for the open expression of dissent. Conciliar demonstrations of harmony and assertions of doctrinal agreement might formalize the alliance and suppress expressions of conflict and divergent interests, but the meticulous and formulaic ritual and language—indeed, the overriding importance of maintaining ceremonial consensus—made the actual resolution of those conflicts and differences all but impossible.

The silencing effects of ritual consensus at church councils is usually magnified by the process of transcribing and redacting conciliar records. Scribes and editors, like the orchestrators of ritual, followed restrictive traditions and formulas in making their inclusions and exclusions. While some of the problems leading to a council's legislation are clear from the content of its canons, only rarely do the records provide a glimpse of procedures of any kind. There are few inklings of any dissension or disharmony that may, in the process of settling a dispute, have made their way past the prescribed ceremonial harmony. Fortunately, the records of Toledo III, opaque as they are, do provide some of those rare glimpses when viewed within the many paradoxes that constitute at least part of their social context: ancient traditions in the hands of neophytes; aggressive disputants vigorously proclaiming their mutual support; individual representatives of holy power wielding collective divine authority; the skillful manipulation of Byzantine rituals of centralized authority in a kingdom long fragmented religiously, culturally, and politically; resounding and formulaic claims for a many-layered social consensus within a context that made its existence highly unlikely.

Because the participants of this council were so aware of the novelty and perhaps even the alien nature of their actions, the council's *acta*, which appear in the seventh-century canonical collection known as the *Hispana*,[18] are more detailed than most council records of the era. They recount the proceedings in

---

18. See intro., n. 51.

a narrative that, although not exactly vivid, reveals a many-sided dialogue among leaders who could no longer rely on overt religious divergence to explain their conflicting interests and contradictory ideas about the exercise of spiritual and governmental power. In exploring this dialogue, however, one must not underestimate the power of the consensus these men had reached on the equality of divinity embodied in the Holy Trinity and on the consequent holy authority of Catholic Church councils and canonical precedent. These concepts were the bedrock of the new alliance, and the records resound with their repeated affirmation. Agreement on them—particularly when formulated in the language of the great ecumenical councils—also involved agreement on such principles as divine guidance for both monarchy and episcopate, secular participation in matters of faith, and the necessity of an exclusively Catholic body of subjects who were unanimously obedient to the legislation of their leaders. The records of Toledo III reveal not only a dialogue but also the constraints that all the involved parties faced in attempting to maintain these principles as they negotiated within the framework delineated by Catholic traditions of conciliar authority and exclusive unanimity.

Interpreting the Conversion

Since the conversion of the Goths from Arianism to Catholicism—their acceptance of the Catholic version of the Trinity—was the premise behind the entire affair, it is not surprising that the council devoted a great deal of attention, ceremony, and rhetoric to its formalization. According to the narrator of the records, the reason the king had convoked the council was so that the kingdom's bishops might "exult in God" and "give thanks for so great a gift" as the conversion of the king and his people.[19] Reccared himself mentioned a number of reasons why he had "judged it necessary to convene [the bishops'] blessedness in one."[20] His own confession and that of his fellow Goths loomed large on the list: the bishops were there to "give eternal thanks to the Lord for the men now coming to Christ,"[21] to examine his own written confession of faith by "synodal judgment"[22] and allow it to be preserved eternally in the canonical records; and to ensure that the Goths would not in the future "avert

---

19. Tol. III, preamble: "ut . . . Domino exsultarent et divinae dignationi pro tanto munere gratias agerent." Rodríguez, 19.

20. Tol. III, *tomus:* "ualde pernecessarium esse prospexi uestram in unum conuenire beatitudinem." Rodríguez, 20.

21. Tol. III, preamble: "ut de hominibus nuper advenientibus ad Christum ipsi aeternas Domino gratias deferatis." Rodríguez, 19.

22. Tol. III, preamble: "iudicio synodali." Rodriguez, 19.

their eyes from the unobstructed light" of truth,[23] since their confession had been witnessed by God, who was, of course, present among the bishops gathered in his name.

Yet even in the highly formalized language surrounding this central item on the council's agenda, one finds varying interpretations of the meaning of the former Arians' public confession of faith. Reccared, for instance, used relatively mild and distancing terms. The king had opened the council by addressing the bishops, calling for them to devote the first three days of the council to fasts, vigils, and prayers in preparation for their deliberations. On the return to the proceedings, the king presented his written confession, or *tomus*,[24] to be read into the records and judged by the bishops, so that "our glory may shine forth, decorated by the witnessing of this faith, through all succeeding time."[25] The *tomus*, which contains lengthy passages on the Trinity and on the authority of church councils, also presented to the bishops the "most noble *gentes*" of the Goths and Suevi as a "holy and pleasing sacrifice" to God.[26] When Reccared specifically discussed the former Arianism of these noble peoples, he attributed it to the "depravity of their teachers" and the infiltration of a "foreign vice."[27] The role of the bishops was twofold. They were to preserve the Goths' confession for future times so that disbelievers might receive the wrath of God and serve as an example to others and to instruct the glorious *gens*, which until now had "erred through ignorance" of the truth.[28] In an earlier part of the *tomus* the king did describe the past suffering of the Catholic Church through the "rather pertinacious animosity" and "molestations" of the heretics.[29] These passages, however, were clearly included in order aggrandize his own role in bringing about the conversion. In discussing the formal confession, his only mention of Arianism was to call it an "ancient error."[30] He did not single out the present converts as responsible

---

23. Tol. III, *tomus*: "a patenti lumine, quod absit, oculos suos auertant." Rodríguez, 20.

24. The *tomus* was a written message from the king to the assembled bishops. On Reccared's *tomus* at Toledo III, see Manuel C. Díaz y Díaz, "Los discursos del rey Recaredo: El *Tomus*," in *Concilio III de Toledo*, in which it is argued that the ideas expressed in both the *tomus* and Reccared's speeches were indeed those of the king. On the general role and significance of the *tomus* in Visigothic councils, see Heide Schwöbel, *Synode und König im Westgotenreich. Grundlagen und Formen ihrer Beziehung* (Cologne, 1982), 81–106; and Gonzalo Martínez Díez, "Los Concilios de Toledo," *Anales Toledanos* 3 (Toledo, 1971), 128.

25. Tol. III, preamble: "per omne succiduum tempus gloria nostra eiusdem fidei testimonio decorata clarescat." Rodríguez, 19.

26. Tol. III, *tomus*: "has nobilissimas gentes . . . quasi sanctum et placabile sacrificium." Rodríguez, 20.

27. Tol. III, *tomus*: "suorum pravitate doctorum a fide hactenus uel unitate ecclesiae fuerit catholicae segregata . . . alieno licet in haeresim deductam uitio." Rodríguez, 20.

28. Tol. III, *tomus*: "nescia hucusque tam clarissima errauerit gens." Rodríguez, 20.

29. Tol. III, *tomus*: "molestiis . . . pertinaciori animositate." Rodríguez, 20.

30. Tol. III, *tomus*: "antiquus error." Rodríguez, 21.

for the evils wrought by that error. Rather, responsibility lay with unnamed teachers and outsiders.

After the *tomus* was read, the assembly heard the creeds of the councils of Nicaea, Constantinople, and Chalcedon, which Reccared and his wife then signed. Following a series of eight acclamations "in praise of God and in honor of the prince,"[31] an anonymous bishop took the floor to address the converts, "with the whole venerable council ordering and prescribing."[32] Speaking for the Catholic bishops, he presented a different view of the meaning of the Goths' ceremonial confession. In inquiring as to what the converts believed, he was impelled, he said, both by the order of the king and by the duty of his own office. He then explained to the former Arians why they should make a public and signed confession, even though God knew they had already converted. It was the best way to "show [themselves] to [their] neighbors by assenting to the holy faith" and to "signify [themselves] to be members of the body of Christ."[33] In this way the bishops would never have doubts or suspect infidelity in the converts' fraternity. Unlike Reccared, who called for the public confession for the sake of his other subjects and future generations, this bishop maintained that a public abjuration of Arianism was necessary for the converts' own status within the Christian community:

> When it is evident that you fully condemn the plague of the Arian perfidy with all its dogmas, rules, offices, communion, and books, and that you are freed from the contagion of the detestable heresy, renewed within the church of God, you will shine splendidly in the habit of true faith.[34]

Thus, the bishop not only reclaimed from Reccared the initiative in calling for the public confession but also asserted the role of the Catholic episcopate in defining the meaning of the confession—in terms quite different from the king's. Emphasizing personal shame and potential suspicion, he did not miss the opportunity to underline the "detestable" nature of Arianism in a manner that implicitly blamed the converts for the contagion it had represented for Catholics.

In their turn, before signing twenty-three anathemas against Arianism,

---

31. Tol. III, preamble: "in laudibus Dei et in fauore principis." Rodríguez, 23.

32. Tol. III, preamble: "Praecipiente autem universo uenerabili concilio iubente." Rodríguez, 23.

33. Tol. III, preamble: "proximis uos fidei sanctae adstipulatione monstretis. Eo itaque fiet ut et uos Christi esse corporis membra significetis." Rodríguez, 23.

34. Tol. III, preamble: "Dum patuerit uos tabem perfidiae Arrianae cum omnibus dogmatibus, regulis, officiis, communione, codicibus praedamnare et a detestandae haereseos exspoliati contagione, innouati quodammodo intra ecclesiam Dei splendide habitu uerae fidei clareatis." Rodríguez, 23–24.

the assembled converts responded to the bishop in unison. Deferring to the superior knowledge of the Catholic bishops, they asked to be instructed in anything the bishops saw as "congruent to the faith."[35] Yet they made a point of remarking that they had already done, at the time of their king's conversion, what was now being asked of them and offered their own version of the purpose of this public abjuration. Acting for the love of right faith, they hastened to do what was asked "out of a desire for concord and because of the devotion we are mindful that we owe to God and the holy Catholic church."[36] While they acknowledged a debt of deference and obedience to the church on account of their previous error, like the king, they portrayed this error as due to their own ignorance—which now they sought to correct through the "charitable persuasion" of the Catholic bishops.[37] The converts saw the proceedings as the fulfillment of a debt through the public repetition of an action already taken, and their appeal for cooperation and teaching from the bishops was tied to that repetition. Their public abjuration of Arianism was part of a covenant, rather than a submission or acceptance of blame.

This interchange seems strangely at odds with the council's rhetoric of consensus and unity. Formulaic as they may be, the words of the different parties reveal important tensions surrounding the conversion. One of the chief tasks facing Toledo III was the transformation of the Iberian bishops from parties in dispute with the Goths into parties allied to them. The ceremonial readings and signings of creeds and confessions, the acclamations and anathemas, could not fully achieve this task, for their social and political meanings were not fully defined. The bishop who demanded the Goths' public confession defined terms for that transformation that were based in the dynamics of local communities: blame for past actions, submission to episcopal authority, and the necessity of the Goths' "neighbors'" certain knowledge of their community standing. In overseeing the Goths' public confession, the bishops might be willing to play the role of teachers and conduits for God's judgment, but they conceived of their position as judges of the Goths' status within the church as part of their continuing role as community advocates.

For their part the Goths, while acknowledging the bishops' superior knowledge, approached them as equals involved in a mutual debt of charity to God and the church. Their language contains no hint of immediate political or social dynamics, other than their reminder to the bishops that they converted along with their king. Reccared, on the other hand, framed his entire discussion of the conversion so as to emphasize the virility, nobility,

---

35. Tol. III, confession of the Goths: "congrua fidei." Rodríguez, 24.

36. Tol. III, confession of the Goths: "propter caritatem et deuotionem quam uel Deo uel ecclesiae sanctae catholicae meminimus nos debere." Rodríguez, 24.

37. Tol. III, confession of the Goths: "de caritate persuadite." Rodríguez, 24.

and general glory of the Goths, to minimize their role in past social evils, and, most of all, to announce his own position as the protector of the church and God's chosen leader of nations. While noting the bishops' "aptness in learning" and calling upon them to instruct the converts,[38] his acknowledgment of their collective power as witnesses, recorders, and voices for the Holy Spirit is all but drowned out by his momentous monologues aggrandizing his own holy authority.

Thus, while the ceremonies and signings did indeed inscribe the Goths' conversion into canonical tradition, witnessed by God for all future generations, they did not create consensus on the nature of the various participants' roles in the new alliance. The varying interpretations of the confession's meaning are mirrored and magnified in other parts of the records, particularly those dealing with the roles of the king and the church in the events leading up to the conversion, and in the future governance of the kingdom.

Reccared and the Mos Canonicus

If another primary task before the council was to instruct the bishops and Goths on conciliar practice and significance, it seems that Reccared seized the pedagogic initiative. He taught a lesson drawn from a clearly Romano-Byzantine curriculum. At the expense of the other players the king's insistence on the importance of his own actions and their significance in the renewal of conciliar authority command the reader's attention. It is tempting to accept his analysis as that of the entire council. In passage after passage the king claimed that, as the agent of God's will, he himself had been the driving force behind the conversion of the Goths and Sueves, the rebirth of synodal activity and ecclesiastic discipline, the reinforcement of his subjects' faith, their future salvation as a result of that reinforcement, the issuing of the canons of the council, and the enforcement of those canons.

In asserting his central role, the king did not deny in any way the importance of conciliar authority. Rather, he claimed it as an expression of his own divine authorization. In convening the council, the king said, he was following God's personal admonition to restore the ecclesiastic institutions to their customary practices. This action was the culmination of a series of past events that had begun when God entrusted "the government of many peoples" to Reccared's care.[39] The king had then gathered the Goths and conquered the

---

38. Tol. III, *tomus:* "docibilitatis." Rodríguez, 20.
39. Tol. III, *tomus:* "moderamen gentium non paucarum." Rodríguez, 19.

"infinite multitude" of the Sueves,[40] so that they might all enjoy the maternal bosom of the church. Reccared had thus eliminated heresy, a point about which he was particularly emphatic. In one passage he implied that it was he, rather than the church or Christ, who had called the nations to one faith:

> God incited me as well . . . kindled by the heat of faith in him, so that having pushed aside the obstinacy of infidelity and having removed the furor of discord I might call back the people, who were serving error under the name of religion, to the recognition of the faith and the fellowship of the Catholic Church.[41]

Reccared's role in these events, he told the council, had brought about the historical turning point being celebrated. Heresy had prevented the holding of synods. By making the council possible, Reccared had eliminated the blockage in the "sacerdotal memory"[42] created by heresy, in order that the bishops might restore the "canonical way of life," or the *mos canonicus*.[43]

Representing the council as the culmination of past events allowed Reccared to assert the necessity of ongoing royal involvement in matters of the faith. Reccared's God-given royal power had forged religious unification in the past, reinforced it through his present confession, and would lay the basis for the future governance of his kingdom. The link between royal action and his subjects' faith resulted in an ongoing double duty to "bridle with the royal power the ravings of the immoderate"[44] and to "regard the sublime with wonder, showing with serene light the truth to people who have been drawn back from error."[45] The king thus claimed authority over the kingdom's future not only by maintaining peace through constraint but also by "making the peoples faithful."[46] According to Reccared's analysis, the fulfillment of this double duty depended upon the bishops' collective authority, which would inscribe the king's prescriptions into eternity through canonical legislation.

---

40. Tol. III, *tomus:* "Sueuorum gentis infinita multitudo." Rodríguez, 20. Reccared did not mention that it was in fact his Arian father Leovigild who had conquered the Sueves nor that Leovigild had turned that people back to Arianism from Catholicism.

41. Tol. III, *tomus:* "Me quoque . . . calore fidei accensum in eo Dominus excitauit, ut depulsa obstinatione infidelitatis et discordiae submoto furore populum qui sub nomine religionis famulabatur errori, ad agnitionem fidei et ecclesiae catholicae consortium reuocarem." Rodríguez, 20.

42. Tol. III, address by Reccared: "sacerdotalibus sensibus." Rodríguez, 19.

43. Tol. III, address by Reccared. Rodríguez, 19.

44. Tol. III, address by Reccared: "insolentium rabiem regia potestate refrenare." Rodríguez, 29.

45. Tol. III, address by Reccared: "inhiare sublimia et ab errore retractis populis ueritatem eis serena luce ostendere." Rodríguez, 29.

46. Tol. III, address by Reccared: "populos fideles efficiunt." Rodríguez, 28.

After the Gothic confessions had been signed, Reccared called for the bishops to legislate. In the only canon he specifically claimed credit for, he sought to fulfill the religious aspects of his royal duties through a measure he had personally designed to maintain his subjects' faith. Instructing the bishops to place his canon "before all the decisions which should be added to the ecclesiastic rules by your holiness,"[47] he proclaimed that all Christians in all the churches of "all the Spains and Gaul"[48] should recite the creed of the Council of Constantinople before taking communion. According to the king, this practice would strengthen the belief of the faithful, confute the perfidy of the infidels, and make it impossible for anyone to claim innocence of heresy due to ignorance.

Fulfilling his religious duty by creating an identifiable body of the faithful would also address his duty for maintaining peace. After his call for the recitation of the creed, the king instructed the bishops to enact other measures directing the behavior of the faithful. "With my clemency in accord with you," he told them,

> in order to constrain the *mores* of the immoderate, end with strict opinions and prohibit with firmer discipline those things which should not be done, and confirm those which ought to be done with an immutable constitution.[49]

In his edict in confirmation of the council's legislation Reccared placed his final seal of authority on the measures he and the bishops had taken. The canons, he decreed, should "remain in eternal stability," on pain of excommunication for delinquent clergy and exile and confiscation of property (which would then accrue to the royal fisc) for laypeople.[50]

By referring to the "*mores* of the immoderate" in his call for the canons, Reccared underlined his own interpretation of the means to restore the well-being of his kingdom and of the meaning and purpose of conciliar legislation. He introduced this concept in his initial speech to the bishops when he referred to the *mos canonicus,* a way of life that had previously been lacking because of the absence of church councils. While the king was concerned with restoring ecclesiastic mores, clerical rectitude was but one element in a larger vision

---

47. Tol. III, address by Reccared: "Omnibus ergo capitulis qui adhuc per uestram sanctitatem regulis ecclesiasticis adiciendi sunt . . . praeponite." Rodríguez, 29.

48. Tol. III, address by Reccared: "omnes Hispaniarum et Gallia." Rodríguez, 29. In this context, "Gaul" refers to Narbonensis, the Visigothic province in southern Gaul.

49. Tol. III, address by Reccared: "autem pro inhibendis insolentium moribus, mea uobis consentiente clementia, sententiis terminate districtioribus, et firmiori disciplina, quae facienda non sunt prohibite, et ea quae fieri debent inmobili constitutione firmate." Rodríguez, 29.

50. Tol. III, *edictum regis in confirmationem concilii*: "manere perenni stabilitate." Rodríguez, 33.

of the future governance of all of his subjects. On the most immediate level the *mos canonicus* was not merely the knowledge of all the decisions handed down from the "holy fathers filled with the spirit of God."[51] For the newly converted king what had been missing in his kingdom because of the "threatening heresy" was the power to order subjects' lives through this knowledge and activity. In Reccared's terminology the *mos canonicus* signified this power.

In his edict in confirmation Reccared delineated the application of the newly restored *mos canonicus:* the decisions of the council were to be obeyed by all those "belonging to our kingdom . . . clerics, laymen, or any type of men."[52] In Reccared's eyes the legislative, moral, and coercive power of the *mos canonicus,* through royal support and the establishment of a kingdom-wide unity of faith, could ensure the inhibition of immoderate human mores throughout the territory he wished to control. Thus, the king claimed a legal jurisdiction over a unified kingdom and body of subjects that could, in theory, redress the current weaknesses of central power and counter any and all conditions of instability, noble factionalism, and potential hostility in the communities of his kingdom.

Reccared's lesson on the meaning of the council, the alliance, and future royal and conciliar governance was essentially a series of claims for his own central authority over the "clerics, laymen, or any type of men" in his kingdom. Viewed within the context of John of Biclar's comparison of Reccared with Constantine[53] or that of Toledo III's repeated invocation of the authority of the great eastern councils, which had been convened and presided over by Roman emperors, this vision does not necessarily look anomalous. Following the turbulent response among some Goths to his conversion, moreover, one can perhaps imagine that the former Arians participating in the council had political reasons for accepting and endorsing the king's claims and visions of central conciliar governance. What is hard to picture, however, is how local bishops like Masona received the king's teachings, which ran counter to their conceptions and exercise of individual and collective holy authority within their own communities.

The Bishops' Response

There is no indication in the council records that any of the church leaders overtly questioned the authority Reccared claimed. The narrator of the

51. Tol. III, c. 1: "sancti patres spiritu Dei." Rodríguez, 29.

52. Tol. III, *edictum:* "omnibus hominibus ad regnum nostrum pertinentibus . . . in omni auctoritate siue clericorum siue laicorum siue quorumcumque hominum obseruentur et maneant." Rodríguez, 33.

53. See chap. 1, n. 4.

records, undoubtedly a cleric, described the king as "filled with the Holy Spirit" as he spoke.[54] The bishops accepted his call to promulgate canons and did so with references to the counsel, command, and consent of the "most pious and glorious lord, king Reccared."[55] Moreover, their eight acclamations in response to the king's confession acknowledged Reccared's role as the "recruiter of new peoples in the Catholic church."[56] They designated him as meriting "the apostolic prize," since he had "fulfilled the apostolic duty."[57] Yet, if one listens to the council records as a dialogue, the acclamations following Reccared's confession can be heard as a measured response to his resounding assertions rather than as a culminating chorus of agreement. Reccared's pretensions of being the restorer of peace to the church were answered first: "Glory to God the Father and Son and Holy Spirit, whose care is to provide the peace and unity of their holy Catholic Church."[58] Reccared as the caller of the nations was replaced by Jesus: "Glory to our Lord Jesus Christ, who with the price of his blood gathered the Catholic church from all the *gentes.*"[59] And Reccared's *inclyta* and *gloriosa gens*—the Goths—became Jesus's *illustra gens:* "Glory to our Jesus Christ, who joined so illustrious a people to the unity of true faith, and instituted one flock and one pastor."[60] Reccared might deserve merit, an eternal crown, and glory from God as the church's recruiter and fulfiller of the apostolic duty, but his claims for personal initiative, even though slightly tempered by references to God's direction, overstepped the bounds of the bishops' vision of human agency in history.

Not only did the bishops disagree with Reccared's version of the past; they do not appear to have been in full agreement with the king's description of the present problems facing the kingdom nor with his vision of future restoration and governance. Although Reccared's voice dominates the records,

---

54. Tol. III, preamble: "divino . . . flamine plenus." Rodríguez, 19.

55. Tol. III, c. 2: "consultu piissimi et gloriosissimii domni Reccaredi regis." Rodríguez, 29.

56. Tol. III, acclamations: "Ipse nouarum plebium in ecclesia catholica conquisitor." Rodríguez, 23. On these acclamations, see Orlandis and Ramos-Lissón, *Historia de los Concilios,* 212; and Jocelyn N. Hillgarth, "Historiography in Visigothic Spain," *Settimane* 17 (Spoleto, 1970), reprinted in *Visigothic Spain, Byzantium and the Irish* (London, 1985), 282–83. On this type of royal acclamation in general, see Eugen Ewig, "Zum Christlichen Königsgedanken im Frühmittelalter," in *Spätantikes und Fränkisches Gallien. Gesammelte Schriften* 1 (Munich, 1976).

57. Tol. III, acclamations: "Ipse mereatur ueraciter apostolicum meritum, qui apostolicum impleuit officium." Rodríguez, 23.

58. Tol. III, acclamations: "Gloria Deo Patri et Filio et Spiritui Sancto, cui cura est pacem et unitatem ecclesiae suae sanctae catholicae prouidere." Rodríguez, 23.

59. Tol. III, acclamations: "Gloria Domino nostro Iesu Christo, qui pretio sanguinis sui ecclesiam catholicam ex omnibus gentibus congregauit." Rodríguez, 23.

60. Tol. III, acclamations: "Gloria domino nostro Iesu Christo, qui tam illustrem gentem unitati uerae fidei copulauit, et unum gregem et unum pastorem instituit." Rodríguez, 23.

the council's legislation contains some clues as to the bishops' point of view on these matters. The bishops' first canon is particularly revealing. Coming soon after Reccared's exposition on the duties and nature of royal authority in both secular and religious human affairs and contravening the king's desire to have his own canon come first, this all-purpose canon in support of traditional ecclesiastic authority has a somewhat dampening effect. Unlike most canons of this period, but very much like the long series of expository canons that would characterize Visigothic conciliar legislation in the seventh century, canon 1 contained a historically descriptive preamble explaining the need for its promulgation. Once again, the bishops' vision was based in the dynamics of local communities as they described the problems engendered by heresy and paganism:

> in some areas in the churches of Spain, because of the pressure of heresy or paganism, the canonical order was laid aside, its violation abounded, the desire for discipline was denied, every excess was fostered by the patronage of heresy, and the constraining power of discipline grew tepid through an abundance of evil.[61]

The canon went on to recount the means by which this situation had been remedied: "the peace of the church [was] restored by the mercy of Christ."[62] The body of the canon was an assertion of traditional ecclesiastic authority as the foundation for the reestablishment of order. Everything prohibited by the "authority of previous canons"[63] should again be restrained by renewed discipline. The acts of all previous councils should remain in force as well as the synodal letters of the popes of Rome. The noncanonical ordination of unworthy persons should be prohibited, and, generally, anyone doing anything "the holy fathers, filled with the spirit of God" had enacted against, should be punished by the "severity of earlier canons."[64]

Unlike the king, the bishops saw the decay of discipline more as a specific, local problem than as a kingdom-wide failure of memory through the absence of synods. Although they undoubtedly agreed with the king that the regular convocation of the councils was necessary, in their eyes the decay of discipline

---

61. Tol. III, c. 1: "in nonnullis uel haeresis uel gentilitatis necessitate per Hispaniarum ecclesias canonicus praetermissus est ordo dum et licentia abundaret transgrediendi et disciplinae optio negaretur dumque omnis excessus haeresis foueretur patrocinio, et abundantia mali teperet districtio disciplinae . . . . Maneant in suo uigore conciliorum omnium constituta, simul et synodicae sanctorum praesulum Romanorum epistolae." Rodríguez, 29.

62. Tol. III, c. 1: "pace ecclesiae Christi misericordia reparata." Rodríguez, 29.

63. Tol. III, c. 1: "priscorum canonum auctoritas." Rodríguez, 29.

64. Tol. III, c. 1: "Nicil ex hoc fiat, quod sancti Patris Spiritu Dei pleni sanxerunt debere non fieri, et qui praesumpserint seueritate priorum canonum distringantur." Rodríguez, 29.

engendered by the ravages of heresy arose from the improper use of worldly power—*patrocinium*—in some areas of the kingdom. The remedy they saw as most important was the application of canonical precedent rather than the holding of new councils. Their focus on the need for the constraints of discipline in particular churches recalls the difficulties in applying canonical precedent to specific incidents and disputes discussed in the previous chapter.

The canon's historical analysis ties this long-term problem to the difficulties of the immediate past. It contains no specifics on the nature of the decay of discipline other than the ordination of unworthy persons. "The patronage of heresy," however, is an apt, if cryptic, description of Leovigild's actions in support of Arians in cities like Mérida. The Arian king's religious activities also included the appointment of possibly "unworthy" Catholic bishops.[65] These problems of the past were compounded by the present situation: the ranks of the Catholic clergy had just been increased by the conversion of Arian clerics, none of whom had been subject to Catholic canonical rules previously. Thus, in their first canon the bishops' analysis of past problems and current complexities in local Christian communities produced an effort to restore order by asserting the jurisdiction and application of canonical precedents. Most specifically, by ensuring the canonical authority of individual clerics' ordinations, the bishops sought to prevent the interference of worldly power in the lives of local churches.

Given their immediate history of conflict with a centralizing king, it is likely that this formulation constituted another attempt by the Catholic bishops to draw a boundary around the aspirations voiced by Reccared. Once again, their depiction of the alleviation of past troubles ran counter to the king's pretensions: peace in the church had come about through the mercy of Christ. Furthermore, in this canon the bishops' resounding reiteration of the primacy of canonical authority in their program for the future restoration of order made no mention at all of royal participation, despite its centrality in the king's call for the canons. For the bishops that future order belonged to the past, to the "holy fathers filled with the spirit of God." The acknowledgment of the king's role in subsequent canons indicates that the bishops accepted some of the general outlines of the king's version of the past, the present, and the future. But in their first act of legislation, they sought to set bounds to his interpretation by confining it within the context of long-standing Catholic tra-

---

65. According to the *VPE*, 5.6.29, Nepopis, the Catholic bishop appointed by Leovigild to replace the exiled Masona, was "a profane man, a slave of the devil, an angel of Satan, a forerunner of Antichrist, and he was bishop of another city" (homo namque profanus servus sane diaboli angelus satanae praenuntius antichristi, et his erat alienae civitatis episcopus), 219. Collins, ("¿Donde estaban," 218) suggests that this appointment was not an isolated case.

ditions of historical interpretation and local ecclesiastic authority. If Reccared's conciliar pedagogy taught the lessons of centralized royal and conciliar governance, the bishops' first canon sought to mediate between those lessons and their own expectations about the exercise of both individual and collective local episcopal authority.

The bishops' assertion of the preeminence of conciliar traditions underlined a central element in the proceedings in Toledo. Through their conversion and its celebration Reccared and his followers had accepted a framework, a context for their actions, that the Catholic episcopate controlled. Certainly, Reccared had at his disposal traditions based on the "Eusebian" identification of the church with the Roman Empire[66] and on the secular powers' participation in great church councils of the past. The realization of those traditions in the present, however, depended on their being recognized within the context of the church's conciliar tradition. Thus, while Reccared expounded so enthusiastically on his own agency, powers, and responsibilities and while the bishops sought to mediate between those claims and their own interests and expectations, there appears to have been little disharmony at the council when it came to exalting the divine power of the church's councils. In this area the bishops and the king were, in fact, mutually dependent.

The bishops controlled conciliar authority in the sense that their participation and expertise were necessary for its ceremonial reenactment, for the attendance of the Holy Spirit at any given gathering, and for the continuing authority of canonical legislation. Yet the centrality given by all parties to the significance of conciliar activity constrained the Catholic bishops, partly because the divine power that flowed through their gatherings depended upon their being allowed to gather. The Arian kings apparently had prohibited Catholic councils since the reign of Agila (549–55).[67] History had proven that kings could and would prevent the gatherings upon which the exercise of conciliar power depended, and therefore the bishops did owe "thanks to God and

---

66. Eusebius of Caesarea made this identification throughout his *Historia Ecclesiastica,* ed. E. Schwartz (Leipzig, 1903), written ca. 325. For general discussions on the "Eusebian tradition," see Arnaldo Momigliano, "The Disadvantages of Monotheism for a Universal State," in *On Pagans, Jews, and Christians* (Scranton, 1987), 150–52; Norman H. Baynes, "Eusebius and the Christian Empire," in *Byzantine Studies and other Essays* (London, 1955), 168; and F. E. Cranz, "Kingdom and Polity in Eusebius of Caesarea," *Harvard Theological Review* 45, no. 1 (1952). On this identification in the Visigothic context, see Hillgarth, "Historiography," 264–65. Hillgarth (282–83) directly ties Toledo III's acclamations for Reccared to a Visigothic interpretation of the Eusebian tradition: "Eusebius' view of Constantine . . . appears again . . . in the Acts of Toledo III. The '*laudes*' (acclamations) the bishops of 589 sing, [are] an example of Byzantine ruler-worship transferred to the West, and probably directly modelled on the '*laudes*' addressed to Marcian at Chalcedon."

67. Thompson, *Goths,* 36.

to the most religious prince"[68] for making the "canonical order" available, on a collective level, once again.

Reccared accepted their gratitude wholeheartedly, and he did not hesitate to use conciliar authority to expand his own. For instance, his vision of the kingdom's future governance as a *mos canonicus* established through conciliar legislation was tied to an expansion of his own legislative powers. His edict in confirmation of the council, which was incorporated into the council's records, contained a preamble that ordered all of his subjects to obey the determinations of Toledo III.[69] The most apparent purpose of the edict was to give the council's legislation the force of civil law. Yet, at the same time, the council's canons supported royal lawmaking. Although by this time promulgating law was by no means a novelty for Visigothic kings, the codes of Euric, Alaric, and Leovigild had been issued according to the principle of "personality"—they were applied according to a person's identity as either Goth or "Roman."[70] By asserting its application to "any type of men" belonging to his kingdom, Reccared's edict constituted the first Visigothic attempt at lawmaking based on the principle of territoriality—application within defined political boundaries rather than by ethnicity—which the king now tied to the transcendent authority of the corpus of canonical tradition. Whether or not this was his conscious aim, it appears that in this instance the king's authority was significantly extended, at least in theory, by his recognition and support for conciliar authority.

Reccared's call for, and full participation in, Toledo III can be seen in a similar light. The council not only provided a public forum for the announcement and formalization of the Goths' conversion, but it also legitimized the authority the king claimed by virtue of his role in that conversion. On the other hand, the king's need for legitimation made it necessary for him to demonstrate an unconditional acceptance and support of the direct access to divine authority that the Catholic bishops, gathered "as one" in a holy synod,

---

68. Tol. III, preamble: "Ad haec autem gratias Deo agente et religiosissimo principi." Rodríguez, 19.

69. Although unprecedented in the history of Iberian church councils, the edict had antecedents in the laws issued by fourth- and fifth-century Roman emperors in confirmation of the great church councils of the eastern Empire. See Orlandis, *Historia de los Concilios,* 191–93; and Schwöbel, *Synode und König,* 139–41.

70. On the principle of "personality" in Germanic law codes, see intro., n. 33. Some historians argue that Visigothic civil law was territorial from the fifth century on. See, e.g., Alvaro d'Ors, "La territorialidad del derecho de los Visigodos," *Settimane* 3 (Spoleto, 1955). The traditional view dates the full territorialization of Visigothic law to the code issued by Recceswinth in 654, the *Leges Visigothorum.* P. D. King ("King Chindasvind and the First Territorial Law-code of the Visigothic Kingdom," in *Visigothic Spain,* 138) presents an argument that Recceswinth's code was based on an earlier territorial code issued by his father, Chindaswinth.

were able to claim. Even though God may have personally selected Reccared as king and guided him in his "apostolic duty" to gather heretics into the church, the king still depended upon the presence of the Lord "wherever there are two or three gathered in my name" to ratify his confession and the actions he had taken on behalf of his subjects and the Catholic faith.

The more emphasis the king gave to the divine power of the holy councils of the church, the more ideological support he granted to the legitimating capacity of the council he had called and thereby to his own position. Reccared did not hesitate in giving this support. There are extensive references to the synodal actions of ancient holy fathers not only in Toledo III's first canon but throughout the king's remarks as well as in the anathemas against Arianism signed by the converting Gothic leaders. A large portion of the king's confession was taken up with his acceptance of the Councils of Nicaea, Constantinople, Ephesus I, Chalcedon, and "all the other councils of the venerable orthodox bishops that are not dissonant from the purity of the faith of these four synods."[71] The creeds of the four major councils were reproduced in full and signed by the king as part of the conciliar *acta*. The emphasis on traditional, orthodox, conciliar authority was carried to the point that we find Reccared and the Gothic converts condemning the Arian Council of Rimini of 359[72] as well as "all the councils of the malignant which stood against the holy synod of Nicaea."[73] In his dependence upon the divinely endorsed authority emanating from the gatherings of Catholic bishops, Reccared gave that authority a central place in his understanding of Catholicism, in his presentation of the alliance with the church and, ultimately, in the definition and governance of his now theoretically unified kingdom.

Provincial Councils and Local Cooperation

While Reccared enthusiastically marshaled the legitimating capacity of conciliar authority to enhance his own, the content of his legislation and the immediate implementation of his *mos canonicus* remained in the hands of the bishops as they made their conciliar decisions. In their first canon the bishops took advantage of their newly won royal support in a narrow way, focusing on

---

71. Tol. III, *tomus:* "Omnium quoque orthodoxorum uenerabilium sacerdotum concilia quae ab his suprascriptis quattuor synodis fidei puritate non dissonant." Rodríguez, 21.

72. Tol. III, anathemas: "Quiquumque Ariminense concilium non ex toto corde respuerit et damnauerit, anathema sit." Rodríguez, 25.

73. Tol. III, *tomus:* "omnia concilia malignantium quae aduersus sanctam synodum Nicaenam exstiterunt." Rodríguez, 21.

reversing the transgression of the canonical order, or *ordo canonicus,* through "revived discipline,"[74] which they defined as unimpeded clerical obedience to the sanctions of previous church councils and papal correspondence. As a whole, all of the council's 23 canons reveal a consistent hesitance among the Catholic bishops when it came to Reccared's vision of ordering an entire kingdom through royally endorsed conciliar authority. Although they accepted certain aspects of Reccared's agenda, they apparently were either unwilling or unable to seize upon the notion of centralized control as precipitously as the king. Their task of mediating between local and central control was complicated by the tensions between their holy authority as individuals and as a collective body. The episcopal consensus asserted in their ceremonies would not support elaborate interference in the power structures of their own dioceses. Their legislation, therefore, is characterized by a noticeable delicacy in its treatment of the mechanisms of their new alliance with the secular authorities and in its implementation of ongoing practical conciliar authority.

In keeping with the limited approach of the first canon, much of the council's legislation addressed the narrow areas of concern that provincial councils traditionally dealt with: the protection and regulation of church property,[75] decorous clerical behavior,[76] procedures for imposing penance,[77] and the rights and responsibilities governing relationships between clerics.[78] It is not clear how or why these particular rulings were made, although some of the language is explicit enough to reflect the disposition of specific disputes.[79] Two further canons on ecclesiastic concerns reflect specific arrangements made in the process of working out the Arians' conversion. One reminds Arian clerics they now must obey the Catholics' celibacy rules and instructs them on how to relate to their wives;[80] another reaffirms the transfer of Arian churches to the Catholics.[81] In all of the canons that fall within the purview of the traditional *ordo canonicus* the king is referred to only once. Other canons do acknowledge his participation in the deliberations or in enforcing the rules in the future. These canons generally contain some elements that relate to specific

---

74. Tol. III, c. 1: "disciplina resurgens." Rodríguez, 29.

75. Tol. III, c. 3, 4, 6, and 19. Rodríguez, 29, 30, and 32.

76. Tol. III, c. 7. Rodríguez, 30.

77. Tol. III, c. 11 and 12. Rodríguez, 30–31.

78. Tol. III, c. 13 and 20. Rodríguez, 31–32.

79. For instance, Tol. III, c. 4 (Rodríguez, 30), gives permission to bishops to convert churches in their dioceses to monasteries and proclaims valid such conversions made in the past if they are not detrimental to the church. Tol. III, c. 13 (Rodríguez, 31), forbids clerics bringing cases against other clerics in public courts, indicates that this has happened in the past, and declares that anyone doing so will automatically lose the case.

80. Tol. III, c. 5. Rodríguez, 30. The canon also reminded those who had always lived under Catholic rules that they should not consort with disreputable women in their cells.

81. Tol. III, c. 9. Rodríguez, 30.

issues of royal property or secular governance. For instance, an anti-Jewish canon was included at the order of the king. It prohibited Jews from purchasing Christian slaves or holding public offices in which they might have the opportunity to punish Christians.[82] Another canon required that bishops request confirmation from the king before accepting donations from royal slaves.[83] The bishops also issued a canon begging the king to keep public officials from forcing ecclesiastic slaves and other clerics to labor in public or private business.[84] Despite the king's appearance in these canons, however, with the exception of the one against Jews, they do not appear to reflect the breadth of his vision of a *mos canonicus.*

Still, the bishops' accommodation of the king's efforts at enforcing strict delineations of religious identity in the anti-Jewish canon and in his creed recitation canon do indicate the bishops' interest in centralized control over religious identities in local communities. Some of the phraseology of the council's legislation also reveals a self-conscious assertion of a kingdom-wide ecclesiastic authority that faintly echoes the king's vigorous demands for his subjects' universal obedience to conciliar authority. A number of canons speak of the territory covered by these decisions as "throughout the Spains" or "throughout all the churches of Spain, Gaul, and Galicia," and so forth.[85] Some canons, moreover, can be read as addressing the opposite of the *mos canonicus,* unrestrained "human *mores.*" The canons on penance were designed to ensure uniformity and discipline for penitents and thus a more rigorous response to "the immoderate." An anti-idolatry measure,[86] like the anti-Jewish measure, was meant to address the continued religious disunity within the kingdom. Canons against infanticide, the forced marriage of religious women, disgraceful behavior at saints' festivals, and unseemly mourning at funerals were all designed to contain the "furor" of undisciplined laypeople.[87]

The canons most obviously reflective of Reccared's call for the conciliar implementation of a *mos canonicus* are those that prescribe a centrally defined and locally implemented cooperation between bishops and secular officials. Four such canons appear in Toledo III's legislation: the anti-idolatry canon, the anti-infanticide canon, the canon on saints' festivals, and the council's most famous canon, canon 18, which called for yearly provincial councils throughout the kingdom. These canons allow a glimpse of the negotiations on governmental practice between the king and the bishops. One can also see,

82. Tol. III, c. 14. Rodríguez, 31.

83. Tol. III, c. 15. Rodríguez, 31.

84. Tol. III, c. 21. Rodríguez, 32.

85. See, e.g., Tol. III, c. 1, 2, 16, and 22: "per Hispaniarum," "per omnes ecclesias Hispaniae, Galliae uel Galliciae." Rodríguez, 29, 31–32.

86. Tol. III, c. 16. Rodríguez, 31.

87. Tol. III, c. 17, 10, 23, and 22. Rodríguez, 30–32.

even more clearly, how the bishops attempted to accommodate the king's vision in applying the concept of a *mos canonicus* to their own communities as well as some of the limitations involved in enforcing a collectively defined consensus in individual dioceses throughout the kingdom. While the bishops clearly welcomed the reinforcement of their individual and provincial leadership entailed in the cooperation with secular officials, they handled the specifics of that reinforcement with kid gloves.

The three canons dealing with individual bishops and the judges in their communities are of particular interest. The anti-idolatry canon begins by bemoaning the fact that "the sacrilege of idolatry is implanted almost throughout all of Spain and Gaul" (i.e., Narbonensis).[88] In response, the canon called upon "every bishop in his locality" to work with the local judge, "inquiring diligently," "exterminating" any sacrilegious practices discovered, and punishing "all those who flock to such error."[89] Bishops and judges neglecting this duty were to be excommunicated, as were any landowners who failed to eliminate idolatry from their possessions or households. The bishops immediately followed their idolatry prohibition with a parallel measure against infanticide. This canon noted that the council had received many complaints that "in certain parts of Spain, fathers, eager for fornication and ignorant of piety, kill their children."[90] After explaining that marriage and copulation are meant only for the propagation of children, the canon pointed out that the king had already directed his judges to investigate with the bishops in those areas. The council therefore gave its consent to the king's initiative by charging the bishops to cooperate, calling on them to inflict "very harsh penalties" against offenders but to avoid capital punishment.[91] The canon on saints' festivals is the council's last canon. It decries an "irreligious custom" among the common people: disgraceful dancing and singing at saints' festivals.[92] Making no mention of the king, or even of joint investigation, the canon ends with the simple statement that the council entrusted the job of expelling such practices from all of Spain to the "priests and judges."[93]

The negotiations involved in this cooperation are only hinted at in the language of the canons. In the first two the king and the bishops asserted their

88. Tol. III, c. 16: "paene per omnem Hispaniam siue Galliam idolatriae sacrilegium inoleuit." Rodríguez, 31.

89. Tol. III, c. 16: "ut omnis sacerdos in loco suo una cum iudice territorii sacrilegium memoratum studiose perquirat et exterminare inuenta non differat. Homines uero qui ad talem errorem concurrunt . . . coerceant." Rodríguez, 31.

90. Tol. III, c. 17: "in quasdam Hispaniae partes filios suos parentes interimant, fornicationi auidi, nescii pietatis." Rodríguez, 31.

91. Tol. III, c. 17: "acriori disciplina." Rodríguez, 31.

92. Tol. III, c. 23: "consuetudo irreligiosa." Rodríguez, 32.

93. Tol. III, c. 23: "ut ab omni Hispania depellatur, sacerdotum et iudicum a concilio sancto curae committitur." Rodríguez, 32.

central power separately, in something of a quid pro quo arrangement: the bishops collectively called upon their own ranks to obey the directives, while the king ordered the judges. Not surprisingly, the bishops appear to have taken the initiative on the idolatry issue. The canon states that the "holy synod" ordered the measure with the king's consent; with this consent established and the authority of the local judges thereby joined to that of individual bishops, the council then attempted to mobilize the independent power of landowners. Thus, the bishops gained Reccared's support in ensuring the participation of local judges in stamping out idolatry. In return, they turned their attention to the "plague" of infanticide, an evil the king had already taken action against before the council. Although the council had received complaints about the problem, the king apparently had seized the initiative on this issue, ordering his judges to work with bishops to investigate and punish offenders. The council gave their support by calling on their own ranks to join in the effort.

In these two canons, then, king and council joined in the centralized direction of local leaders to uncover and punish crimes that would seem obvious examples of the "ravings of the immoderate" and the elimination of which would contribute significantly to establishing a kingdom-wide community of obedient faithful. In the canon on saints' festivals the bishops applied these principles without comment on consent or initiative. The issue in question, however, makes it safe to assume that in this case the bishops used the mechanisms established in the previous canons as a model for dealing with their own particular interest in orchestrating local saints' cults. Agreement achieved at the highest level, instituted through conciliar authority, would be administered by local leaders working in harmony to maintain Christian obedience at all levels of society: Reccared's *mos canonicus* in action, Toledo III's vision of consensus realized.

Yet, given the bishops' interpretation of the king's claims and the Goths' confession, along with their first canon's limited means for the restoration of order, these canons merit careful analysis for their application in local communities. Their details indicate conscientious planning, some of which probably involved preliminary agreements made before the council met. It is revealing, therefore, to consider what details were left out. Although the measure against idolatry included excommunication for bishops, judges, and landowners who neglected their duty, the infanticide canon contains no such provision. Other than the exclusion of capital punishment, neither measure contains specific penalties for those found to have committed these crimes. Most significantly, perhaps, although both canons called for diligent cooperative investigations by local bishops and judges, neither one addressed in any way how those investigations were to be carried out, what judicial practices were to be used, what tribunals would decide cases or impose penalties, or, generally, what the legal relationship between individual judges and bishops was to be.

Apparently, the bishops' acceptance of the king's vision did not encourage a willingness to dictate these matters. The council clearly saw the central recognition of their roles as local investigators and collaborators as an acceptable and undoubtedly desirable affirmation of the holy authority of individual bishops. Collectively, however, the episcopate did not wish to infringe so fundamentally on the various and complex judicial arrangements and relationships of power in local communities. In the one instance where the bishops did address such details in these canons, they did so with noticeable delicacy. The idolatry canon's clause on landowners apparently excluded these powerful men and their household members from the investigations of the bishops and judges. They were, however, made subject to excommunication by the local bishop if they did not themselves investigate the matter on their own estates.

It is highly unlikely that the bishops, the king, or his agents were not concerned with the specific mechanisms by which their shared duties were to be carried out. Their concern is evident in the council's eighteenth canon, which contains many of the details left out of these other measures. This canon called for the renewal of yearly provincial councils,[94] which were to be summoned by the metropolitan bishop and held in November. At these tribunals local judges and royal fiscal agents—at the order of the king—were to meet with the province's bishops in order to learn "how they should piously and justly act with the people—both private people and fiscal slaves—lest they burden them with demands or superfluous impositions."[95] The bishops were to investigate the judges, "according to the royal admonition," either correcting those abusing the people or bringing news of their activities "to the ears of the prince."[96] Judges who refused to change their behavior were to be excommunicated, leaving the bishops and the community elders to decide on the tribunal that would take responsibility for the province "without detriment."[97]

---

94. Because of the "distance and poverty of the churches of Spain" ("itineris longitudine et paupertate ecclesiarum Spaniae"), Tol. III, c. 18, reduced the number of councils ordered per year to one. Rodríguez, 31. Some historians describe canon eighteen as institutionalizing provincial councils and the "representative" role of the local bishops, singling it out as Toledo III's central political development and the core of the new alliance between Gothic and ecclesiastic leaders. See, e.g., Orlandis, *Historia de los concilios,* 224–25; and Ramon D'Abadal, "Els concilis de Toledo," in *Dels Visigots als Catalans* (Barcelona, 1968), 71.

95. Tol. III, c. 18: "quam pie et iuste cum populis agere debeant, ne in angariis aut in operationibus superfluis . . . gravent." Rodríguez, 31

96. Tol. III, c. 18: "ut aut ipsos praemonitos corrigant aut insolentias eorum auditibus principis innotescant." Rodríguez, 31–32:

97. Tol. III, c. 18: "quid provincia sine suo detrimento praestare debeat iudicum." Rodríguez, 32. On the office of *iudex,* the local royal agent who heard civil court cases, made arrests, judged, carried out sentences in criminal cases, and was often seen as susceptible to bribery, see Thompson, *Goths,* 139–42. Thompson argues that until 654 the *iudex* had authority only over the Gothic population.

Although the language still leaves room for interpretation, this canon is much clearer than the others on questions of procedure and the distribution of power within the province. Central authority was still exercised according to a division between the king's enforcement of his agents' attendance at these councils and Toledo III's call to the bishops. On the provincial level, however, the episcopate appears to have had collective authority over individual judges and fiscal agents, even in regards to the treatment of fiscal slaves. Although the process of investigation is not specifically laid out, the role of the council in the procedure is obviously central. One can assume that the bishops' duties as *prospectatores* were to be exercised at their provincial tribunals, in the presence of the Holy Spirit. The procedures for dealing with abusive agents are relatively specific; the bishops had the choice between informing the prince of individual abusers or exercising their collective voice of admonition, warning those "brought forward" in their investigation.[98] While it is not clear what powers the king might exercise against these men, the bishops' power to excommunicate those who refused to reform themselves appears to have been considered enough to depose them. On the other hand, the bishops' collective authority was not sufficient for choosing the new secular "tribunal" for the province. In this decision they had to consult with other local powerful men—the *seniores*.

The bishops, hesitant to interfere too closely in the dynamics of individual dioceses, were more methodical in implementing their collective power on the provincial level. Their collective ability to educate and investigate, based in their Christian learning and dignity and their access to divine judgment, were recognized and ratified as the highest local authority, on some issues, at least. Yet even canon 18, with its careful provisions for the conciliar control of secular agents, left many key details unaddressed. For instance, while the conciliar collectivity was given supervisory power over individual royal agents, the specific activities to be supervised were not made completely clear. The primary issues in question seem to have been financial ones: the elimination of "superfluous impositions and demands" made by fiscal agents. Yet some of the language—for example, the directions for bishops to investigate "how the judges act with the people"—is general enough to cover a wide array of abuses, including judicial ones. It may be that provincial councils were envisioned as the tribunal to which individual bishops could bring any disputes with local agents that might arise in working out the mechanisms of their community cooperation. This is not made clear in canon 18, however, and provincial councils are not mentioned in the three other canons on local collaboration. Again, when it came to specific local judicial mechanisms, the bishops

---

98. Tol. III, c. 18: "ipsos praemonitos." Rodríguez, 32.

were unwilling to prescribe too closely, and they left ample room for adjustment according to local situations.

Indeed, the bishops at Toledo III left the role of provincial councils in the future governance of the kingdom largely undefined. Aside from canon 18, only one canon mentions local councils at all.[99] Moreover, while canon 18 included instructions on the timing, location, and notification for provincial councils and the metropolitan bishops' leadership in their convocation, the remainder of the measure is entirely devoted to supervising royal agents. Unlike Martin of Braga, who emphasized conciliar pedagogy at the Galician council in 572,[100] the bishops at Toledo III did not fully delineate or explain the particular purpose or competence of provincial councils, despite all the participants' acknowledgment that the preceding years of heretical rule had blocked "synodal business"[101] and the knowledge of "discipline."[102] Thus, it seems that, while the drafters of these canons were willing to apply the larger principles behind the *mos canonicus* to some issues involving lay behavior in local communities, and though they were apparently eager to assert their collective power over secular officials, they were not willing to implement central ecclesiastic control in a systematic way. The mechanisms of provincial conciliar judicial authority, like those of the joint local powers of bishops and judges, were left open to interpretation, depending on specific circumstances—which frequently did not include a shared clerical knowledge of conciliar ceremony, precedent, and procedure.

In principle there would have been very little reason for the bishops to reject most of the key elements in Reccared's vision of a *mos canonicus*. These bishops had behind them years of community leadership without the benefits of support from the secular government. They had worked under the conditions of violence and instability arising from the territorial expansion and consolidation of Visigothic rule as well as from the competition presented by Arian congregations. There is no reason to believe that they would not have supported the establishment of a new community of the faithful made obedient to the traditions, and thus to the leaders, of orthodox Christianity. Nor would they have objected to the legitimation of conciliar authority as the legislative power behind the ordering of that community and the constraint of its human *mores*. This once again enabled them to lay claim to a collective access to divine judgment.

Most important, Reccared's vision incorporated the centralized recogni-

---

99. Tol. III, c. 4: bishops converting churches of their dioceses into monasteries were to obtain the consent of their councils. Rodríguez, 30.

100. See chap. 1, n. 62.

101. Tol. III, address of Reccared: "synodica negotia." Rodríguez, 19.

102. Tol. III, c. 1: "optio disciplinae." Rodríguez, 29.

tion and institutionalization of the individual episcopal leadership that had long provided the underpinnings for the organization and daily life of many Hispano-Roman communities.[103] The men at Toledo III, however, were faced with the task of mediating between the local position and holy authority of individual bishops, the episcopate's collective access to the Holy Spirit, and the king's centralizing aspirations. Highly sensitive to the dynamics of local communities, in terms of both the conflicts of the immediate past and the longer-term difficulties involved in applying canonical precedents, the bishops in 589 stepped lightly around many areas of potential judicial conflict and contradiction that were embedded in the establishment of kingdom-wide consensus, or Reccared's *mos canonicus.*

The king desired and received conciliar confirmation for his legislative powers, along with practical assistance in the oversight of his governmental agents. In this sense, the council's legislation can be read as the bishops' accommodation of the kingship's need for centralized control and thus of his overall agenda. The actual implementation of some key aspects of the alliance in local areas, however, was left to the discretion of provincial episcopates as they began to establish their own versions of conciliar authority and procedure. To an even greater extent that implementation was left to the now officially recognized holy authority of individual bishops, navigating their own way through existing power relationships in their various communities. For the time being the exercise of governmental power, for all its lack of local definition, was weighted away from the centralizing inclinations of the Visigothic kingship.

Catholic Consensus and Unresolved Differences

Toledo III left major questions unresolved. To be sure, Reccared's claims for royal initiative in history, as well as for royal responsibility for the future maintenance of the people's faith through the establishment of a *mos canonicus,* were inscribed into the council records and thus into canonical authority. Yet the same is true of the Catholic bishops' more limited views—the assertions of the church's primacy in the triumph over heresy and in the reestablishment and enforcement of the *ordo canonicus* based on the primacy of canonical precedent in local areas. Although contained within the unanimous support for conciliar authority and its judicial capacity, these differences do not appear to have been settled in any programmatic way. If one returns to Leander's closing homily, reading it as the final words of the leading church

---

103. On one such community in the sixth century, see Collins, "Merida and Toledo."

representative in response to the council's dialogue, it can also be read as an answer to the potential for confusion and dissension arising from the council's lack of explicit definitions.

Leander made no reference to either royal or conciliar authority nor to the actions of the king or the former Arians, aside from their conversion. Rather, he offered a broad interpretation of the historical sufferings of the church at the hands of heresy. His theological argument was meant to show how the mystery of salvation had been realized in the Goths' conversion,[104] and his presentation was aimed at evoking exultant joy in his audience at the reunification of the peoples divided at the Tower of Babel.[105] Yet in his "resolute optimism,"[106] Leander presented an ideal vision of the unity of the worldwide church that distanced his audience from any possibility of future suffering within the church and from personal responsibility for past depredations. Consequently, Leander's homily, intentionally or not, removed the significance of the conversion and its celebration from the arena of the immediate present and so from the contradictions implicit in the words of his contemporaries.

Leander's entire speech was a eulogy to Catholic unity—a unity foretold in Scripture, a unity prescribed by nature, a unity defined by its opposition to the divisions of heresy. According to Leander, those who did not participate in the shared sentiment and love of unity, those who did not partake of the single heart and soul of the Lord's one possession, the Catholic Church, would not survive. God had foretold what would happen to these deviants when he said, "the nation or kingdom that does not serve you will perish."[107] Leander's own words made the fate of nonparticipants more immediate and more individual: "Since Christ wishes to have one church from all the nations, whoever is a stranger from it, although he may be called by the Christian name, is not held by the union of Christ."[108] A stranger to the church was a stranger to unity and was therefore excluded from the community.

Leander's homily provided a context for the actions and words of his contemporaries that evoked human unity on a scale far outreaching, both geographically and chronologically, the history of disunity they were seeking to

---

104. Jacques Fontaine, "La homilía de San Leandro ante el Concilio III de Toledo: temática y forma," in *Concilio III de Toledo*, 250.

105. Fontaine, "La homilía," 253

106. Fontaine, "La homilía," 256: "optimismo resoluto."

107. Leander, *homelia*, quoting Isaiah 60.12: "Qui, ut notesceret quae uentura essent genti uel populo quae ab unius ecclesiae communione recessissent, secutus est: 'Gens enim et regnum quod non seruierit tibi, peribit.' " Rodríguez, 37.

108. Leander, *homelia*: "Dum ergo ex omnibus gentibus unam uult Christus habere ecclesiam, quicumque extraneus est ab ea, licet Christiano nomine nuncupetur, Christi tamen compage non tenetur." Rodríguez, 37.

redress. It also posed that unity against any conflict they might have encountered in the council itself or in the future. Leander ended the homily with an
exhortation that suggests that he conceived of this naturally prescribed, God-
given, worldwide and exclusively Catholic unity as a means for creating harmony out of the dissonance he faced at the council:

> Let us all say: Glory to God in the highest, and on earth peace to men
> of good will, for there is no gift to compare with the gift of love.
> Therefore it is above all other joys that peace and love have been
> made, which take first place of all virtues. It remains that unanimously
> made into one kingdom, we should attend God with prayers, as much
> for the stability of the earthly kingdom as for the joy of the celestial
> kingdom, so that the kingdom and the nation that glorify Christ on
> earth should be glorified by Him not only on earth but also in
> heaven.[109]

In the only explicit reference he made to the kingdom in which he lived, Leander finally brought the weight of his praise of unity to bear on the future of his
society. The Catholic unity of humanity had been made concrete in the community consensus of the Visigoths' kingdom, and that unity and consensus
made possible the unanimous prayers to God that would ensure the stability
of their leadership. Dissension, disharmony, conflict, and contradiction could
not survive in a community whose very definition was grounded in the exclu-
sivity of its unanimity; dissent marked one a stranger to the body of Christ, to
the church, and to the providential history that had produced the conversion
of the Visigoths and the unity now embodied in the alliance among the community's leaders.

Toledo III's agreement on these broad and distancing concepts allowed
all concerned to recognize and support one another's authority. It also allowed
the articulation and celebration of an ideal Christian consensus to drown out
the disharmony implicit in its various participants' words. Yet, despite Leander's vivid vision of Catholic unity, in many senses Toledo III failed at its most
important tasks. The canons did address some local issues arising out of the
recent conflicts between Catholics and Arians, and the council gave the bishops a platform from which to express their collective grievances. At the same
time, however, it also allowed the former Arians, including the king, to put

---

109. Leander, *homelia:* "Dicamus ergo omnes: 'Gloria in excelsis Deo et in terra pax
hominibus bonae uoluntatis.' Nullum enim praemium caritati compensatur. Inde omni gaudio
praeponitur, quia pax et caritas facta est, quae omnium uirtutum obtinet principatum. Superest autem ut unanimiter unum omnes regnum effecti tam pro stabilitate regni terreni quam
felicitate regni caelestis Deum precibus adeamus, ut regnum et gens, quae Christum glorificauit
in terris, glorificetur ab illo non solum in terris, sed etiam in caelis." Rodríguez, 38.

forth their own analyses of the past and its meaning for the present and future, undermining the consensus necessary for the transformation of these aggrieved community advocates into allies. That transformation was further compromised by the lack of definition concerning the bishops' new role as local collaborators and judicial authorities. Their individual leadership might be recognized by the king and his agents, but the process of working out the mechanisms for cooperation in local communities could easily produce new grievances as various bishops and judges vied for power and influence. Likewise, as a lesson on the meaning and purpose of conciliar authority, the council focused heavily on centralized authority and the role of divinely elected rulers, leaving provincial conciliar practice and the application of canonical rules in local communities vague and open to interpretation. This contradictory pedagogy also left unexplained the potentially problematic relationships between central royal authority, central ecclesiastic authority, and individual bishops. Rather than mediating these complex configurations of holy power, the council sidestepped the issues.

Indeed, the only consistent response in the council records to the varying views, the potential for conflict, and the threat these might pose to the alliance was the continuing reiteration of the sanctity of Catholic unity—the only explicit definition of which seems to have been an unqualified universal acceptance of the authority of orthodox tradition. Any future conflict would have to be worked out within the limited, and idealized, foundations of the alliance: the unity of the Catholic Trinity, kingdom-wide Christian consensus, and the holy authority derived from both. The alliance celebrated at the council represented a balance of powers made precarious by the history of cultural, political, and religious divisions that preceded it—a balance too precarious to support a kingdom-wide consensus on the local exercise of holy authority in resolving conflicts. Yet, despite the variance between the different parties' visions, Reccared's ideals for the centralized imposition of a kingdom-wide, episcopally led *mos canonicus* as one of the means for the territorialization of Visigothic rule were in many ways complementary to, and indeed dependent upon, the narrower vision of the bishops. In the long run the complementary lack of explicit definition in these varying visions may have helped lay the basis for seventh-century ideological expansions and symbolic redefinitions in the language and practice of conciliar and governmental authority. In the short run it stimulated a wide variety of interpretations and contradictions in the implementation of the new alliance in local communities.

CHAPTER THREE

Collaboration, Suspicion, and Innovation in the Provinces

In 589 the leaders of the Visigothic kingdom had reached an agreement on the equality of the Catholic Trinity. In doing so, they had settled on the outlines of a new, more limited framework within which they would carry on future struggles over holy authority. Over the next forty years the terms and arenas of conflict shifted within that framework. The decade after Toledo III was a period of particular fluidity in ideas and practice. Provincial councils met in most of the kingdom's provinces, developing various interpretations of individual and collective episcopal authority. Meanwhile, the king issued three secular laws. While asserting the sacred authority of church councils and of royal lawmaking, these leaders continued to face the resistance that had existed prior to the Visigoths' conversion. During this period neither episcopal consensus nor divinely elected kingship appears to have wielded the holy authority necessary to overcome this resistance. By the end of the 590s the absolute Christian consensus that would have endowed either type of legislation with the force of effective divine sanctions was still alive as an ideal. But that ideal was perhaps even farther from realization than it had been in 589.

After the men in Toledo dispersed, local leaders and common people had to deal with the nuts and bolts of Toledo III's contradictory vision and, in doing so, faced a number of vital practical questions. How were local secular authorities—judges, counts of cities, and the provincial *duces* who were their superiors—to cooperate with ecclesiastic leaders in judicial processes? How would that cooperation be complicated by the incorporation of Arians—powerful secular men, bishops, lower clergy, and common laypeople—into the Catholic community? How were individual bishops to mediate between their own interests and those of their provincial episcopate as a collectivity? How were councils going to exercise their holy power in ways that would demonstrate and sustain the authority to enforce their decisions? How were local authorities to mediate between their own claims to holy power and the divine authority claimed by the king? And, ultimately, how was local consensus on the divine authority of bishops, councils, and kings, if and when it was established, to be translated into unanimous obedience and kingdom-wide Christian consensus?

As is usual in dealing with the Visigothic evidence, there is very little datable material of any kind from this period, let alone sources that would reveal a variety of local responses to these questions. In order to coax from the existing material a better understanding of the circumstances within which Iberian communities confronted the questions raised by Toledo III, this chapter will begin by looking at one incident that occurred prior to 589: a rebellion in Mérida in 588, which was described in detail in the *Vitas patrum emeritensium.*[1] This episode offers a glimpse into the community dynamics to which the men at Toledo III were responding in 589 and with which they were still confronted after they returned home. While leaders in other communities faced different configurations of power and loyalty, the dynamics in Mérida provide a general framework for considering the variety of measures taken as local leaders throughout the kingdom tried to implement the new alliance during the decade after the council.

In 588 Masona, that dignified Gothic bearer of the Holy Spirit and metropolitan bishop of Lusitania, still held office in Mérida. Although the Arians of the city had lost their royal support when Reccared converted to Catholicism in 587, they still held the basilicas and privileges that Leovigild had given them. They also continued to wield enough influence in the community that their bishop, the "scabrous" Sunna, could call on their support in his effort to resist conversion to Catholicism. Together with a group of wealthy Gothic nobles, some of whom were counts appointed by Reccared, Sunna hatched a plot to kill Masona and the province's Hispano-Roman *dux,* Claudius. The conspiracy was apparently aimed at seizing royal power in the area and thus was also an attack on the king.[2] According to the *Vitas,* after Reccared's conversion Sunna, "urged on by the devil," convinced the group of Gothic counts, along with "an innumerable multitude of the people," to apostatize from the new faith.[3] He "devised deceitful plans against the servant of God, Masona, to kill him."[4] Under the guise of friendship Sunna sent emissaries to Masona with an invitation to come to his house. The Catholic bishop, immediately wise to the plot, demurred; he was busy with church matters, he said, and invited the conniver to come to his house instead. Sunna called together his coconspira-

---

1. *VPE,* 5.10.1–11.21, 233–45.

2. The *VPE* presents the episode as an attack specifically on Masona; John Bicl., *anno VI Mauricii,* 218, however, describes it briefly as one of three rebellions against the king prior to Toledo III.

3. *VPE,* 5.10.1–2: "iritatus a diabolo . . . cum innumerabili multitudine populi," 233.

4. *VPE,* 5.10.2: "contra famulum Dei Masonam episcopum fraudulenta consilia qualiter eum interficerent commentavit," 233.

tors, assigning one of them—a youthful noble named Witteric—the task of running Masona through with his sword.

When the group, now accompanied by "huge crowds" of supporters,[5] arrived at the episcopal abode, Masona made them wait outside while he sent word to the *dux*, Claudius, who lived close by. Claudius arrived on the double, also bringing along a "huge multitude," and everyone entered Masona's house, greeting the holy man "according to custom."[6] After the nobles and bishops had taken their seats and talked for a while, Witteric prepared to make his move and kill the *dux* and Masona. Unfortunately for the conspirators, the young man was prevented from doing so by "the judgment of God":[7] no matter how hard he tried, he could not draw his sword. After futilely casting shifty-eyed glances of encouragement at the impotent swordsman, the Arians abruptly took their leave and went home in disgust.

Utterly undone by the miracle, Witteric stayed behind, threw himself at Masona's feet, and confessed. Not only did he admit his own evil intentions, but he revealed the conspirators' contingency plan: they were preparing to ambush Masona and the entire Catholic community during the customary Easter procession from the cathedral church to Eulalia's basilica outside the city walls:

> As you are unsuspectingly proceeding unarmed, the whole mass of them will suddenly rush upon you and, drawing their swords and clubs, will kill everyone indiscriminately, men and women, the old and the children, with cruel death.[8]

Witteric begged for the bishop's mercy, telling Masona to take him prisoner and to "investigate everything diligently and know the truth for certain."[9] "Always illustrious for the virtue of compassion,"[10] Masona soothed Witteric's fears, incarcerated him, and informed Claudius of the new developments. Pursuing the investigation, the *dux* found Witteric was speaking truthfully and, on the designated day, foiled the ambush. After killing some attackers and taking others prisoner, he went to Sunna's house and arrested

---

5. *VPE*, 5.10.9: "cum ingentibus catervis," 235.

6. *VPE*, 5.10.8–9: "cum ingenti multitudine . . . . salutato viro sancto ex more," 235.

7. *VPE*, 5.10.14: "divino iudicio," 237.

8. *VPE*, 5.11.3: "Cumque vos inermes simpliciter processeritis, omnis eorum repente super vos irruat multitudo arreptisque gladiis vel fustibus omnes pariter, viros ac mulieres senes vel parvulos, crudeli morte interimant," 239.

9. *VPE*, 5.11.5: "omnia strenue perquiras ac certissime cognoscas," 239.

10. *VPE*, 5.11.6: "semper virtute pietatis enituit," 239.

him as well. Imprisoning the counts, Claudius put Sunna in Masona's custody and set Witteric free.

With the situation under control, the *dux* reported the events to Reccared, suggesting that he "immediately pronounce sentence and tell him what to do with the enemies of the Lord Jesus Christ."[11] Reccared sentenced the lay conspirators to exile and the loss of their property and, apparently, of their hands.[12] Showing his mercy toward clerics, the king authorized the community to try converting Sunna so that he might do penance and then be made bishop in another city. The ever-willful Sunna refused, offering to die for his lifelong religion. The Catholics of Mérida drove him into exile, clearing the way for the king not only to return to the Catholics the Arians' basilicas and privileges but also to grant to Masona all of Sunna's personal property.

The final episode in this drama involved the fate of Vagrila, a conspirator who had avoided exile by taking refuge in the basilica of St. Eulalia.[13] Claudius again reported the situation to the king, who decreed the following sentence:

> Vagrila, with his wife, his children, and all his patrimony shall serve forever as a slave of the most holy virgin Eulalia. And by this decree we ordain that as the lowest slaves are wont always to go on foot before the horse of their masters, so he is to walk before the horse of his master, the superior of St. Eulalia's and, laying aside his pride and glory, perform in all humility every service that the lowest slave is accustomed to perform.[14]

Masona, however, chose to be more compassionate. The bishop ordered Vagrila to vacate the basilica and had him symbolically enact the king's sentence:

---

11. *VPE,* 5.11.11: "Omnia igitur quae gesta fuerant orthodoxo principi Reccaredo Claudius dux intimavit atque ut, porrectam confestim decretus sui sententiam, ei praeciperet quid de hostibus Domini Ihesu Christi fieri deberet suggessit," 241. On Claudius and the office of *dux* (duke) in the structure of offices under Leovigild and Reccared, see E. A. Thompson, *The Goths in Spain,* (Oxford, 1969), 143–44.

12. John Bicl., *anno VI Mauricii,* 218.

13. On sanctuary in churches and bishops as mediators during this period, see Edward James, "*Beati Pacifici:* Bishops and the Law in Sixth-Century Gaul," in *Disputes and Settlements: Law and Human Relations in the West,* ed. John Bossy (Cambridge, 1983), 37–42.

14. *VPE,* 5.11.17–19: "Inimicus summi Dei miror cum qua facie atria eius sancta ingredi praesumpserit, ut quem hactenus insaniendo frustra persecutus est nunc ad eum percipiendi causa remedii confugium facit. Sed quia multae miserationis novimus esse Deum et nullum despicere, quamvis delinquentem, ad se convertentem ambigimus, ob hoc ita decernimus: Ut ipse Vagrila cum uxure filiis et omni patrimonio suo perpetim sanctissimae virginis Eulaliae servus deserviat. Nam et hoc praesenti decreto sancimus ut sicut ultimi pueri ante equum dominorum suorum absque aliquo vehiculi iuvamine ambulare soliti sunt, ita ante caballum domini qui praeest cellae sanctae Eulaliae ambulare debeat et omne servitium quod infimum consuevit peragere mancipium coram eo deposito cothurno vel fastu cum omni humilitate deserviat." 243–45.

In obedience . . . to the order of the king, he commanded [Vagrila] for the sake of obedience to walk before the horse of the deacon Redemptus from the church of St. Eulalia to the episcopal residence that is built within the walls of the city. When [Vagrila] had taken the staff of the deacon and with it in his hands had come to the bishop's house, the holy man at once released him with his wife and children and all his lands and permitted him to go free. He laid upon him this one injunction, to preserve his Catholic Faith pure and immaculate in every detail all the days of his life.[15]

With peace returned to the community, Masona and his people chanted psalms, clapped hands, sang hymns, and, "rejoicing after the manner of the ancients with great uproar in the streets," made their way once again to their cherished saint's basilica.[16]

The author of the *Vitas* assured his readers that after the rebellion, with "storms being put down everywhere, the Lord vouchsafed to grant the Catholics abundant peace."[17] Claudius, according to John of Biclar, went on to lead a tiny but triumphant army against sixty thousand more rebels and Franks in Narbonensis the next year.[18] Reccared went on to call Toledo III and then ruled peacefully until 601. After attending the great council and being its first episcopal signatory, Masona continued to govern his diocese for ten or fifteen more years. And Sunna, put to sea in a little boat by the Catholics of Mérida, ended up in North Africa, where he infected new communities with his "pestilential disease" before finally being "punished by the judgment of God" and dying a "cruel death."[19]

With the exceptions of Claudius' victory in Narbonensis and the scalped *dux*'s attempt at usurpation after Toledo III, there were no more incidents of organized violence against the kingship until after Reccared's death in 601.

---

15. *VPE,* 5.11.20–21: "ut iussioni principis obtemperans causa oboedientiae de ecclesia sanctae Eulaliae usque ad atrium quo est fundatum intra muros civitatis ante caballum Redempti diaconi pergeret ordinavit. Arreptoque baculo supradicti diaconi manibusque gestans ad atrium pervenisset, statim eum vir sanctus cum uxore et filiis et omnibus praediis absolvens liberum abire permisit. Hoc solum illi praecepit ut omnimodis catholicam fidem integram et immaculatam cunctis diebus vitae suae conservaret." 245.

16. *VPE,* 5.12.7: "celebrantes more priscorum platearum fragore magno," 247.

17. *VPE,* 5.12.8: "Posthaec, remotis ab omni parte tempestatibus, copiosam Dominus populo Catholico largire dignatus est pacem," 249.

18. John Bicl., *anno VII Mauricii,* 218. John's contention that Claudius' army of three hundred men defeated a sixty thousand–man army is an exaggeration meant to enhance the religious aspects of the struggle; he draws a parallel between those numbers and the fact that "in a like manner, many years ago, God is known to have destroyed, at the hand of the general Gideon and only three hundred men, many thousands of Midianites who were attacking the people of God" (deus . . . similiter ante multa temporam spatia per manum Gedeonis in CCC viris multa milia Madianitarum dei populo infestantiam noscitur extinxisse). Wolf, 77–78.

19. *VPE,* 5.11.14–15: "pestifero morbo . . . . Deinde divino protinus mulctatus iudicio crudeli exitu vitam finivit," 243.

According to Isidore of Seville, Reccared's military successes from this point on were so easily won that his army appeared to be doing wrestling exercises rather than waging wars.[20] For their part the kingdom's bishops did begin to hold provincial councils, attempting to put into practice Toledo III's directives for local governance. The last decade of Reccared's reign apparently was a time of relative peace and stability.

Nevertheless, the complex array of local judicial relationships and tensions at work in Sunna's downfall cannot have been simply swept out to sea with the unrelenting heretic or sent into exile with his accomplices. Nor is it likely that the measures taken at Toledo III were adequate to address these dynamics in all the communities of the kingdom. The efforts of leaders to put ill-defined ideals into practice during this key period produced mixed results: a variety of interpretations of conciliar authority, of the distribution and social meaning of holy power, and of the means by which to transform those abstractions into ongoing community governance. This variety represents continued dialogue and disagreement in the development of the Visigothic vision of Christian consensus. The problems and diversity they reflect would remain to confront succeeding generations of Iberian leaders.

"Priests and Judges"

The hesitation of the bishops at Toledo III in accepting Reccared's *mos canonicus* was partly based in their unwillingness to interfere in the relations among bishops, "judges," and other powerful people. Consequently, the council did not legislate the details of the new judicial collaboration, nor those of provincial councils. The story of Sunna's downfall, although almost completely lacking in specific legal details, depicts the permutations of personal power among various claimants to judicial authority and divine endorsement—the networks of loyalty, privilege and conflicting interests that made the bishops so hesitant about centralized, legislated collaboration and supervision.[21]

In 588 the hostile situation in Mérida encouraged cooperation between the bishop and the *dux*. When danger first arose, Masona was able to summon Claudius and his entourage at a moment's notice and enjoyed the *dux*'s full support in investigating and foiling the conspiracy. The division of responsi-

---

20. HG, 55, 266.

21. Other evidence for the official delineation of the authority of various governmental offices during the Visigothic period is rather murky; it is difficult to see human faces and interests in the abstractions of the law codes and legal formulas. On the administration of secular government and law, see Thompson, *Goths*, 114–47 and 252–73; and P. D. King, *Law and Society in the Visigothic Kingdom* (Cambridge, 1972), 23–121.

bilities between the two Catholic leaders was in many respects straightforward. Masona, merciful and compassionate, received Witteric's confession. While protecting the repentant conspirator, he turned the entire affair over to the secular authority, Claudius, for investigation and the use of coercive force. The *dux* oversaw the fates of the lay offenders, while the Catholic bishop and his community took charge of the episcopal conspirator, Sunna, and the refuge seeker, Vagrila.

In this case so smooth a collaboration is not surprising. The conspiracy had threatened the lives and faith of both men, each one a longtime Catholic leader in a city riven by religious hostility. Yet this episode illustrates areas of potential contention that in a different community, under different circumstances, might have stood in the way of such effective cooperation. Masona, for instance, was obviously dependent upon Claudius for protection and enforcement. Given a different configuration of local loyalties, Claudius could have chosen to ignore the bishop's summons when the counts arrived at his house—with disastrous consequences for Masona and his followers. The same is true for the investigation into the conspirators' contingency plan. A successful outcome depended upon Masona being willing to turn the responsibility over to the *dux* and upon Claudius carrying out a legitimate investigation, despite the fact that those involved were his subordinates and also might have had claim to his protection.[22] There were no guarantees that in other communities the mutual interests of the *dux* and bishop would outweigh their individual desire to define and wield their own authority over their various underlings.

Nor was there any guarantee that centralized efforts to dictate collaboration between local leaders would overcome conflicting interests and personal loyalties. The inexpedience of such interference is well illustrated in Masona's response to Reccared's orders concerning the refugee Vagrila. The bishop took pains to obey the king by having Vagrila publicly display his servitude to the deacon Redemptus. But Masona directly contravened the practical effects of Reccared's sentence by allowing Vagrila and his family to retain their freedom, property, and thus their position in the community. In this instance the local bishop's desire to protect and define his church's sanctuary rights and to assert the superiority of his own merciful authority over the king's justice overrode the need for smooth collaboration between local ecclesiastic and central secular leadership.

---

22. According to Thompson (*Goths,* 143–44), little is known of the administrative duties of *duces* in the Visigothic kingdom. *Duces* ranked above *comites;* they were the royal officials responsible for an entire province, while counts were active in single cities and the neighboring rural areas. The case of Claudius makes it clear that *duces* had some military responsibilities as well.

Masona's interest in limiting royal authority in his see was mirrored by the attitude of the bishops at Toledo III the following year. Focusing on the dynamics in their own communities, the bishops at that council circumscribed Reccared's pretensions by leaving much of the practical meaning of their alliance open to local definition. At the same time, the king and bishops agreed on the basic principle of provincial conciliar governance as a means for regulating relations between secular officials, clerics, and their communities. In 588 Masona and Claudius had successfully collaborated without such regulation; indeed, the bishop had resisted the king's efforts in that direction. After Toledo III, as the bishops returned to their dioceses, they and their secular collaborators had to navigate the ill-defined connection drawn in Toledo between the principle of conciliar governance and the flexibility necessary for accommodating local balances of power. In many communities these were undoubtedly as complex, though differently configured, as those in Mérida in 588.

In November 589 the Council of Narbonne—the first provincial council held after Toledo III—confronted the issue of collaboration in particularly volatile circumstances. Like Mérida, Narbonensis had seen a rebellion following Reccared's conversion. It was here that Claudius had won his miraculous victory over sixty thousand rebels and Franks. Unlike the episode in Mérida, however, the rebellion in Narbonensis had caused far-reaching disruption. The leading rebels—two Gothic nobles and a Gothic bishop—had gained the support of the Catholic Frankish king Guntramn, who dispatched an army to assist them.[23] According to the *Vitas,* "in this endeavor they killed a large number of clerics, religious, and Catholics of all ranks, and made an immense slaughter."[24] While this description is no doubt exaggerated, the rebellion, the invasion of the Franks, and the arrival of the defending army must have caused considerable chaos. According to the *Vitas,* the rebels wanted to bring back Arianism by deposing Reccared. The rebellion is still generally seen as an Arian reaction to the king's conversion. The participation of the Catholic Franks, however, and the necessity of calling in a military leader from Lusitania indicate that religion may not have been the only source of division in the province. In any event any collaboration among local clerical and secular leaders had failed to contain the disruption.[25]

---

23. *VPE,* 5.12.1–5, 245–47. See also Garvin, Commentary, *VPE,* 511–13; and Thompson, *Goths,* 103.

24. *VPE,* 5.12.4: "Interim per idem tempus innumerabilem clericorum religiosorum et omnium Catholicorum interficientes multitudinem, immensam fecerunt stragem," 247.

25. Thompson, *Goths,* 104, concludes from this, and the other rebellions immediately following Reccared's conversion, that "Spanish and Septimanian Catholics assisted the protest of the Gothic Arians."

The sources offer little detail for this episode.[26] The records of the council in Narbonne, however, shed light on some of the circumstances and consequences of the rebellion. At the same time, the rebellion provides an immediate context for the provincial council, helping to explain its unusually harsh interpretation of the local meaning of the new alliance. This council stands out for its legislation on lay behavior, the rigor of its punishments, and its systematic reliance on secular coercive force. For a number of lay transgressions the bishops levied fines to be paid to the local count and called for the beating of slaves and others who could not pay the fines. Yet, despite this apparent eagerness to adopt the principle of collaboration, these bishops limited its effective use to the arena of coercion. There is no trace of any discussion about the financial and judicial alliance outlined in Toledo III's canon 18. Judges and fiscal officers do not appear to have attended the council.

Indeed, this council also stands out among the provincial gatherings of this period for its concern with limiting contact between clerics and networks of secular influence, or, as the council put it, "the power of patronage."[27] In their preamble, using language very similar to that of Toledo III's first canon, the bishops in Narbonne blamed the power of patronage for preventing the enforcement of previous canonical legislation. Reiterating the Council of Nicaea's prohibition against clerical conspiracies, their fifth canon explicitly blamed such plots on "the patronage of lay people."[28] In order to discourage clerical participation in the networks of lay power, they forbade clerics from wearing purple, because "the purple is owed above all to those who exercise the power of lay people, not to the religious."[29] They also barred clerics from loitering and conversing on city streets[30] and ordered abbots, whose monasteries served as jails for convicted clerics and important laymen (*honorati*), to cease their practice of wining and dining their prisoners.[31]

Both this overarching concern with controlling contact with lay patronage as well as the council's assertive reliance on secular coercion to control lay communities probably came in response to the rebellion of 588. Threatened from within their province by social instability and uncertain loyalties and

---

26. The story can only begin to be reconstructed by combining the accounts of John of Biclar, who describes the events as arising solely from the Frankish invasion, and the *VPE*, which does not mention Claudius' participation.

27. Narbonne, preamble: "patrocinationis potestatem." Vives, 146.

28. Narbonne, c. 5: "concinnabula vel coniurationes non fiant clericoum quae sub patrocinio solebant fieri laicorum." Vives, 147.

29. Narbonne, c. 1: "quia purpura maxime laicorum potestate praeditis debetur, non religiosis." Vives, 146.

30. Narbonne, c. 3. Vives, 147.

31. Narbonne, c. 6. Vives, 147.

from without by neighboring kings, the bishops sought to consolidate the church's position—and thus their own—by aggressively defining and defending the boundaries of their traditional jurisdictions. The strength they drew from the mandates of Toledo III, from the support of the monarchy, and from the recent victory over the rebels allowed them to act immediately and with unusual force. They struck while the iron was hot. The dangers associated with intimate involvement in secular affairs, however, forced them to be cautious about relying upon royal officials for anything but the most clearly defined tasks: collecting fines and meting out punishments. The bishops' individual and collective positions were best protected by sharply delineating the separation between clerical and royal authorities, rather than by marshaling the holy power of church councils to supervise and thus to legitimate the agents of centralized royal governance.

Only two other provincial councils during this period even touched on the issue of collaboration, and both did so less elaborately than the council in Narbonne. The First Council of Seville in 590 gave detailed instructions to secular judges on how they were to restrain clerics who consorted with serving girls. The canon criticized Baetican bishops for failing to deal with the impure clerics and directed secular judges to remove the women from the clerics' houses and to add them to their own households: "so that when the bishops do not succeed in inhibiting this vice, the judicial power shall use coercion."[32] The only evidence for a council attending to the fiscal aspects of the governmental alliance is a letter known as *de fisco barcinonensi,* which was signed by a group of bishops in Tarraconensis who were presumably in attendance at the Second Council of Saragossa held in 592.[33] The letter informed the treasury agents in Barcelona of a fixed rate of public tribute and called upon the agents to refrain from demanding more than that amount. With these instructions the letter gives explicit and detailed voice to the role of councils in ensuring the fair fiscal treatment of the king's local subjects.

There is no indication, however, that any provincial councils during this period served as public forums for hearing complaints against abusive agents or for instructing secular officials about how they should "act with the peo-

---

32. Seville I, c. 3: "ut vitium hoc, dum sacerdos inhibire non praevalet, potestas iudicialis coerceat." Vives, 158. The canon also outlined the supervisory power of individual bishops; the judges were to act "with the will and permission of the bishop" (cum volumtate et permissu episcopi) and were directed to render an oath promising that they would find no excuse to return the women to the unchaste clerics.

33. The text of this letter appears out of chronological order in the manuscripts, and thus in Vives, 54, following the records of Barcelona I, held in 540. Its signatories, however, are among those who signed the acts of Saragossa I in 592; the letter is therefore generally associated with that provincial council. On the letter's contents, see José Orlandis and Domingo Ramos-Lissón, *Historia de los Concilios de la España romana y visigoda* (Pamplona, 1986), 239–45.

ple." In Narbonne, Seville, and Saragossa provincial councils appear to have been more willing than the bishops in Toledo to issue detailed rules about specific instances of collaboration. Yet, despite this attention to detail, the provincial councils—if they dealt with the issue at all—apparently were even more reluctant than the bishops at Toledo III in giving their wholesale endorsement to collaborative judicial mechanisms or to the systematic use of conciliar authority in support of centralized governance.

Reccared's laws contain further indications of the various local dynamics that placed roadblocks in the way of collaboration.[34] One law addressed a continuing difficulty with controlling personal profiteering by local tax collectors, judges, provincial governors, and fiscal agents. Clerics were not providing the necessary supervision of these men, and city officials were neglecting to fulfill their terms of office.[35] The law required clerics to fulfill their supervisory duties: they were to report any abuses by judges or governors or "be punished by the judgment of a council."[36] Evidently, the personal benefits and influence tied to exercising fiscal authority, or the desire to evade the burdens associated with city offices, carried more weight with leading men in local communities than did Toledo III's mandates. Local clerics were also unwilling or unable to accept the burden of challenging the power of these men and reporting their abuses. It would appear that provincial councils, as the silence of their records implies, were not playing their supervisory role.

Another of Reccared's laws prohibited marriages to virgins and widows who had taken chastity vows as well as marriages that would be considered incestuous due to consanguinity.[37] The law was particularly intrusive: it called for "priests and judges" to nullify marriages, exile people from their properties and homes, and dictate inheritance matters. It specifically disallowed any appeal based on the marriage being of long standing and called for the separation of spouses even when no one had come forward to accuse them. Apparently, Reccared was aware of the difficulties in enforcing such intrusive measures. Here the king abandoned the idea of holding clerics accountable to councils and instead levied a heavy fine on local authorities who would not

---

34. These laws are undated, and so it cannot be known for certain whether they were issued before or after Toledo III. All three laws deal with issues that were addressed at the council in 589, and their clearly Catholic nature indicates that they appeared after Reccared's conversion from Arianism. It is unlikely that Reccared's position during the two years between his conversion and Toledo III was strong enough to support kingdom-wide lawmaking; therefore, I assume that Reccared's legislation postdates the council.

35. *LV*, 12.1.2, 407–8. The evasion of civil offices was widespread in the late antique period. For further discussion of the phenomenon in the Roman and Byzantine Empires, see A. H. M. Jones, *The Later Roman Empire, 284–602*, 2 vols. (Oxford, 1964), 737–66. On the same subject in the Visigothic kingdom, see Thompson, *Goths*, 118–21.

36. *LV*, 12.1.2: "concilii iudicio esse plectendos," 408.

37. This law, *LV*, 3.5.2, 159–61, was an elaboration of Tol. III, c. 10.

enforce the measure. Although the law's language emphasizes the ecclesiastic nature of its content and intent,[38] Reccared's efforts to compel enforcement called for obedience to royal, rather than conciliar, authority. The king could not rely on provincial councils to enforce the cooperation of local clerics and secular officials any more than he could rely on those men to enforce the law without the threat of a heavy fine.

The texts of these laws open with grandiose rhetoric announcing the royal responsibilities to legislate, uphold justice, protect subjects, and promote good *mores*. Clearly, Reccared had not relinquished his claims to royal holy authority and the royal duty to maintain a *mos canonicus* throughout the kingdom. The king continued to demand collaboration between royal agents and clerics in administering royal justice in local communities. Like the councils in Narbonensis and Baetica, he also saw a need to address specific details of collaboration in order to override local interests and loyalties and thus to gain obedient enforcement. Yet all of these laws, secular and ecclesiastic, indicate that Toledo III's call for collaboration had, for the most part, gone unheeded. Although provincial councils met, they did not wield the authority necessary for supervising or punishing secular officials or for settling disputes between local inhabitants and royal agents. Nor could their authority be assumed to command clerical obedience. The power of influential individuals like Masona or Claudius was more likely to be an effective means for enforcing order and obedience than a still ill-defined conciliar tradition or a newly Catholic lawmaking king. Yet the cooperation of such individuals could not be counted on either. It could, in fact, be seen as a danger, as it apparently was in Narbonensis.

Arians and Authentic Christian Identity

While the bishops at Toledo III had been hesitant about legislating detailed judicial mechanisms, they had shown no trepidation when it came to condemning the Goths' Arianism and the troubles it had caused in their communities. The former Arians may have tried to distance themselves from their heretical pasts, but the Catholic bishops had insisted on defining their public confessions as a submission to Catholic scrutiny. They called on the converts to prove to their "neighbors" that they had been "freed from the contagion of the detestable heresy."[39] This attitude may have originated in part from the long-term persecution of the church at the hands of Arians that John of Biclar

---

38. According to the law, the king was seeking to support "the admonitions of divine law" (divinae legis monita) and the "canons of the Church" (canonum sententia), 160–61.

39. See chap. 2, nn. 33 and 34.

and Leander of Seville described so eloquently. The extent and severity of such persecution, however, is debatable.[40] Since the bishops in Toledo were generally concerned with the dynamics of their communities, their wariness was more probably based on their experiences during the years immediately prior to Toledo III, when after Reccared's conversion Arians like Sunna and his followers had been called upon to follow their king's lead and reject their ancestral religion. The Catholic bishops' suspicion about the authenticity of their new allies' faith was another factor complicating the establishment of local collaboration and collective episcopal authority.

In describing the conspiracy in Mérida, the *Vitas* made much of the Arians' deceptive displays of fraternity and reverence toward the Catholic leaders. When, for instance, the conspirators came in false friendship to Masona's house and paid him and the *dux* Claudius the "customary" homage, they were so cunningly "fraudulent"[41] that the Catholics would never have known that an attempt had been made on the men's lives if Witteric had not unmasked himself. Later, the conspiring counts did not hesitate to defile the city's Easter celebration by disguising their wagon-load of weapons as a customary offering of grain.[42] Such a flair for dissemblance was a stereotypical attribute of heretical villains in Catholic polemics; the Arians in Mérida may not actually have been the willful charlatans the author describes. Still, it is clear that this period saw profound confusion in defining and determining religious fidelity. Leovigild's innovations of the early 580s had blurred the distinguishing features of religious identity while at the same time making doctrinal difference a more urgent distinction in local communities. Reccared's conversion had further muddied the waters—particularly for longtime Catholics. If Arian Goths had been known to venerate Catholic saints and worship in Catholic basilicas even before their king's conversion,[43] how were Catholics to know if any Goth who followed Reccared's lead out of ethnic loyalty or political expedience had in fact also accepted the holy authority of their new church's leaders and traditions? Although the stereotypical heretics in works like the *Vitas* may cast doubts on the accuracy of such portrayals, they do reflect some of the prejudices not only of the authors but also of their audiences.

Sunna's obstinacy may also be a stereotype, but the circumstances of his

---

40. Collins, "¿Donde estaban," 215, argues that, up until the reign of Leovigild, Arians and Catholics enjoyed a long period of "convivencia"; Thompson, *Goths,* 31–37, describes a high level of tolerance for Catholics by the Arian kings.

41. See n. 4 of this chapter.

42. *VPE,* 5.11.3–8, 237–41.

43. In addition to reporting that Leovigild prayed at Catholic martyrs' tombs and churches (see chap. 1, n. 118), Gregory of Tours (*LH,* 6.40, 310–11) also describes attending a Catholic mass with an Arian envoy named Oppila; the Arian, however, did not participate in Communion.

final refusal to convert make clear some of the central issues about authentic conversion and Catholic authority. After Sunna's arrest Reccared called upon the Catholics of Mérida to try to convert the "false bishop" one last time and have him do penance for his sins. This way, "when he had done penance and they knew him to be a good Catholic, they might make him bishop in some other city."[44] This was one charade, however, that the Arian bishop would not perpetrate. He repeatedly refused the Catholics' entreaties, finally declaring:

> I do not recognize penance and shall never be a Catholic. But I shall either continue to live in the rite in which I have lived or gladly die for the religion in which I have persevered from the beginning of my life until now.[45]

Penance was one of the few punishments that the church could impose upon its members without recourse to secular coercion. In traditional practice penance was a public affair, through which the penitent expected to gain the support of the entire Catholic community in seeking divine mercy.[46] In order to so do, the repentant sinners publically submitted to the local bishop, who would assign the term of penitence, lay hands on the penitent, and place a cloth of goat's hair on his head—the *cilicium*.[47] After this ceremony the sinner was tonsured and joined the ranks of the community's other penitents, all of whom were considered suspended from communion. They could be subjected to a number of ritualized humiliations, including frequent attendance at services to "receive the imposition of hands,"[48] sitting as a group in the back of the church, kneeling while the rest of the congregation was standing, and in some cases being assigned duties such as cleaning the church building.[49] According to one canon, some penitents were considered to be—metaphorically, at least—"lying at the door of the Catholic church."[50] Some canons

44. *VPE*, 5.11.12: "pseudoepiscopum . . . ut acta poenitude cum eum iam cognoscerent perfectum esse catholicum eum postmodum in quacumque alia civitate ordinarent episcopum," 241.

45. *VPE*, 5.11.13: " 'Ego quid sit poenitentia ignoro. Ob hoc compertum vobis sit quia poenitentiam quid sit nescio et catholicus numquam ero, sed aut ritu quo vixi vivebo aut pro religione in qua nunc usque ab ineunte aetate mea permansi liberter morior,' " 241.

46. Henry G. J. Beck, *The Pastoral Care of Souls in South-East France during the Sixth Century* (Rome, 1950), 194–95.

47. See the First Council of Toledo (400), c. 2; *La colección*, 328–29; and Braga II, Eastern canon 23: "sub cilicio." Vives, 93. On this and other practices of public penitence in Gaul during this period, see Beck, *Pastoral Care*, 192–98. For specifically Iberian practices, see Justo Fernández Alonso, *La cura pastoral en la España romanovisigoda* (Rome, 1955), 521–26.

48. Tol. III, c. 11: "ad manus impositionem." Rodríguez, 30.

49. Beck, *Pastoral Care*, 194–95.

50. Braga II, Eastern canon 77; "ad ianuam ecclesiae catolicae . . . subiaceat." Vives, 104.

assigned specific periods of penance for different crimes,[51] but this detail was often left undefined, apparently leaving the sentence up to the bishop imposing penitence, along with the decision about when the penitent was ready for reconciliation.[52] Sunna's refusal to subject himself publicly to this process, particularly given the fact that he would be placing himself under Masona's powers of reconciliation, is not surprising. Furthermore, his forthright denial of the validity of penance was also a rejection of the entire community's role in gaining divine mercy, making plain Sunna's utter irredeemability as a participant in the community's consensus. He and his infectious obstinance had to be put to sea in a little boat.

Given the Arians' reputation for deception, the Catholics in the kingdom could not rely on all the heretics to come clean as Sunna finally had. Moreover, it appears that some Iberian bishops, like those in other areas of the West during this period, had been using their penitential prerogatives to make the process less rigorous and less public.[53] The bishops at Toledo III addressed problems with penance in their eleventh canon, which complained that "in certain churches" men were not practicing penance "according to the canons, but most abominably": they sinned at will, demanding reconciliation every time.[54] Under such circumstances former Arians could almost be expected to accept penance fraudulently. While the canon did not single out former Arians as the source of the problem, it did go on to reiterate and describe the process by which penance ought to be administered: publicly, "according to the canonical form of the ancients."[55] Penance, moreover, was not the only potential problem. If a heretic could falsely accept penance, they might also feign submission to the entire body of canonical legislation; hence, Toledo III's concern with former Arians clerics not practicing celibacy[56] and, for that matter, its insistence on the overarching authority of all traditional orthodox sources of church law.[57]

To appreciate the local consequences of the Arians' conversion during

51. See, e.g., Braga II, Eastern canons 77, 78. Vives, 104. The first of these assigned ten years for abortion or birth control, the second assigned lifelong penitence for intentional homicide, and five or seven years for accidental homicide.

52. See, e.g., Lérida, c. 5; La colección, 301; and Tol. III, c. 11. Rodríguez, 30. See Beck, Pastoral Care, 196–97, who also points out that reconciliation did not end a person's penitential status, as can be seen in Barcelona I, c. 6 (Vives, 53), which calls for penitents to devote the rest of their lives to fasting and prayer.

53. On the trend toward easing the rigor of public penance and the increasing reliance on either deathbed penance or less public forms of penitential discipline in Gaul during the sixth century, see Beck, 199–209.

54. Tol. III, c. 11: "quasdam Hispaniarum ecclesias non secundum canonem sed foedissime pro suis peccatis homines agere paenitentiam." Rodríguez, 30. On this canon, see Fernández Alonso, La cura, 571–72.

55. Tol. III, c. 11: "secundum formam canonicam antiquorum." Rodríguez, 30.

56. Tol. III, c. 5. Rodríguez, 30.

57. Tol. III, c. 1. Rodríguez, 29.

this period, it is not necessary to judge the authenticity of the new converts' Catholicism. What is important here is that upon their return from Toledo III, Catholic bishops were charged with more than the problematic task of collaborating with secular officials whose local interests could easily diverge from their own. They were also expected to wield holy authority through conciliar consensus with newly converted bishops whose genuine acceptance of doctrinal brotherhood was in their eyes questionable. Their holy collectivity, moreover, was supposed to administer divine justice to clerical and lay communities whose membership included people who did not necessarily accept the basis of its sanctions and authority.

Lingering suspicions about former Arian clerics could have repercussions on individual clerics and entire provinces. An atmosphere of continuing distrust about former Arians' commitment to the rules of celibacy in Lusitania, for instance, goes far in explaining one of the more obscure letters among the few remaining from Reccared's reign. Addressed to the king from a monk by the Germanic name of Tarra, the letter is an appeal for help in clearing the cleric of false rumors that he had consorted with a "harlot" in Mérida.[58] The letter reflects a particularly tense situation, in which the expected avenues of investigation had been ignored. Apparently, Tarra was exiled without being directly accused or having confessed,[59] solely on the basis of gossip circulating in his monastery, which he labeled "an assembly of filthy turpitude."[60] Tarra's account is filled with recriminations against those who had "fraudulently" ruined his reputation,[61] including an unnamed "pontiff"—possibly Masona, still in office when the letter was written—who had banished him for "unnatural exploits."[62] Lacking a witness to testify to his purity, Tarra supported his case to the king by emphasizing his orthodoxy. He asserted that it was the "Spirit of the Father" who spoke through him in denying the rumors.[63] He offered Reccared an oath in the name of the "the Father, the Son, and the Holy Spirit"—the faith by which he claimed to be "always commanded"—to ensure that his assertions of innocence would "not be judged useless and fraudulent."[64] The monk ended his letter by urging the king that during his reign those "oppressed" by false charges should rejoice in having their names cleared and those "made haughty" by feigned virtues should be bridled and

---

58. *EW*, 9.31: "scortum," 29.
59. *EW*, 9.27–30, 29.
60. *EW*, 9.22: "maculosi turpitudinis coitum," 29.
61. *EW*, 9.24: "fraudulenter," 29.
62. *EW*, 9.10–11: "a pontifice templi . . . facta infanda . . . proiectus," 28.
63. *EW*, 9.21–22: "Spiritus Patris qui loquitur in nobis," 28–29.
64. *EW*, 9.35–39: "profero testem Fidelem presentem, quo semper iubor, obtestantem per Patrem et Natum et Spiritum Sanctum . . . quod pagina presens omneque taxatur nec fraude frustratum," 29.

restrained.[65] Tarra's language is notably arcane,[66] and it cannot be known whether he was, in fact, a former Arian. His Germanic name does not necessarily indicate any doctrinal background. Given the insistence upon his own orthodoxy, however, it is probable that this exiled monk had been the victim of his community's general hostility toward ex-Arian Goths. If this were the case, it would appear that, in Lusitania at least, Catholics' suspicions of their new brothers' purity and obedience to canon law had begun to compromise the equitable exercise of ecclesiastic justice.

Tarra's closing exhortation implies that in his own eyes he was not the only one suffering because of this atmosphere of distrust. The records of Saragossa II—held in 592, on the opposite side of the peninsula from the monk and his troubles—give further testimony to a widespread skepticism, if not outright antagonism, toward the new members of the Catholic clergy. The council's three canons reflect a "rigorous attitude" toward the converted Arians, setting guidelines for integrating them into the Catholic community that were notably more restrictive than those enacted at Toledo III.[67] The bishops in Saragossa addressed fears of clerical misbehavior on a province-wide level, singling out former Arians for particularly close supervision. They called for the reordination of ex-Arian clerics who lived "utterly chaste" lives and for the deposing of those who did not.[68] The council expanded the notion of ceremonially ensuring religious purity to apply to the cult of relics. Any relics found in ex-Arian churches were to be brought to the local bishop, who would subject them to trial by fire.[69] Fearing interference from closeted Arians, the council also provided that anyone who was discovered hiding Arian relics should be "separated from the assembly of the sacrosanct church."[70] Their final canon again affirmed the principle of reordination, and extended it yet further: any churches consecrated "in the name of the Catholic faith" by bishops who hadn't yet "received benediction from a Catholic bishop" were to be reconsecrated.[71]

The idea of reordination contrasts rather starkly with the Western

---

65. *EW,* 9.43–44: "hac temporibus tuis, glorificentissime princeps, letentur emersi fraudibus pressi fraudeque erecti frenetur repressi," 29.

66. Thompson, *Goths,* 109.

67. José Orlandis, "Zaragoza, ciudad conciliar," *Hispania y Zaragoza en la antigüedad tardia. Estudios varios* (Saragossa, 1984), 67.

68. Saragossa II, c. 1: "castissimam . . . vitam." Vives, 154. Tol. III, c. 5, had made no such demand; it only admonished the converts to refrain from sleeping with their wives and provided for demoting to the rank of lector those who didn't do so. Rodríguez, 30.

69. Saragossa II, c. 2. Vives, 154.

70. Saragossa II, c. 2: "a sacrosanctae ecclesiae coetu segregentur." Vives, 154.

71. Saragossa II, c. 3: "episcopi de Arriana haerese venientes si quas ecclesias sub nomine catholicae fidei [consecraverint] necdum benedictione a catholico sacerdote percepta, consecrentur denuo." Vives, 154.

church's expressed tradition against rebaptism.[72] By flirting with doctrinal deviation, however, the council was able to place each ex-Arian cleric, including the bishops, under the scrutiny of the Catholic episcopate. Their lives would have to be individually investigated to determine which converts merited ceremonial endorsement through reordination. Each Arian relic would be evaluated, while the willingness of converts to allow their holy objects to be subjected to possible destruction could function as a test of their fidelity. The canon on reconsecration rested on the principle that the ritual power of ex-Arian bishops depended upon the authorization of their long-term Catholic colleagues. By nullifying their previous consecrations, the council publicly denied the independent authenticity of their new episcopal brothers' holy authority.

Of all the provinces in the kingdom Tarraconensis, Saragossa's province, had the strongest traditions of conciliar activity. In 592, however, the provincial episcopate appears to have been unwilling to extend their collegiality to ex-Arian bishops. Given the attack on those bishops' authority, it is not surprising that the only see not represented at Saragossa II was the city of Barcelona, whose bishop was Ugnas, a prominent former Arian. The other ex-Arian bishop known to have governed in the province at the time, Fruisclus of Tortosa, was also absent, although the Catholic with whom he shared the see, Julian, was present.[73] Ugnas' absence from Saragossa becomes even more significant if one considers the signatories to the *de fisco barcinonensi*—the letter traditionally associated with that council, which informed the treasurers of Barcelona of a fixed rate of public tribute.[74] The letter contained the declaration that it had been signed by "all the bishops who contribute to the fisc of the city of Barcelona,"[75] yet it does not bear the signature of Ugnas, who surely should have been counted among that number. Thus, while this letter constitutes the only evidence for the implementation of the fiscal aspects of canon 18, it also indicates that by 592 the level of tension and alienation among the bishops of the province was undermining the very foundation of conciliar governance: episcopal collectivity and consensus.

Aside from the four rebellions in the years 588 and 589, once their king had converted most Arians appear to have come quietly into the new religion.

---

72. Orlandis, "Zaragoza," 67. Paul Séjourné, *Le dernier père de l'Église. Saint Isidore de Séville* (Paris, 1936), 193–95, argues that canon 2 does not actually call for reordination; rather, the *benedictio* to which the former Arians were to submit was "une simple formalité de réconciliation à l'Église catholique." The severity of the canons concerning Arian churches and relics, however, does not support such a mild interpretation.

73. Orlandis, "Zaragoza," 68.

74. See n. 33 of this chapter.

75. *de fisco barcinonensi*: "omnes episcopi ad civitatem Barcinonense fiscum inferentes." Vives, 54.

Sunna, who was apparently willing to be martyred rather than forsake his life-long religion, is the only Arian known to have taken such a publicly rigorous position. The threat his rejection of penance posed to the enforcement of ecclesiastic justice may have been a real danger embodied in all the converting Arians, but it did not become a rallying point for open opposition. The Catholics' distrust of the converts' sincerity and obedience to the church's traditions and rules probably constituted a greater obstacle to collaboration and conciliar governance. The existence and significance of a general atmosphere of suspicion are impossible to prove. What is readily evident in the conciliar evidence, however, is a continuing, almost obsessive concern among Iberian leaders with authentic Catholic identity and obedience. Their vision of social consensus and conciliar governance depended upon establishing that authenticity. In later years the full weight of their concern came to rest on the lives of another group of suspect subjects: the Jews. The period surrounding Toledo III, when leaders like the bishops in Saragossa addressed their suspicions about their new colleagues, contributed significantly to the development of this fundamental element in the Visigothic vision of consensus.

Innovations and Anomalies in Conciliar Practice

Dedicated as he was, Sunna may have had a more practical reason for refusing to convert to Catholicism: if he had done so, he would have had to leave Mérida. Although the agreement between Reccared and the Catholics apparently provided for Arian bishops to remain in their sees even if it meant sharing the diocese with a Catholic bishop, Mérida was the metropolitan see in Lusitania. Such a sharing of preeminent provincial power does not seem to have been part of the bargain.[76] Another problem with sharing power—along with the two men's history of antagonism—may have been that Masona was, apparently, something of an autocrat. This paragon of sacred dignity had publicly berated Leovigild, contravened Reccared's sentencing of Vagrila, and at Easter paraded like a king through the streets of his city, receiving homage from silk-clad attendants.[77] It is hard to imagine him willingly sharing power with any cleric, let alone his longtime enemy. In any case, as it turned out, Masona did not have to accept Sunna as co-metropolitan. Nor does it appear that he accepted any form of collective episcopal governance in his province. There is no evidence of any provincial council meeting in Lusitania during Masona's episcopacy—something the author of the *Vitas* would surely have

---

76. See chap. 2, n. 15. It was part of Reccared's sentence against Sunna that, if the Catholics succeeded in converting him, he would be sent to another diocese. See n. 44.

77. *VPE*, 5.3.12, 197.

mentioned in his detailed description of Masona's career. It seems that Masona dealt with Toledo III's lack of definition of conciliar practice by ignoring canon 18 altogether. Perhaps his wealth and prestige were more effective means of wielding provincial leadership than the risky and complicated business of cultivating episcopal consensus.

The difficulty of establishing this source of holy authority may have discouraged provincial councils in Galicia as well. There are no conciliar records from that province during this period. Although the other provinces did gather their bishops, aside from Tarraconsensis, none of them appears to have done so more than once throughout the years of Reccared's reign. Of course, assuming a lack of councils based on the absence of provincial council records is a particularly problematic proposition during this decade. The records of all these councils, with the exception of Seville I, were excluded from the *Hispana* and are extant in only one manuscript.[78] Still, in some ways it is surprising that bishops gathered as many times as the records indicate during this period. The holy authority that Toledo III had attributed to councils was foreign to traditional ways of governance in all parts of the peninsula. Moreover, the records from Tarraconsensis illustrate that cooperation among provincial bishops could be as much of a problem as collaboration between secular and ecclesiastic leaders or between former Arians and Catholics.[79] The lack of a living conciliar tradition must have exacerbated these problems. Yet these men's conciliar inexperience also prompted improvisation. The meetings that did occur offered diverse and sometimes innovative models for conciliar competence and ceremony.

The council in Narbonne in 589, for instance, was unusual not only in the harshness of its punishments for lay transgressions—the beatings and fines to be inflicted by the secular authorities—but also in the penalties meted out to clerics. Lower clergy were disciplined particularly stringently: one canon called for them to either lose their stipends or be beaten for the crime of failing to open the door for their superiors.[80] This council also conceived of its jurisdiction in unusually broad terms. In addition to being the only council

---

78. Martínez Díez, "Concilios españoles," 303–4. The manuscript containing the provincial conciliar records in question is the *Codex Emilianense,* or Escorial D-I-1. According to Martínez Díez, *La colección, Estudio,* 117, this "conocidísimo" codex originates from the monastery of San Millán de la Cogolla (near Logroño), dates from the late tenth century, and includes, in addition to the Julian recension of the *Hispana,* a copy of the corpus of Visigothic laws known as the *Liber Judicorum* as well as various chronicles and other "diversas piezas." While some manuscripts of the *Hispana* include a section of "extravagant" councils, the *Codex Emilianense* is the only one that follows these with the records of the provincial councils of Narbonne, Saragossa II, Huesca, Toledo (597), Barcelona II, and Egara (614), along with the letter *de fisco barcinonensis.* Martínez Díez, 119, suggests an independent source for these and other sections of the codex.

79. See n. 85 of this chapter.

80. Narbonne, c. 11. Vives, 148.

during this period to directly address lay behavior, that is, human *mores,* its legislation specifically asserted its authority over all of the diverse lay communities of its province. Many canons addressed every "Goth, Roman, Syrian, Greek and Jew" in the region.[81] Even in his most expansive rhetoric at Toledo III, Reccared had addressed only "Goths, Romans, and Jews." It may be, however, that the breadth and rigor of the council's legislation undermined the acceptance of conciliar governance in this province. Despite their eagerness in 589, there is no evidence that the bishops of Narbonensis ever met in a provincial assembly again.

A sharply divergent interpretation of conciliar practice appears in the records of Seville I, which met in 590 under Leander's leadership as metropolitan of Baetica.[82] Here, in an agenda confined to ecclesiastic matters, the bishops relied heavily on the moderate language and concepts of Roman legal tradition. The council's decisions read like court records. The primary case at hand had been brought by an absent coprovincial bishop, Pegasius of Ecija, who challenged the legality of his predecessor's manumission of some church slaves. In contrast to the bishops of Narbonne, the Baetican bishops made their decision "using good will more than severity."[83] They heard the facts in the case, consulted canonical precedent, made their determination, and instructed Pegasius on how to proceed.

The legalistic simplicity of these proceedings, which were recorded as a letter to the plaintiff, is somewhat surprising when one considers that Leander had been responsible for orchestrating the Byzantine-flavored ceremonial grandeur of Toledo III. The dramatic difference between that ornate event and his modest provincial council suggests a conscious decision to differentiate two types of conciliar authority—the solemn, epoch-making, doctrine-defining "ecumenical" council and the local forum for ecclesiastic dispute settlement, the provincial council. In the heavily Romanized province of Baetica, with its long history of local governmental independence and conflict with the Visigothic kingship, it is not surprising to find such legalistic delicacy in the introduction of this unfamiliar source of judicial authority.[84] By associating

---

81. Narbonne, c. 4: "omnis homo tam ingenuus quam servus ghotus, romanus, syrus, graecus vel iudaeus." Vives, 147.

82. On this council, see Orlandis, *Historia de los Concilios,* 233–35. According to Orlandis (233), Pegasius of Ecija was the only nonattendee among the bishops residing in the Visigothic portion of the province.

83. Seville I, c. 1: "Propterea ergo de uno consensu omnes significamus magis humanius quam severius cogitantes." Vives, 152.

84. In maintaining a continuity in Baetican political particularism from the time of Agila (549–54) to Hermenegild, Rafael Gibert ("El reino Visigodo y el particularismo Español," *Settimane* 3 (Spoleto, 1956), 573–75) argues that the landholding "senators" of the province maintained a level of romanization, order, and security throughout the sixth century that was significantly higher than the other provinces. On the Hispano-Roman landholding aristocracy and urban leadership throughout sixth-century Iberia, see Thompson, *Goths,* 115–21.

their limited version of conciliar governance with the practices of secular law, Leander and his colleagues made their actions more accessible, less threatening, and perhaps more immediately authoritative in a potentially volatile political situation. The fact there are no more Baetican councils recorded until 619 may indicate a less than enthusiastic response on the part of both ecclesiastic and secular leaders.[85]

Paradoxically, the province that seems to have come closest to developing ongoing conciliar governance during this period, Tarraconensis, also saw a tendency in its conciliar legislation to enhance the individual power of bishops at the expense of collective, conciliar episcopal authority. Councils met in the province at least three times between 592 and 599. At the first of these, Saragossa II, the Catholic bishops asserted their collective power in order to police the authenticity of their new ex-Arian colleagues' faith. By placing each convert under the scrutiny of their local bishop, the Catholic episcopate strengthened the diocesan control exercised by those individual bishops. At the same time, even though this action was taken by the episcopate as a collectivity, the process of examining and reordaining the Arian bishops must have weakened episcopal harmony. In any case the episcopal consensus at this council was compromised by the absence of the ex-Arian bishops of the province.

It is not clear whether or not relations between former Arians and their co-clerics had improved by the time of the Council of Huesca in 598. The records of this council bear no signatures.[86] Whether or not the divisions of 592 had been mended, the bishops of Tarraconensis now devised a new means to maintain and enhance the individual authority of every provincial bishop over his own subject clergy. They called for yearly diocesan synods, at which the bishop was to show all his clerics

> the way to regulate their lives, and to caution them to submit themselves to the ecclesiastic rules, and to commend each one to a reputation of moderation, sobriety and true chastity, verified by men of good standing.[87]

---

85. Since the redactor of the *Hispana*'s first recension, which was compiled in Seville, did include Seville I, it seems probable that the meeting in 590 was the only Baetican council during this period.

86. The records of the Council of Huesca were not written down until 614, at which point the action taken there seems to have been ratified by the Council of Egara. See Orlandis, *Historia de los concilios*, 242–43.

87. Huesca (598): "omnibus regulare demonstret ducendi vitas, cunctosque sub ecclesiasticis regulis adesse praemoneat quousque etiam parsimoniae et sobrietati atque veridicae castimoniae honestorum vivorum testimonio fama conmendet." Vives, 158.

In addition to exhorting his clergy as a group, the bishop was to examine the lives of every cleric individually. "If, God forbid, rumor says anything evil about anyone," he was to

> find out everything with great care, validating it with the true and certain testimony of clerics or secretaries, and also of those very women about whom the evil report circulates, as well as with the other proofs through which the traces of adulterers are customarily discovered with certainty.[88]

The investigation of the lives of former Arians mandated in 592 would have put them under episcopal scrutiny only once. Now individual bishops were authorized to conduct yearly inquisitions, extracting testimony from clerics and others and employing public means of investigation apparently drawn from local secular legal practices—the "proofs through which the traces of adulterers are customarily discovered with certainty." These episcopal powers were not mitigated by any mention of conciliar oversight or appeal or any admonitions against bishops abusing or tyrannizing their clerical subjects.[89]

When the bishops of Tarraconensis met again the following year in Barcelona, the ex-Arians Ugnas and Fruisclus were present. Perhaps by now the province's bishops were so secure in their individual power that the converts no longer were seen as a threat. In any case this council does reflect an effort by the Tarraconese episcopate to police itself, rather than focusing entirely on maintaining episcopal control over either ex-Arians or lower clergy. The council's first two canons dealt with episcopal simony. The third canon was also inspired by a desire to ensure an honorable episcopate, this time by instituting specific rules for electing bishops. Though framed in an appeal to canonical tradition, the canon is another innovation, deviating significantly from the practice of election by co-bishops that had been sanctioned at the Council of Nicaea, reaffirmed at the First Council of Toledo in 397, and included in the Eastern canons translated by Martin of Braga in

---

88. Huesca (598): "quod si, quod absit, quicquam malum de quoquam fama dictaverit, per veram et certissimam clericorum probatione vel virorum admanuensium vel certe illarum foeminarum de quibus fama percurrit atque etiam diversis argumentis ex quibus adulterorum indicia certissime suspicari solent." Vives, 158.

89. For the most part, similar canons from other councils provided measures for countering the abuse or neglect of such individual episcopal powers, measures that generally involved recourse to the conciliar collectivity. See, especially, the Eastern canons translated by Martin of Braga. Vives, 86–106. Among them, canon 18 specifically prohibited the holding of diocesan councils, a prohibition previously issued by the Council of Antioch in 341. On diocesan synods in Merovingian Gaul, see Odette Pontal, *Clercs et laïcs au Moyen Âge d'après les statuts synodaux* (Paris, 1990), 11–13.

572.[90] The council explicitly disallowed the selection of new bishops by fellow bishops or "by the consent of the clergy or people" or by royal appointment.[91] Instead, the canon established a new procedure, modeled on the one followed in the election of the Apostle Matthew in the Acts of the Apostles.[92] First, two or three qualified candidates were to be selected by the "consensus of the clerics and people."[93] Those names would then be submitted to the provincial episcopate. This body's role was now limited to fasting and then turning the final choice over to Christ; the new bishop would be selected from among the candidates by lot (*sors*). Apparently, no body of human electors, including the conciliar repository of sacred episcopal consensus, was reliable enough to make the final choice in so important a matter.

In the early medieval West episcopal elections were opportunities for the expression of community consensus. At the same time, however, they were often fraught with social tensions.[94] The authority of the office could engender power struggles involving powerful families, kings, commoners, and ecclesiastic factions. By leaving the final choice up to chance, or Christ, the bishops at Barcelona were able to minimize the obligations or loyalties a successful candidate might owe to other powers and groups. In practice the elections probably remained manipulable by various parties and individuals.[95] Later evidence shows that, at least in eliminating royal participation, the measure was ineffectual.[96] Still, the canon reflects a problem in the province with the authority of councils. Like the prerogative of the king or the consensus of the people, the collective will of the episcopate was not considered immune from human manipulation. The improper election of unworthy individuals—those who had not come up through the ranks and were beholden to the influence of other powers—could compromise the holy power of the entire group. In order to achieve authoritative consensus, each bishop had to be free from the taint of ambition or dependence. Yet, in order to achieve such individual purity, the council had to acknowledge the fragility of its own consensus, its susceptibility to human networks of power and influence. The new election procedure did recognize the symbolic importance of both community and episcopal consensus, but ultimately it sacrificed the episcopate's claims to overarching group

---

90. Orlandis, *Historia de los concilios*, 245–46, and n. 65.

91. Barcelona II, c. 3: "per sacra regalia aut per consensionem cleri vel plebis vel per electionem assensionemque pontificum." Vives, 159.

92. *Acts* 1, 21–26. Orlandis, *Historia de los concilios*, 246.

93. Barcelona II, c. 3: "quos consensus cleri et plebis selegerit." Vives, 160.

94. Brown, "Relics," 246. For a discussion of different methods of episcopal election in various communities in the later Roman Empire, see Jones, *Later Roman Empire*, 2:915–20.

95. On various avenues of manipulation, see Jones, *Later Roman Empire*, 2:918–19.

96. See Orlandis, *Historia de los concilios*, 245.

authority for the sake of ensuring the unassailable purity and independence of its individual members. Once again, the Tarraconese episcopate collectively tinkered with traditional ecclesiastic procedures in order to support the individual authority of local bishops.

Like the bishops at the council in Seville, the bishops of Tarraconensis adapted their interpretation of conciliar authority to already existing forms and procedures of local governance, both secular and ecclesiastic. Like the bishops in Narbonne, they also used this new source of social authority to define and defend their traditional hierarchies and jurisdictions more aggressively. And, like Masona of Mérida, their primary concerns continued to lie in maintaining their own, individual, authentic holy power.

It is unlikely that many of the bishops of Tarraconensis or the rest of the peninsula were able to exhibit or exercise that power as ostentatiously as Masona. The history of religious antagonism in his city, his decisive victory over the local Arians, the wealth of his see, and the enthusiasm of his congregation allowed this holy man to make public gestures of personal authority that could rival those of a king. As civic patron, educated orator, leader of processions and demonstrations, divinely inspired community advocate, and public provider of peace, mercy, and divine justice, Masona acted as the focus of his community's consensus in a manner that was familiar and accessible to the people of his city. He did give his prestigious support to the ideal of conciliar governance and consensus. Not only was he the first episcopal signatory at Toledo III, but he also traveled to Toledo again in 597 to attend another council.[97] In his own province, however, there was little practical reason for Masona to adapt his own brand of episcopal authority to a new, unfamiliar form of community governance and consensus.

Less prominent, wealthy, or popular bishops in other provinces may have been more eager to take advantage of their newly reaffirmed collective access to divine justice. Yet the tension between that access and their personal holy authority ultimately made it impossible to carry through on the efforts to define the practical role of episcopal consensus as a source of justice for either lay or clerical communities. Without the consistent, ongoing application of conciliar governance, the interests of individual bishops and their communities continued to weigh against a general acceptance of the authority of its decisions and legislation. With the council in Barcelona in 599, this period of provincial conciliar activity drew to a close. There are records for only four other provincial councils in the entire kingdom during the next thirty-three years.

---

97. Masona signed the acts of a pluri-provincial council held in the royal city that year. See n. 104; and Vives, 157.

In 633 the first compilation of Iberian church councils, the *Hispana,* was assembled in Seville.[98] The fact that of these six councils the editor included only the records of Seville I indicates that these provincial interpretations of conciliar practice and authority were not recognized as authoritative precedents among the conciliar cataloguers and practitioners during the last two-thirds of the seventh century. Whatever the reason they were excluded from the systematization projects of that later time, however, the attitudes, ideas, and practices first developed during this period of experimentation saw continued life and development in seventh-century struggles over the meaning and mechanisms of holy authority in Visigothic Iberia. The harsh penalties and broad sweep of the Narbonese interpretation, for instance, came to characterize much Iberian canonical legislation in the seventh century, particularly in its anti-Jewish measures. The legalistic approach to clerical dispute settlement and the pedagogic purposes evident in the records of Seville I also saw new life and elaboration, particularly under Leander's successor and brother, Isidore. The Tarraconese episcopate's fascination with special procedures to preserve clerical hierarchies, purity, authentic faith, and the preeminent power of individual bishops was also a central preoccupation of council goers of the next century as they continued to wrestle with the contradictory nature of conciliar consensus.

The Failure of Centralization

In 588 consensus was finally achieved in Mérida when "all the enemies of the Catholic faith" had been "overthrown" through a combination of divine judgment, secular coercion, royal justice, and episcopal mercy.[99] Despite the river of rhetorical consensus that flowed from Toledo III, such a winning combination of recognized powers eluded the men seeking to achieve kingdom-wide consensus in the ensuing decade. Various parties continued to try to assert their divine authorization in guiding the kingdom to consensus, but those attempts were subdued, compared to the rhetoric of Toledo III and to the more fully articulated vision of legislated consensus that emerged in later years. The king's legislation, for instance, contained language that echoed his speeches of 589, and, as territorial rather than personal lawmaking, these

---

98. See intro., n. 51. According to Martínez Díez, *Estudio,* 306–25, Isidore was probably the editor of the *Hispana*'s first recension, the *Isidoriana.* For arguments against Isidore as editor, see Charles Munier, "Nouvelles recherches sur l'*Hispana* chronologique," *Revue des Sciences Religieuses* 40 (1966), who offers a critiquè of Martínez Díez's *Estudio.* For further bibliography, see Hillgarth, "The Position of Isidorian Studies: A Critical Review of the Literature, 1936–1975," *Studi Medievali,* ser. 3, 24 (Spoleto, 1983), reprinted in *Visigothic Spain, Byzantium and the Irish* (London, 1985), 56–57.

99. *VPE,* 5.12.6: "prostratis . . . universis fidei Catholicae inimicis," 247.

laws—like his edict in confirmation of Toledo III's canons—reflected an ambition for rulership over a united body of subjects.[100] Yet they were all elaborations on canons from Toledo III. Reccared did not assert his territorial lawmaking capacity on any untrodden jurisdictional turf. Perhaps the most noteworthy aspect of these laws is that there were only three of them. By the 580s lawmaking—with the aid of clerical advisors—had become a traditional activity of image-conscious Visigothic kings.[101] Reccared's Arian father, the active self-promoter Leovigild, had fully revised the existing Visigothic code,[102] despite his hostile relationship with many of his leading subjects. Reccared, who received glowing rhetorical endorsement from Toledo III, John of Biclar, and even the pope, Gregory the Great,[103] does not seem to have gar-

---

100. See chap. 2, n. 70.

101. Visigothic royal lawmaking apparently began in Toulouse during the reign of Theodoric I (419–51). See Sidonius Apollinaris, *Epistulae*, II, 1, ed. and trans W. B. Anderson, *Sidonius, Poems and Letters* (Cambridge, 1965). The earliest extant Visigothic legislation consists of a fragment of the code issued c. 476 by the king Euric (466–84), in the *Codex Euricianus*, ed. Karl Zeumer, *MGH Leges* I.3–27 (Hannover, 1902). Both this code and Alaric II's *Breviary* (or *Lex Romana Visigothorum*), promulgated in 506, were produced with the help of Gallo-Roman clerical advisors. On the image-making purposes of these and other "barbarian" law codes, see Patrick Wormald, "*Lex Scripta* and *Verbum Regis*: Legislation and Germanic Kingship, from Euric to Cnut," in *Early Medieval Kingship*, ed. P. H. Sawyer and Ian N. Wood (Leeds, 1977).

102. Leovigild's code is known as the *Codex Revisus*. According to Isidore, *HG*, 51, 258, Leovigild "corrected those [laws] which seemed to have been irregularly promulgated by Euric, adding many that had been left out and removing many superfluous ones" (In legibus quoque ea quae ab Eurico incondite constituta uidebantur correxit, plurimas leges praetermissas adiciens plerasque superfluas auferens). Wolf, 103. These laws are now found in the code of Recceswinth (the *LV*, or the *Forum Iudicum*, promulgated in 654), included under the headings "*Antiquae.*" See P. D. King, "King Chindasvind and the First Territorial Law-code of the Visi-gothic Kingdom," in *Visigothic Spain, New Approaches,* ed. Edward James (Oxford, 1980), 132.

103. In 599 Gregory gave confirmation to Reccared's claims for personal credit for the conversion of the Goths in a congratulatory letter, *Epistola* 9.228, ed. Paulos Ewald and Ludo Hartman, *MGH Epistolarum* II (Berlin, 1894). Gregory termed it a miracle "that through your excellence the whole nation of the Goths has been brought over to the solidity of right faith from the error of the Arian heretics" (per excellentiam tuam cuncta Gothorum gens ab errore Arrianae hereseos in fidei rectae soliditate translata est). The pope tied this accomplishment to Reccared's own salvation in terms that must have supported the king's claim that his conversion necessitated further royal responsibility for his subjects' faith: "I confess that I often tell of these things that have come about through you to my gathered sons . . . and for the most part these things arouse myself against myself, because I, lazy and useless, am inactive in idle leisure while kings take pains with the congregations of souls on behalf of the riches of the celestial fatherland. And thus what shall I say to the coming judge at that tremendous examination, if at that time I arrive empty-handed, whereas your excellence leads the flocks of the faithful behind you, the flocks that you have brought together just now to the grace of true faith through zealous and continuous preaching?" (Haec me, fateor, quae per vos acta sunt saepe convenientibus filiis meis dicere . . . haec me plerumque etiam contra me excitant, quod piger ego et inutilis tunc inerti otio torpeo, quando in animarum congregationibus pro lucro caelestis patriae reges elaborant. Quid itaque ego in illo tremendo examine iudici venienti dicturus sum, si tunc illuc vacuus venero, ubi tua excellentia greges post se fidelium ducit, quos modo ad verae fidei gratiam per studiosam et continuam praedicationem traxit?), 222.

nered the practical or technical support necessary to follow in his father's legislative footsteps.

While church leaders may have been reluctant to give their help to a royally legislated consensus in these years, this was not because they intended to legislate consensus themselves. The provincial episcopates, perhaps with the exception of the bishops at Narbonne, did not show any more enthusiasm for centralized legislation than the bishops at Toledo III had. Furthermore, the mandates of canon 18 appear to have faded rapidly from memory. Kingdomwide episcopal consensus did not flow naturally from a provincial conciliar practice that was itself diverse and discontinuous. Neither the king's claims for religious leadership nor the church's assertions of a historical turning point were capable of providing an accepted centralized authority for the kingdom's clerical communities, let alone for the entire population.

The Toledan see did make a stab at using provincial procedures to assert a kingdom-wide preeminence at a council in 597. Despite an unremarkable agenda of ecclesiastic concerns,[104] the acts were signed by fifteen bishops from all the provinces except Galicia—including such luminaries as Masona of Mérida and John of Biclar (now bishop of Gerona in Tarraconensis). It seems that the Toledan church was using what was essentially a provincial council to promote the city's contested status as the metropolitan see of Cartaginiensis and as the central "holy city" of the entire kingdom.[105] During this uncertain

---

104. Orlandis, *Historia de los concilios,* 241, characterizes the canons of this council as "paltry" or, at best, "modest."

105. Confusion and contention surrounding the composition of the province of Cartaginiensis, and the privileges of Toledo as its metropolitan see, date from as early as the Second Council of Toledo of 527. During Roman times the province had been clearly defined politically and ecclesiastically, but during the fifth and early sixth centuries provincial boundaries had become increasingly blurred. See Antonino González Blanco, "El decreto de Gundemar y la historia del siglo VII," *Los visigodos. Historia y civilización,* Antigüedad y Christianismo 3 (Murcia, 1986), 162; and Thompson, *Goths,* 34. Toledo II identified the interior part of the province as "Carpetania and Celtiberia." See the letter from the metropolitan Montanus; *La colección,* 365. During the Byzantine occupation the traditional metropolitan see of "Cartaginiensis"—Cartagena—became part of the Byzantine territories; the bishop of Toledo signed the records of Toledo III as the metropolitan of "Carpetania." During the seventh century efforts to establish Toledo as the metropolitan see of "Cartaginiensis" rather than "Carpetania" became closely tied to efforts to establish Toledan prominence as the ecclesiastic center and royal city of the kingdom. On this complicated process, see chap. 4, n. 13; and González Blanco, "El Decreto," 159–69; Eugen Ewig, "Résidence et capitale pendant le Haut Moyen Age," *Revue Historique* 230 (1963): 31–33; José María Lacarra, "Panarama de la historia urbana en la Península Ibérica desde el siglo V al X," *Settimane* (Spoleto) 6 (1959): 339; and "La Iglesia visigoda en el siglo VII y sus relaciones con Roma," *Settimane* 7, no. 1 (Spoleto, 1959): 375–78; Juan Francisco Rivera Recio, "Encumbramiento de la sede toledana durante la dominación visigótica," *Hispania Sacra* 8 (1956); Fernández Alonso, *La cura,* 237–41; and Manuel C. Díaz y Díaz, "La obra literaria de los obispos visigóticos toledanos: supuestos y circunstancias," *La Patrología Toledano-Visigoda* 27, Semana Española de Teología (Madrid, 1970).

decade, however, the royal city's prestige was not compelling enough, or conciliar authority not well-enough established, to inspire much interest in the effort. Most of the kingdom's bishops failed to attend the council or sign the records, including the influential Leander of Seville. Nor did the episcopate of Cartaginiensis conclusively endorse this interpretation of their own collective authority. Only five bishops from the province signed the records, compared to fifteen who had been present in 589. Without the acceptance of provincial leadership, neither the city of Toledo nor any other potential source of centralized authority could hope to tie the unrealized ideal of provincially guided ecclesiastic unity to a practical, centrally defined kingdom-wide Christian consensus.

The intricate obstacles to collaboration between Christian leaders extended from the daily life of individual cities like Masona's, through the intermittent efforts at province-wide episcopal harmony, to the ongoing relationship between the parties that had fashioned the alliance between *regnum* and *sacerdotium*. Much as local relationships of power and influence discouraged legislated interference from the center, so it was at the highest levels of social and religious leadership. The mutual suspicions and disagreements masked by Toledo III's ostentatious claims for unity did not evaporate on any level. The relative peace, benevolent kingship, and renewal of church discipline achieved in the years after 589 did not constitute the turning point in Visigothic history that would have allowed the kingdom's leaders to reach a consensus on the meaning of their alliance or to work out the local mechanisms and meanings of conciliar governance. While this important decade saw numerous experiments and contributions to the development of both the ideals and practices of Christian consensus, it did not see the fundamental social changes necessary for any of those measures to take root.

CHAPTER FOUR

Culture, Coercion, and
the Corruption of Justice

In 588 the Catholics of Mérida celebrated their victorious consensus with chanting, clapping, singing, and rejoicing "after the manner of the ancients with great uproar in the streets."[1] Masona already had demonstrated his leadership over this unanimity. By freeing Vagrila from Reccared's sentence, the bishop displayed his own independence and mercy, while at the same time he orchestrated a demonstration of symbolic submission and reintegration that probably helped to heal the divisions in the community. But such mercy could not be shown to everyone involved without continuing the conditions of uncertainty and suspicion. The dissenters from Mérida's consensus—the conspirators who lost their lands and hands and Sunna in his little boat—had been forcibly excluded from the community. Later events proved that even a very limited range of episcopal mercy could be a dangerous path to community fence mending and consensus building. After the defeat of the conspirators, Masona and Claudius had freed the would-be assassin, Witteric. This man was not sufficiently impressed by his experience with divine judgment to mend his ways permanently. In 603, two years after Reccared was succeeded by his son, Liuva, Witteric assassinated the young king, seized the throne, and went on to rule until 610.

Little is known about Witteric's reign other than that he won no significant military victories,[2] failed to enforce Reccared's anti-Jewish legislation,[3] became embroiled in a dispute with the Frankish king Theuderic,[4] and

---

1. See chap. 3, n. 16.

2. *HG*, 58.

3. According to a law promulgated by Sisebut (611/12–620), *LV*, 12.2,13; 418, Jews had succeeded in evading Reccared's measure against owning Christian slaves by bribing previous rulers—presumably Witteric and his successor, Gundemar (610–611/12). See E. A. Thompson, *The Goths in Spain* (Oxford, 1969), 165.

4. This was due to the fact that Theuderic reneged on a marriage commitment to Witteric's daughter. Witteric tried to put together a coalition against Theuderic with two other Frankish kings and the Lombard king Agilulf, but this too seems to have fallen apart. See the *Chronicle* of Fredegar, 4.30–31, in *The Fourth Book of the Chronicle of Fredegar*, ed. and trans. J. M. Wallace-Hadrill (London, 1960), 20–21.

inspired the intense dislike of clerical leaders.[5] The usurper was himself assassinated in 610 and buried without ceremony.[6] He was succeeded by an unremarkable king, Gundemar, who ruled to 611 or 612. It may be that the usurpation in 603 represented an Arian reaction to Reccared's conversion, hence the clerical hostility toward Witteric.[7] A more likely scenario, however, is that the power struggle arose out of noble hostility toward the dynastic aspirations of Leovigild's family,[8] a phenomenon that tended to repeat itself in hereditary royal successions, particularly when the intended heir was young or militarily untried.[9] Reccared's son was an infant when he became king in 601. Clerical antipathy toward a usurper who murdered his legitimate king does not require an explanation based in dogma. Witteric's actions and his subsequent failure to seek legitimacy by currying favor with the episcopate—as later usurpers did—would have been enough to turn church leaders against him.[10] At the same time, his unsuccessful warfare and fruitless diplomacy probably encouraged the Gothic nobility to question his suitability as their military leader and thus his divine endorsement as king. A noble Goth named Bulgar attributed Witteric's downfall to divine judgment: "pierced by a sword more celestial than human," the usurper was condemned to be tortured in hell.[11]

The lack of sources makes it difficult to know much more about how contemporary leaders interpreted this interlude of instability and disunity. Yet these years constitute the immediate backdrop for the ideas and actions of a new generation of Christian leaders in the kingdom. By the end of Witteric's reign, Leander, Masona, Reccared, and probably most of the other signatories to the acts of

---

5. See Thompson, *Goths,* 157. Isidore of Seville, *HG,* 58, reported that "in his life [Witteric] did much that was unlawful" (in uita plurima inlicita fecit), 268. Aside from the usurpation, this king's specific crimes are unclear. The king apparently caused some trouble for the bishop of Toledo at the time, Aurasius. See Ildefonsus of Toledo, *De viribus illustribus* 5, *PL* 96, 195–204, and Thompson, *Goths,* 157. Another contemporary commentator on Witteric was a Gothic royal official named Bulgar, who in one of his letters dubbed him an "impious tyrant" (impii tiranni). *EW,* 13, 39.

6. *HG,* 58, 270.

7. This explanation has been suggested by several modern historians. See bibliography in Garvin's commentary on the *VPE,* 497.

8. Thompson, *Goths,* 157; and José Orlandis, *Historia del reino visigodo* (Madrid, 1988), 98.

9. See chap. 1, n. 16.

10. Witteric was not without clerical supporters, however. Bulgar, *EW,* 13, 39, refers to one bishop, Elegius of Egara, who, following Witteric's orders, held Bulgar confined without light or "human consolation" (humana consolatione).

11. *EW,* 14: "celeste magis quam humano . . . gladio perfosus," 39. Isidore (*HG,* 58) gives another version of the king's death: because Witteric "had lived by the sword, he died by the sword," being killed at a banquet in 610 "as the result of a conspiracy of certain men" (quia gladio operatus fuerat, gladio periit . . . inter epulas enim prandii coniuratione quorundam est interfectus), 270, trans. K. Wolf, *Conquerors and Chroniclers of Early Medieval Spain,* (Liverpool, 1990), 106.

Toledo III had died. The new leaders cannot have been unaware of the failure of much of these men's work. Witteric's career not only illustrated the dangers of misapplied judicial mercy and the possibility of the kingship losing its divine endorsement through the misuse of armed force; his reign also served to underline the inability of previous royal lawmaking and provincial councils to overcome the obstacles standing in the way of consensus. The limited efforts made during the 590s in both arenas apparently came to a halt with Reccared's death in 601. The questions left open by Toledo III remained unanswered, while the issues at stake became even more pressing. Whether Witteric threatened an Arian revival or not, the prospects for kingdom-wide consensus and the divine favor it signified must have looked dimmer during the first decade of the seventh century than at any time since Reccared's conversion.

Thus, it is not surprising that when kings and bishops again took up the issues of holy authority, Christian consensus, and conciliar governance, the scope of the debate had shifted. What is surprising, perhaps, is that, despite the setbacks under Witteric, the terms and arenas of dialogue were now more clearly defined and articulately advocated. In fact, the difficulties actually may have encouraged Christian leaders to close ranks behind particularly able spokesmen. In any case, in the decade following Witteric's death the multiplicity of viewpoints in the sources from the earlier period narrowed to the visions of two men: the bishop of Seville, Isidore, and the most literate of Visigothic kings, Sisebut (611/12–621). Both men assumed positions of leadership in a conscientious renewal of Christian culture, which they both saw as a key to wielding legitimate authority and to creating an orderly, God-pleasing Christian society.

Despite their shared appeal to the authority of literate culture, however, the men's views and policies differed significantly. The king advocated royally legislated forced conversion as the means to establish and maintain Christian consensus, while Isidore's vision of social order was centered on clerical education and discipline. After Sisebut's death, in 621, the contradictions between these two visions, their internal weaknesses, and the chasm between such ideals and the social dynamics in the kingdom's communities contributed to new conflicts and confusion. Nevertheless, from this point on, legislated religious uniformity, clerical discipline, and Christian cultural renewal became the defining terms of ideological and practical development in the struggle to locate and exercise holy authority and establish Christian consensus in the Visigothic kingdom.

Royal Education and Forced Conversion

Witteric's successor, Gundemar, does not seem to have impressed his contemporaries. Only the noble Goth Bulgar expressed an absolute contrast between the two kings. According to this man's letters, Gundemar was as pious and benevolent as Witteric had been evil and insanely cruel. Bulgar's effusiveness no doubt was inspired by ties of personal loyalty and duty. Exiled and imprisoned by Witteric, he had been recalled to service by Gundemar. Isidore of Seville, in his *History of the Goths,* has very little to say about Bulgar's royal patron.[12] Gundemar's relations with church leaders were probably an improvement over Witteric's; a church council may have been held in Toledo during his reign.[13] But the new king's reputation perhaps was enhanced by the ill will toward his predecessor; his own accomplishments were minimal. Although he won a battle against the Basques, Gundemar was not notably suc-

---

12. *HG,* 59, 270.

13. The authenticity of this council's records and a decree issued by Gundemar and bearing the signatures of Isidore and twenty-five other bishops has been questioned by some modern historians, beginning with Mansi in his *Conciliorum omnium maxima collectio,* 10.511. Suspicions voiced by Felix Dahn (*Die Könige der Germanen,* 5 [Leipzig, 1885], 175) are amplified with complex argumentation into outright rejection of the documents by Antonino González Blanco ("El Decreto de Gundemaro y la historia del siglo VII," *Los Visigodos. Historia y civilización,* Antigüedad y Christianismo 2 [Murcia, 1985]; and "La historia del S.E. peninsula entre los siglos III–VIII d.C. (Fuentes literarias, problemas y sugerencias)," *Del Conventus Carthaginiensis a la Chora de Tudmir. Perspectivas de la Historia de Murcia entre los siglos III–VIII,* Antigüedad y Christianismo 2 [Murcia, 1985], 71). On the other hand, the documents are used without question by Paul Séjourné, (*Le dernier père de l'Église. Saint Isidore de Séville* [Paris, 1936], 86–88); and E. A. Thompson (*The Goths in Spain,* [Oxford, 1969], 159–60). José Orlandis and Domingo Ramos-Lissón (*Historia de los concilios de la España romana y visigoda* [Pamplona, 1986], 248–52), acknowledge but dismiss the charges of forgery. The documents in question are published in Vives, 403–10; they were found in manuscripts containing the *Juliana* recension of the *Hispana,* which was compiled c. 681 in Toledo. They were not included in the earlier *Isidoriana* recension. See Gonzalo Martínez-Díez, *Estudio, La colección,* vol. 1, 209–20. The "Edict of Gundemar," the conciliar *acta,* and three letters concerning the election of a bishop were inserted into the *Juliana* out of chronological order, as what Martínes Díez calls "suplementos" to the Twelfth Council of Toledo, held in 681. Toledo XII was concerned primarily with legitimizing a problematic succession; however, it included a canon asserting the primacy of the Toledan see in episcopal elections throughout the kingdom. Gundemar's Edict and the conciliar *acta* accompanying it were both assertions of Toledo's metropolitan status within the province of Cartagena and thus can be seen as supporting the claims to kingdom-wide primacy made at the council in 681. The documents from Gundemar's council are a clear rewriting of the history of the province of Cartaginiensis, claiming that the signatory from Toledo at Toledo III was "ignorant," because he signed as the metropolitan of a province called Carpetania (Vives, 405; see chap. 3, n. 105). If genuine, this material shows a reassertion not only of the Toledan see's power but also of the king's; his edict is framed in language making claims to religious direction similiar to, if not stronger than, Reccared's. Moreover, it would appear that the rewriting of history in favor of Toledo was carried out at Gundemar's behest, and with the support of Isidore, whose signature appears first after the king's, and before those of the metropolitans from all the kingdom's provinces. Séjourné (88–100) argues that Isidore's willingness to discredit a previous bishop (the signatory in 589 from Carpetania) in support of a king was in keeping with his "loyalisme" to the Visigothic monarchy, as well as his continuing agenda for the establishment of an "église nationale." Even if Gundemar did not actually participate in these activities and Isidore's signature is inauthentic, it seems probable that the king's reign was known as one supportive of the Toledan Church; otherwise, the later forgers would not have chosen to attribute their work to this particular kingship.

cessful at war; he failed to win any victories against the Byzantine occupation in the southern peninsula. His reign was apparently troubled by disturbances in Narbonensis, possibly related to a complex diplomatic venture into internal Frankish power struggles.[14] Finally, like Witteric, Gundemar did not issue any legislation and apparently failed to enforce Reccared's anti-Jewish law.[15] All in all, the most important feature of Gundemar's reign seems to be that his lack of achievements highlighted the self-promotion of his more successful and much more effectively propagandized successor, Sisebut.

The most obvious contrast between Sisebut and his two predecessors was his military success. He personally led his army in two important victories against the Byzantines, paving the way for his successor Swinthila's (621–31) expulsion of the Byzantines from the peninsula in 624. Sisebut furthered his military reputation by suppressing a rebellion in the North and by building the first Visigothic fleet.[16] The war with the Byzantines also allowed the king to exhibit his diplomatic expertise—another area in which his predecessors seem to have been lacking—in an exchange of letters with the Byzantine commander, Constantius. Visigothic relations with the Franks probably improved during his reign as well. The two monarchs against whom Witteric and Gundemar had maneuvered without success, Theuderic and his notorious grandmother Brunhild, met their deaths in 614 at the hands of the Merovingian king Clothar, who unified Gaul in that year. Sisebut tied himself to the downfall of these enemies by publishing a saint's life, the *Vita Desiderii*, which described the martyrdom of a Gallic bishop at the hands of the evil monarchs. The work was partly intended as a justification for Clothar's gruesome torture of Brunhild—a Visigothic princess who had been given by her father, Athanagild, in marriage to the Frankish king Sigebert (561–75).[17] Through this and other writings Sisebut also expressed another quality in contrast to his predecessors: his extravagant piety. His aggressive religious devotion is particularly evident in his two extant laws.[18] They are both detailed elaborations of Reccared's law against Jews owning Christian slaves. One of them explicitly poses Sisebut's

14. Bulgar, *EW*, 11, 12, and 13, 31–40. According to Bulgar, the inhabitants of the region were agog over the activities of Theuderic and his mother Brunhild, who had incited the Avars against another Frankish king, Theudebert. Gundemar entered into an alliance with Theudebert, involving the transfer of envoys and money—the subjects of Bulgar's correspondence with certain bishops in Frankish territory.

15. *LV*, 12.2.13, 418.

16. *HG, Recapitulatio*, 70, 286.

17. Sisebut, *Vita Desiderii*, 21, in *MW*, 67–68. On the political meanings of this piece, see Jacques Fontaine, "King Sisebut's *Vita Desiderii* and the Political Function of Visigothic Hagiography," in *Visigothic Spain. New Approaches*, ed. E. James (Oxford, 1980); on Sisebut's rendition of the torture of Brunhild—according to the king, she was torn to pieces while tied between two "untamable steeds" (sonipedum indomitorum)—see 118–19 and 124–25.

18. *LV*, 12.2.13 and 14, 418–23.

rigorous anti-Judaism against the laxity of previous kings.[19] Indeed, the king carried this sinister aspect of his piety to new, precedent-setting extremes: he issued a law ordering the forced conversion of all the Jews in the kingdom.[20]

Sisebut's image-making efforts were quite successful. His reputation was still strong outside his kingdom later in the century, when the Burgundian chronicler known as Fredegar reported that the king was "a wise and most pious man, much admired throughout Spain."[21] For modern historians the reign of this pious, victorious, diplomatic, lawmaking king is most noticeably set off from the troubled years under Witteric and Gundemar by the fact that it coincided with a conscientious movement for cultural renewal. To this day Sisebut is credited with a kind of coleadership of the "Isidorian Renaissance."[22] Spearheaded by Isidore of Seville, this movement saw an outpouring of literature aimed at regenerating clerical culture and addressing the contemporary needs of both the church and the kingship through the systematization and dissemination of classical and patristic knowledge.[23] Sisebut embraced

---

19. *LV,* 12.2.13, 418.

20. The law is not extant. It is known through Isidore's commentary in *HG,* 61, and through Tol. IV, c. 57. See n. 66 of this chapter, and chap. 5, n. 37.

21. Fredegar, 4.33: "vir sapiens et in totam Spaniam laudabelis ualde, pietate plenissemus." Wallace-Hadrill, 20–21. In the same passage Fredegar also related that the king bemoaned the number of enemy dead after a battle with the Byzantines: "Woe is me, that my reign should witness so great a shedding of human blood!" (Eu me misero, cuius tempore tante sanguis humanae effusio fietur; Wallace-Hadrill, 23. Isidore, *HG,* 60–61, 270–74, also noted this merciful aspect of Sisebut's character.

22. Fontaine ("Political Function," 99) describes the "Isidorian Renaissance" as being understood by contemporaries "at one and the same time as an intellectual renaissance, a moral rearmament, a religious revival and as a construction of a new political, royal, and national ideology." Sisebut's participation, he says (98), provided to his age "a royal example of the return to the refinement of ancient culture." Quoting L. J. Van der Lof ("Der Mäzen König Sisebutus und sein 'De eclipsi lunae'," *Revue des Études Augustiniennes* 18 nos. 1–2 [1972], 150) Fontaine argues that Sisebut's writings were all animated by a faith in "'the possibility of a cultural policy directed by the king'" and that the royal author "actively pursued" his personal duty of the "education of Spain." Sisebut has also been described as a "Byzantine type of ruler, above all concerned with orthodoxy" (Jocelyn N. Hillgarth, "Historiography in Visigothic Spain," *Settimane* 17 [Spoleto, 1970], reprinted in *Visigothic Spain, Byzantium, and the Irish* [London, 1985], 285); as seeing himself as a theologian on a par with the emperor Justinian (Jacques Fontaine, *Isidore de Séville et la culture classique dans l'Espagne wisigothique* [Paris, 1959], 868, n. 1); as a "patron of the Isidorian age," (Walter Stach, "König Sisebut ein Mäzen des isidorischen Zeitalters," *Die Antike* 19, no. 1 [1943]); and as an "Alfonso the Wise of Visigothic Spain" (Fontaine, in his edition of Isidore's *de naturam rerum: Isidore de Séville. Traité de la nature suivi de l'épitre en vers du roi Sisebut à Isidore* [Bordeaux, 1960], 152).

23. Although Isidore traditionally has been seen as a derivative compiler of ancient knowledge whose works symbolize the cultural poverty of early medieval Europe, recent scholars—particularly Fontaine (*Isidore de Séville*)—have sought to rehabilitate his intellectual reputation by recontextualizing his thought within his contemporary society, rather than simply within the intellectual traditions of classical culture. Thus, Isidore's emphasis on the encyclopoedic assembling of classical and patristic knowledge and terminology is seen as part of a conscious—rather than random—gathering of classical artifacts and concepts applicable to the

cultural renewal wholeheartedly, presenting himself to the world and to posterity as a patron of and a participant in the literary arts. Royal education and cultural leadership were central elements in his conception of royal authority and Christian consensus. In Sisebut's view cultural leadership enabled kings (most notably himself) to determine the correct royal laws and procedures for fulfilling their duties for religious leadership; it also made it possible to teach the meaning of royal authority to others. As his many writings show, Sisebut took up these tasks with vigor.

For Sisebut the creation of Christian consensus involved eliminating all forms of doctrinal diversity among all of his subjects. Such was the personal, familial, political, and religious duty of all Christian kings. In his view the safety and survival of the kingship, the Gothic *gens,* its subjects, and the church depended upon the correct use of royally directed legal procedures (such as forced conversion) to achieve a uniform Christian identity among his subjects. The literate king articulated these principles particularly clearly (while at the same time demonstrating his leadership in international affairs) in one of his more elaborate letters, which was addressed to Adalwald, the Arian king of the Lombards.[24]

Sisebut began the letter by urging Adalwald to convert to Catholicism himself and then advised him on how to bring the rest of his subjects into the orthodox faith. According to Sisebut, it was a king's duty, as the glorious head to the body of subjects, to "slice off putrid errors with the cutting knife of proof."[25] If he failed in that duty he would bring so much damage to himself and his people that he would have to "show the reason to the pastor of pastors."[26] In order to perform this necessary amputation, Sisebut suggested that some subjects might be converted to Catholicism by "promising that which they desire," while "the gentle threatening of a rule should subdue certain ones," and "a harsher rebuking should direct others."[27] The king went on to explain that

---

practical and political needs of both the Iberian Church and the Visigothic monarchy. Isidore's modern reputation has recently achieved new heights through a movement to have him designated as the patron saint of the Internet. On Isidore's life as an active educator, see Jacques Fontaine, "Fins et moyens de l'enseignement ecclésiastique dans l'Espagne Wisigothique," *Settimane* 19 (Spoleto, 1972), reprinted in *Culture et spiritualité en Espagne du IVe au VIIe siècle* (London, 1986), with bibliography on 145 n. 1. Modern Isidorian scholarship is evaluated in detail by Jocelyn N. Hillgarth in "The Position of Isidorian Studies: A Critical Review of the Literature 1936–75," *Studi Medievali,* ser. 3, 24 (Spoleto, 1983), reprinted in *Visigothic Spain, Byzantium and the Irish;* and in "Isidorian Studies, 1976–85," *Studi Medievali,* ser. 3, 31, no. 2 (Spoleto, 1990). A more recent treatment of Isidore's work is Pierre Cazier, *Isidore de Séville et la naissance de l'Espagne catholique* (Paris, 1994).

24. *EW,* 8, 19–27.

25. *EW,* 8.64–65: "errores putridos cultro . . . resecando absciderit," 22.

26. *EW,* 8.66: "pastori rationem pastorum exhibeat," 22.

27. *EW,* 8.82–85: "Plectendi sunt pollicitatione qua cupiunt . . . quosdam lenis debet comminatio regule subdere, quosdam asperior increpatio flectere," 22.

the eager ones are easily drawn along by an offered gift, and the stubborn are driven away from the depraved sect by severe deprivation. These things should be carried out calmly, according to place, time, and person, until at length the gleaming torch of faith's ardor, growing strong with Catholic vigor, reflects the firm, light-streaming hearts of the believers, while the putrid remainder of the heretics are drawn into the ashes.[28]

In this letter the king did not go into detail about the exact definition of "a harsher rebuking" or "severe deprivation," but his surviving legislation makes his meaning much clearer.

Sisebut's law forcing the conversion of the Jews in Spain no longer survives.[29] But another law, forbidding Jews to employ or be patrons to Christians, lays out his conception of the role of royal legislation in establishing religious unity. According to the king, the law was "conceived out of the love of piety and religion" and for the health of his kingdom: "We seek out a healing remedy for ourselves, our *gens,* and all the peoples pertaining to the provinces of our kingdom, when we gently snatch those joined to our faith from the hands of the infidels."[30] The measure established complicated procedures and penalties for the removal of all Christians from "the deadly dominion of Jews."[31] It invoked the death penalty against Jews who converted Christians to their faith as well as public beatings, scalping, and enslavement for any Chris-

---

28. *EW*, 8.85–91: "nam facile cupidus porrecto munere trahitur et contumax districtionis seueritate de praua secta repellitur. Hec quidem equanimiter pro loco, pro tempore, pro persona gerenda sunt, donec ardor fidei conualescens uigore catholico, lampade corruscante, fundata corda credentium luciflua reddat et putridas hereticorum reliquias de fumosis orta materiis exurens in fauilla reducat," 22.

29. Sisebut's exact requirements for the Jews' conversion are unknown. According to Ramon Hernández ("El problema de los judios en los PP. Visigodos," *Patrología Toledano-Visigoda,* 27, Semana Española de Teología [Madrid, 1970], 107 n. 50) "El edicto de Sisebuto debió venir expresado . . . en los términos de conversión o destierro . . . ; pasado un plazo para dar tiempo a los hebreos a tomar su decisión, se les amenazaría seguramente con la pena de muerte." For varying views on Sisebut's action, see also Thompson, *Goths,* 166–67; James Parkes, *The Conflict of the Church and the Synagogue: A Study in the Origins of Antisemitism* (London, 1934), 355–56; Solomon Katz, *The Jews in the Visigothic and Frankish Kingdoms of Spain and Gaul* (Cambridge, 1937), 11–12; Bernard Bachrach, "A Reassessment of Visigothic Jewish Policy, 589–711," *American Historical Review* 78 (1973): 18–19; A. Lukyn Williams, *Adversos Judeos: A Bird's Eye View of Christian Apologiae until the Renaissance* (New York, 1935), 215–16; Jeremy duQuesnay Adams, "Ideology and the Requirements of 'Citizenship' in Visigothic Spain: The Case of the *Judaei,*" *Societas* 2 (1972): 321; Bernhard Blumenkranz, *Juifs et Chrétiens dans le monde occidental* (Paris, 1960), 110–11; Orlandis, *Historia de los concilios,* 288–89; Bat-Sheva Albert, "*De fide catholica contra Judaeos* d'Isidore de Séville: La polémique anti-Judaïque dans l'Espagne du VIIe siècle," *Revue des Études Juives* 142 (1982): 304–5.

30. *LV*, 12.2.14: "Universis populis ad regni nostri provincias pertinentibus salutifera remedia nobis gentique nostre conquirimus, cum fidei nostre coniunctos de infidorum manibus clementer eripimus," 420.

31. *LV*, 12.2.14: "funesta Iudeorum imperia," 420.

tians who, having been converted to Judaism, wanted to remain "in that perfidy."[32] Sisebut's claims for the power of royal legislation extended to the final judgment—he personally sentenced anyone who violated the law to be "separated from the manifest flock of Christ and, at the left hand with the Jews, consumed by atrocious flames with the devil as his companion."[33] Sisebut saw legal procedures and harsh secular punishments as effective tools for caring for his kingdom's religious well-being. If they were not adequate, however, royal religious legislation also carried the force of graphically expressed divine sanctions.

The king's vision of the role of the church and its episcopate in Christian governance and the establishment of unity is harder to discern. He has been described as exhibiting a strong "clericalism" in his denunciation of Theuderic and Brunhild in the *Vita Desiderii*.[34] The *Vita* was also intended as a lesson on evil kingship. Sisebut labeled the two rulers as the exact opposites of what has come to be recognized as the Isidorian model of correct kingship: rather than ruling, they destroyed, rather than advancing, they perished.[35] The royal author illustrated their evil policies by narrating their persistent persecution of a particularly holy bishop, Desiderius of Vienne.

Sisebut's description of the Frankish monarchs' anticlerical abuses reads like a laundry list of possible episcopal complaints against secular interference in church governance. The rulers began their campaign by encouraging, if not actually soliciting, false witnesses against the bishop. They manipulated a church council into stripping Desiderius of his office and condemning him to exile.[36] The monarchs then investigated the exile's miracle working, hoping to disprove his powers. Eventually, according to Sisebut, Theuderic and Brunhild, rebuked unrelentingly by Desiderius, were convinced by the devil to "extract the soul of the soldier of Christ from the corporeal chains."[37] In order to achieve this end the royal pair further abused their judicial powers, issuing a "noxious" edict: "'It is pleasing that Desiderius, dangerous to our *mores* and the enemy of our works, be punished, beaten with blows, and afflicted with

---

32. *LV*, 12.2.14: "in ea perfidia stare," 422.

33. *LV*, 12.2.14: "discretus a Christi grege prespicuo, ad levam cum Hebreis exuratur flammis atrocibus, comitante sibi diabulo," 423.

34. Fontaine, "Political Function," 126.

35. *Vita Desiderii*, 15: "non prodesse, sed obesse et magis perdere quam regere . . . ," 62. See Fontaine, "Political Function," 126. On the Isidorian conception of kingship, see Marc Reydellet, *La royauté dans la littérature latine, de Sidoine Apollinaire a Isidore de Séville* (Rome, 1981), 505–97; and "La conception du souverain chez Isidore de Séville," in *Isidoriana*, ed. Manuel C. Díaz y Díaz (Leon, 1961).

36. The Council of Chalon (603). See Fredegar, *Chronicle*, 4.24. Wallace-Hadrill, 15.

37. *Vita Desiderii*, 16: "a corporeis uinculis Xpi militis animam . . . extrahere," 63.

many kinds of penalties.'"[38] This inimical sentence was enthusiastically carried out. Sisebut claims that Desiderius was seized "from the bosom of the
church" and led "like a condemned prisoner" to be stoned to death by a
depraved crowd.[39]

In narrating the story, Sisebut hammered home his message by consistently manipulating the facts in the case.[40] For instance, the king's story does
not mention that one of the most important figures behind Desiderius' martyrdom was in fact a prominent bishop: Aridius of Lyons.[41] No other source
mentions a royal edict or the sentence it contained. A much less spectacular
version of the bishop's death appears elsewhere.[42] The king's liberal doses of
artistic license served to emphasize his condemnation of Theuderic and Brunhild's misuse of specific royal powers—judicial, conciliar, and legislative. Sisebut made his abstractions of evil rule concrete in the procedural abuses the
Frankish monarchs made at the expense of the church and its own legal procedures: false witnesses, biased investigations, inimical judgments, abominable
edicts, malicious manipulations of conciliar power, and the final irony of treat-
ing a miracle-working bishop as a common condemned criminal.

Yet, despite this careful condemnation of Frankish royal interference in
episcopal affairs, Sisebut's vision of his own religious responsibility included
the duty to oversee the pastoral duties of bishops. For instance, in a letter to
Eusebius of Tarragona he raked the prelate over the coals for attending the-
atrical spectacles. The king used this metropolitan's sinful reputation as an
excuse for demanding the confirmation of a royal episcopal appointee to the
see of Barcelona.[43] In another letter he chastised Cicilius of Mentesa for
neglecting his responsibilities by entering a monastery, ordering him to present
himself in person to be reprimanded by the king and a group of bishops.[44] This
royally convened episcopal gathering indicates, if not his convocation of an

---

38. *Vita Desiderii*, 16: "Desiderium moribus nostris infestum et operibus inimicum
lapidum ictibus uerberatum multoque genere penarum afflictum animaduerti complacuit," 63.

39. *Vita Desiderii*, 17–18: "gremio raptim eclesie tollitur et quasi reus indemnes occisurus
ad supplicium ducitur," 64–65.

40. Fontaine, "Political Function," 111–15.

41. On Aridius, see Fredegar, *Chronicle*, 4.24; Wallace-Hadrill, 15; and Fontaine, "Political Function," 112 and n. 2.

42. In another *Life* of Desiderius by a cleric in Vienne, in *MGH, scriptores rerum
merovingicarum*, ed. Bruno Krusch, 3.638–645. See Fontaine, "Political Function," 114. For
comments supporting this *Life*'s authenticity against Krusch's arguments that it is a forgery, see
Ian N. Wood, "Forgery in Merovingian Hagiography," *Fälschungen im Mittelalter* V, *MGH,
Schriften* 33 (1988): 373–76.

43. *EW*, 6, 14–15.

44. *EW*, 1, 3–6. According to Fontaine ("Political Function," 126 n. 1) this letter illustrates
Sisebut's intention to "govern the Church just as much as the State."

actual church council, a group of bishops supporting the king's interference in episcopal discipline.

The combination of this interference with the king's harsh criticism of Theuderic and Brunhild's meddling in church affairs might seem paradoxical, or perhaps hypocritical. Sisebut, however, criticized those evil rulers not for their meddling but for their motives, and particularly for their methods. The correct use of royal and ecclesiastic procedures was, for Sisebut, one of the central responsibilities of Christian kings. In the king's eyes Theuderic and Brunhild had revealed their evil rulership when they had abused those procedures in their criminal persecution of Desiderius. Likewise, previous Visigothic kings had reneged on their religious duty by abusing accepted judicial procedures when they failed to enforce Reccared's anti-Jewish law. Adalwald would risk eternal damnation and personal and collective shame through his own failure to convert; he would multiply the risk through failing to fulfill correctly his religious responsibility to implement the mass conversion procedures so carefully laid out by the expert, Sisebut.

By casting himself as a scholar, a teacher, and a preacher, Sisebut paid tribute to the traditional authority of the church and to the cultural programs of its contemporary leaders, especially Isidore of Seville. In so doing, the king also presented a case for his own status as a learned authority on Catholic governance. This status allowed him to define royal religious duties and to institute the correct methods for fulfilling them. In honoring the church and its cultural traditions, he asserted his right and duty to guide and amend them. By leading the Visigothic kingship out of the quagmire created by previous kings' neglect, incompetence, and faithlessness, Sisebut laid the basis for a series of claims for holy authority that outstripped the ones made at Toledo III by that new Constantine, Reccared. The fact that Sisebut's interpretation of that authority transgressed the bounds of much of the church's teachings on the role of secular powers and on the efficacy of forced conversion was drowned out by the king's loud claims to personal piety and learning.

Clerical Education and Conciliar Practice

Given his aggressive vision, not to mention the precedents for royal participation in conciliar governance so vigorously reaffirmed in 589, one might expect Sisebut to have been particularly enthusiastic about promoting royal control over conciliar justice and its procedures. Yet there are records of only two provincial councils during his reign.[45] Outside of using "the most glorious

---

45. The Council of Egara, in 614, and the Second Council of Seville, in 619.

king's" regnal year for dating purposes, neither mentions Sisebut, or his royal permission for the gathering. While the king may have surrounded himself with a coterie of bishops who would gather at his command in order to rebuke one of their colleagues, it does not appear that his vision of royal holy authority mixed well with the by now rather frayed concepts of conciliar governance from 589. It may be that this was either because Sisebut recognized the practical pitfalls that had emerged in the 590s or because the troubles under Witteric had increased the episcopate's wariness about exercising their collective capacity for dispensing justice, particularly in concert with a Visigothic king. It is easy to imagine that Sisebut's interventionist attitudes would make at least some bishops hesitant to open up another avenue for royal interference if they were not compelled to do so.

Isidore of Seville, however, was not one to be put off by the pretensions of this image-making king, no matter how victorious or literate he might be. The learned bishop was, after all, the metropolitan of his province, Baetica. As an active Christian leader and educator, his literary recovery of the past had immediate practical meanings, particularly in governing and educating clerics.[46] In 619 Isidore brought his cultural expertise to bear on the question of conciliar governance when, twenty-seven years after the last such meeting, the bishops of Baetica gathered at the Second Council of Seville.[47] Here, in canons overflowing with references to a variety of ancient legal precedents and principles, Isidore presented to his contemporaries a carefully crafted practical application of cultural renewal. Like Sisebut, Isidore placed adherence to clearly delineated procedures at the center of his program for correct Christian governance. Other than that, however, the bishop's views had little to do with Sisebut's grandiose vision. In the face of the king's enthusiastic combination of culture, coercion, and consensus, Isidore may not have withdrawn into an ivory tower of erudition, but he did limit his definition of conciliar authority to ecclesiastic dispute settlement, clerical discipline, and Christian education.

One of the problems that had confronted the kingdom's leaders in the 590s had been episcopal inexperience and ignorance of conciliar tradition. Toledo III had presented conflicting and vague lessons on the competence and procedures of provincial councils, and the councils of the 590s had not estab-

---

46. See Cazier, *Isidore de Séville,* 55–57; more generally, see Fontaine, "Fins et moyens."

47. Isidore had succeeded his brother as metropolitan sometime before Reccared's death in 601. The province's geographical territory had also changed since 590; some of the territory recovered from the Byzantines had been reincorporated into Baetica. Although the exact timing and territory of Sisebut's campaigns against the Byzantines are not known, the coastal Baetican city of Málaga had come into Visigothic hands by 619—the city's bishop signed the acts of Seville II. See Vives, 185. On the Visigoths' reconquest of the Byzantine province, see Thompson, *Goths,* 331–34. On the character and content of Seville II, see Orlandis, *Historia de los concilios,* 252–60.

lished any lasting precedents. The twenty-seven-year hiatus since the only previous council in Baetica meant that Isidore and his colleagues at Seville II confronted similar conditions of ignorance and potential confusion. For Isidore
the issue of cultural renewal would have made the problem of conciliar pedagogy even more pressing. If one of the purposes of recovering ancient knowledge was to address contemporary social needs, then church councils, as
forums for applying the decisions of the past to present-day problems, were
the perfect vehicle for putting Isidore's educational ideals into practice. Yet, in
the eyes of this meticulous educator, enforceable conciliar authority depended
upon a faithful, deliberate—educated—appeal to the authority of conciliar
tradition, rather than the ad hoc interpretations that had failed in the recent
past. In 619, as the Baetican bishops heard and decided cases, the council's
proceedings and record keeping were molded into a detailed lesson on the correct way to wield collective episcopal authority.

Isidore and his council approached the task of rendering ancient tradition
into contemporary pedagogy with characteristic subtlety. Seville II taught by
example, not by prescription. The bishops issued no rules on conciliar procedure. Instead, the records began by describing the membership, setting, seating, and general agenda of the gathering—modestly characterized as "some
ecclesiastic business."[48] Many of the following canons, rather than simply
announcing the rule being invoked, as one finds in most provincial conciliar
records, instead rendered detailed case-by-case accounts of the names, dioceses, and legal issues involved in disputes over such questions as the territorial
rights of dioceses, errant clerics, noncanonical ordinations, and the unjust
ejection of priests from office.[49] Although they include no detailed narrative of
the proceedings, the canons often refer to the process by which the bishops
heard arguments and witnesses, ordered investigations, and, most important,
applied legal precedents. Once inscribed into canon, these details and descriptions provided a divinely endorsed conciliar exemplar that could serve the educational and judicial needs of succeeding generations.

By marshaling the precedents of the past to authorize a redefinition of
ancient tradition, Isidore was following the lead of his brother and predecessor, Leander of Seville.[50] Leander had orchestrated the reconfiguration of the
"ecumenical" conciliar tradition to formalize the alliance of 589. In 590, under
his leadership, Seville I had evoked the measured language of Roman legal traditions in its interpretation of provincial conciliar practice. Seville II amplified
that Romanized voice into a resounding chorus of Roman legal citations, in

---

48. Seville II, c. 1: "pro aliquibus ecclesiasticis negotiis." Vives, 163.

49. Seville II, c. 1 and 2, diocesan rights; c. 3, errant clerics; c. 4 and 5, noncanonical ordinations; c. 6, unjust clerical deposings. Vives, 163–66.

50. On Leander as Isidore's "éducateur," see Fontaine, "Fins et moyens," 153.

combination with any mixture of conciliar, papal, or scriptural law that might be applied to any given case.[51] Indeed, Seville II's canons contain numerous comparisons between the council's own activities and the activities of secular courts. For instance, in response to the case of a priest in Cordoba whose bishop had unjustly ejected him from his office and condemned him to exile, the sixth canon decried the "tyrannical power"[52] of bishops who ousted priests and deacons on the basis of rumors "without a conciliar investigation."[53] While the canon's demand that all such cases be decided by "synodal judgment" was based on conciliar precedent,[54] the explanation of the principle involved compared the matter to secular practice: if freed slaves could not be returned to servitude "unless they were publicly accused before the praetors' tribunal,"[55] then how could clerics be condemned by only one judge? The council's overall emphasis on legal precedents, investigations, and proper procedures enhances such comparisons to secular justice.

Seville II's appeal to secular legal traditions indicates that in 619 Isidore was explicitly seeking to establish what Leander had hinted at in 590: the association of conciliar holy authority with the prestige, procedures, and jurisdictions of Roman law.[56] Yet, although two royal agents were in attendance,[57] as far as the records reveal the council did not deal with the activities of secular officials or the lay population of Baetica. Isidore's redefinition of conciliar tradition included legal territories usually associated with secular governance, but, like his predecessors in the 590s, he did not see councils as a means for supervising a working alliance between local secular and ecclesiastic leaders or as an expression of centralized royal and ecclesiastic authority. On the other hand, the records of this model council do reflect a remarkable confidence in the efficacy of conciliar judicial procedure in ordering the local churches of Baetica. There is no trace here of the tension between collective and individual

---

51. See, e.g., Seville II, c. 2, in which the bishops referred a territorial dispute to further investigation after the applicable canons had been brought forth and "the synodal decrees were read through" (prolatis canonibus synodalia decreta perlecta sunt). Vives, 164. The same decision also invoked the rule of thirty years' possession (tricennalis obiectio) taken from "the edicts of the secular princes and the authority of the Roman pontiffs" (saecularium principum edicta praecipiunt et praesulum Romanorum decrevit auctoritas). See also canon 7, which cites God's instructions to Moses and Aaron in *Exodus* on priestly power then turns to "the authority of ancient law" as well as "recent ecclesiastic rules" (quaedam tamen auctoritate veteris legis, quaedam novellis ecclesiasticis regulis sibi prohibita noverint). Vives, 167.

52. Seville II, c. 6: "potestate tyrannica." Vives, 166.

53. Seville II, c. 6: "sine concilii examine." Vives, 166.

54. Seville II, c. 6: "synodali iudicio." Vives, 167.

55. Seville II, c. 6: "nisi publice apud praetores tribunali foro fuerint accusati." Vives, 167.

56. That is, "vulgar" Roman law. See intro., n. 33. On the legal sources used at Seville II, see Séjourné, *Le dernier pére*, 104–10.

57. Seville II, c. 1: Sisiclus, "rector rerum publicarum," and Suanila, the "rector rerum fiscalium." Vives, 163.

episcopal authority that lingers below the surface of some of the records from the 590s. Nor is there any indication of the possibility that these procedures might be abused.

This confidence stemmed in part from the fact that, by limiting the scope of his conciliar vision to dispute settlement among clerics, Isidore sheltered his version of conciliar procedure from involvement in networks of secular power. At the same time, this limited clerical jurisdiction meant that the participants in provincial councils would be the same people who were the immediate targets of Isidore's larger educational agenda. Isidore assumed that properly educated clerics would understand and accept the divinely endorsed authority of church councils—particularly if it were carried out in procedures stamped with the "authority of ancient law,"[58] including the precedents of scriptural, conciliar, and especially Roman law. Thus, Isidore's vision of conciliar authority—like Sisebut's conception of royal authority—was inseparable from his vision of cultural renewal. For Isidore ongoing clerical education made possible the successful exercise of conciliar authority, while, at the same time, correct conciliar procedures—and their records—were a means for ongoing clerical education.

Conflicting Visions

Sisebut's literary relationship with Isidore has enhanced the king's long-standing image as a cultural patron and coleader of the Isidorian Renaissance. The Sevillan bishop, most of whose writings date from Sisebut's reign, dedicated two works to the king,[59] who reciprocated by dedicating to Isidore a poem of his own on lunar eclipses.[60] Yet, despite the apparent endorsement of the king's cultural aspirations in Isidore's dedications, the bishop's attitude toward the king, and his ideas about consensus, was ambivalent. Of course, while the triumphant king was still alive, Isidore kept his criticisms to himself. In his *Chronicon,* written in 615, Isidore described Sisebut's conversion policies without comment, nor did he mention coercion: the king "captured certain cities of the Roman army and converted the Jewish subjects of his king-

58. Seville II, c. 7: "auctoritate veteris legis." Vives, 167.

59. The first was the *De natura rerum,* written during the first years of Sisebut's reign, between 612 and 615. See Fontaine, *Traité de la nature,* 1. The second was a preliminary version of the *Etymologies* in 620. See Luis Cortés y Góngora, in the introduction to his Spanish translation, *Etimologías* (Madrid, 1951) 3.

60. Traditionally entitled "The letter of Sisebut, king of the Goths, addressed to Isidore on the subject of his 'Book of Wheels' (meaning the *de natura rerum*)" (Epistula Sisebuti regis Gothorum missa ad Isidorum de libro rotarum), in Fontaine, *Traité de la nature,* 328–35.

dom to the faith of Christ."[61] Sisebut's victories, particularly those won against the Byzantines, must have lent an authority to his teachings on royal religious responsibility that Isidore was not in a position to question. For nine years during this period of ascendent kingship and cultural revival, the king, in all his ponderous erudition, held an uncontested platform from which to preach his sermons on culture, consensus, and royal holy authority.

Once the king had died, in 621, Isidore allowed himself a bit more freedom of speech. At the end of Sisebut's reign the bishop published the first version of his glorification of the Visigoths, the *Historia Gothorum*. Following Swinthila's final victory over the Byzantines in 624, he produced an even more laudatory version.[62] Isidore's praise for Sisebut's military successes in this work was unequivocal.[63] The bishop's remarks on the image-making king's piety and education, however, were less than enthusiastic.[64] Compared to the

---

61. Isidore, *Chronicon*, 120, *PL* 83, 1017–58: "quasdam ejusdem Romanae militiae urbes cepit, et Judeos sui regni subditos ad Christi fidem convertit." This work, written in 615, was a history of the world, with the Christian era marked mainly by the episcopacies of famous bishops, the military fortunes of the Roman emperors, and the periods of prevalence of various heresies. See Hillgarth, "Historiography," 289–92.

62. For an analysis of the two editions, with arguments in favor of the shorter version preceding the more propagandistic long version, see Cristóbal Rodríguez Alonso, *Las Historias de los Godos, Vandalos y Suevos de Isidoro de Sevilla* (León, 1975), 26–56. On the "patriotism" of the piece, see Hillgarth, "Historiography," 295–99.

63. Isidore (*HG*, 60–61, 270–74) commented on Sisebut's military triumphs against the Basques and Byzantines as well as his merciful attitude after his victories.

64. Most authors attribute to Isidore a much more enthusiastic torrent of praise for Sisebut than I do. For instance, Fontaine ("Political Function," 95 n. 2) quotes the "portrait of the king painted by Isidore of Seville in *Historia Gothorum*, 60," as evidence for Sisebut's unanimously voiced reputation for piety among his contemporary authors. However, the passages Fontaine cites—"Sisebutus christianissimus . . . in iudiciis iustitia et pietate strenuus ac praestantissimus . . . cuius exitus non solum religiosis, sed etiam optimis laicis extitit luctuosus"— are interpolations found in only three related, and relatively late (thirteenth- and fourteenth-century), manuscripts of the longer version of the *HG*. See Rodríguez Alonso, *Las Historias*, 149–51 and 154–56. Rodríguez Alonso attributes the similarities between these manuscripts (including their many interpolations) to a lost manuscript dating from the ninth century, which served as their model. Other authors, such as Wolf (*Conquerers and Chroniclers*, 25) attribute to Isidore the same appreciation for Sisebut's piety. Hillgarth ("Historiography," 288) describes the "Recapitulatio" that concludes the *HG* as ending with an "outburst of praise for Sisebut" and maintains that Isidore also ended his *Chronicon* with "high praise" for the king. The passages in question can only be read as high praise, however, if one is already assuming an unequivocally positive attitude on the part of the bishop. The passage ending the *HG* concerns Sisebut's activities in building a fleet, and, while it presents this positively, its tone is in keeping with the entire "Recapitulatio," which asserts the military prowess of the Goths as a historical *gens*—the description of Sisebut is no more of an outburst than the rest of the section. The sentence in question in the *Chronicon* is either the one quoted in n. 61 of this chapter or *Chronicon*, 121, which refers to Sisebut as "gloriosissimi principis." Neither of these seem overly effusive for a piece written while the king was living. While I do not mean to question Sisebut's piety or justice, I do believe that Isidore's relative reticence is significant, and that Isidore's "friendship" with the king has colored both ninth-century interpretations and modern readings of the *HG*. The entire question is further complicated by modern confusion surrounding the sequence and significance of the two different versions of the *HG*.

praises heaped on Reccared and Swinthila, the passage on Sisebut is quite low-key. It contains no hint of the two men's relationship nor of the king's "patronage" of culture. Although Isidore acknowledged Sisebut's learning, he qualified the extent of his education. The king, he wrote, was "somewhat instructed in the knowledge of letters."[65] What Isidore objected to most explicitly was the use to which Sisebut had put this partial knowledge. The description of the king in the *Historia* began with a well-known criticism of Sisebut's attempts at forced conversion:

> At the beginning of his reign he forced the Jews into the Christian faith, indeed acting with zeal, "but not according to knowledge," for he compelled by force those who should have been called to the faith through reason.[66]

Sisebut's policy of forced conversion and his advocacy of "the severity of difficult circumstances" as a means for Adalwald to convert the Lombards had plunged into the murky waters of traditional Christian teaching on the efficacy of religious coercion. Ancient authorities like Saint Augustine, in response to the needs of their own societies, had attempted to negotiate their way around a traditional understanding: any Christian's salvation depended on that individual having accepted faith freely.[67] While he equivocated on forced conversion for heretics, Augustine, and Gregory the Great after him, had explicitly rejected the coercion of Jews, a position that Sisebut directly contravened.[68]

---

65. *HG*, 60: "scientia litterarum ex parte inbutus," 272. Wolf, 106.

66. Isidore, *HG*, 60, quoting Romans 10.2: "qui initio regni Iudaeos ad fidem Christianam permouens aemulationem quidem habuit, 'sed non secundum scientiam': potestate enim conpulit, quos prouocare fidei ratione oportuit," 272. Wolf, 106.

67. Emilien Lamirande, *Church, State and Toleration: An Intriguing Change of Mind in Augustine* (Villanova, 1975), 73.

68. According to Jeremy Cohen (*The Friars and the Jews* [Ithaca, 1982], 20) Augustine argued that the Jews were preserved by God for the sake of the Church, "so that in adhering to the Old Testament they might witness the truth of and historical basis for christological prophecy, and so that they might ultimately accept the implications of this prophecy by converting to Christianity at the end of days." According to Robert A. Markus ("Gregory the Great and a Papal Missionary Strategy," in *The Mission of the Church and the Propagation of the Faith*, ed. G. J. Cuming, 29–38, Studies in Church History 6 [Cambridge, 1970]; reprinted in *From Augustine to Gregory the Great. History and Christianity in Late Antiquity* [London, 1983], 30) Gregory I's attitude toward the Jews involved a "scrupulous concern for justice and humanity." Markus quotes Gregory's *Epist.* 1.34 on the issue, in which the pope laid down a general principle: "those who do not agree with the Christian religion should be brought to the unity of faith by mildness and generosity, by admonition and persuasion; otherwise men who might be won to believing by the sweetness of preaching and the fear of the coming judgment will be repulsed by threats and pressure." The attitudes of these two authorities were more open to reconfiguration when it came to converting pagans and heretics. Augustine, for instance, apparently changed his mind on the question of coercing heretics, moving from an

Thus, by forcing the Jews into Christianity, Sisebut had violated one of the central principles of Isidore's educational program: the faithful application of ancient knowledge to present-day Christian governance. Sisebut's incomplete education had resulted in a royal procedure that overtly transgressed the prescriptions of past Christian teachers. For Isidore this failure was so fundamental that, once the king had died, he withdrew his implicit endorsement of Sisebut's efforts at religious direction and his attempts to present himself as a pious patron of Christian culture.[69]

Despite their confidence in culture and correct procedure, both Isidore and Sisebut were keenly aware that their own society still posed obstacles to the effective enforcement of Christian authority. Isidore's magisterial display of correct conciliar procedure and his confidence in the obedience of an educated clergy were based on disengaging conciliar justice from the networks of secular authority and the interests of the king, a precaution also taken by many bishops in the previous generation. Isidore's later criticisms of the king indicate a likely source for his jurisdictional conservatism: he feared the dangers posed to authentic Christian consensus, and thus to lay acceptance of conciliar holy authority, by the interference of a zealous but ill-educated king attempting to assert his own centralized holy authority through the intemperate use of coercive force. For his part Sisebut, despite his enthusiastic assertion of the efficacy of correctly implemented judicial procedures, acknowledged in the *Vita Desiderii* a host of possible abuses and loopholes in their administration. The only remedy Sisebut seems to have imagined for these dangers was a continuing concentration of authority in the hands of educated Christian

---

advocacy of relative tolerance to the active support of legislated coercion sometime around the year 405, in an effort to eradicate the Donatist Party in North Africa. See Lamirande, *Church, State and Toleration;* Peter Brown, "St. Augustine's Attitude to Religious Coercion," *Religion and Society in the Age of St. Augustine* (London, 1972); and W. H. C. Frend, *The Donatist Church* (Oxford, 1952), 239–41. Augustine does not seem to have advocated imperially sponsored coercion against the pagans of his day; see Lamirande, *Church, State, and Toleration,* 29–32. Gregory's position changed during the course of the Roman mission to the Anglo-Saxons of Kent; see his letters to Mellitus and to Ethelbert recorded by Bede, *Historia Ecclesiastica gentis Anglorum,* 1.30 and 1.32, in *Bede: Ecclesiastical History of the English People,* ed. and trans. B. Colgrave and R. A. B. Mynors (Oxford, 1969); and Markus, "Gregory the Great," 34–38.

69. Isidore's description of the king's demise, *HG,* 61, 274, also indicates an equivocal evaluation of the monarch. Apparently, rumors circulated on the cause of Sisebut's death. In the earlier version of the *HG* Isidore noted that some people attributed it to illness, while others asserted that poison was involved. In the later version he recounted a further theory under popular discussion: that the king had died from an overdose of medicine. Wherever the circumstances allowed, Isidore made a point in the *HG* of noting the violent ends that overtook bad kings; the idea that evil royal actions provoked evil royal deaths was a recurring message. In a work so clearly designed for polemical purposes the choice to include such questionable information about Sisebut—what one might even call rumormongering—cannot have been without symbolic value.

kings, who would ensure their own divine support through fulfilling their responsibilities for maintaining Christian consensus. Divine support gave kings the authority to assert divine sanctions for their legislation and decisions; Christian consensus would ensure obedience to those sanctions. The misuse of royal justice and religious power, as in the case of Theuderic and Brunhild, would ultimately result in divine judgment against the offending monarch. The years between 621 and 633 proved both Sisebut and Isidore correct on the dangers underlying the other's ideas about Christian governance.

The Consequences of Coercion

Sisebut's attempt at coerced consensus created uncertainties over the religious loyalties of converted Jews that were similar to the suspicions surrounding former Arians after Reccared's conversion. This time the judicial and social repercussions were apparently much more far-reaching. Of course, Sisebut's concern with the status of Jews was not exactly innovative. Limiting the power of Jews over Christians had been an item on the Visigothic agenda since Toledo III. That council's canon prohibiting Jews from buying Christian slaves or marrying or consorting with Christian women also excluded Jews from holding public offices through which they might punish Christians.[70] One of Reccared's laws had expanded the prohibition on Jews buying Christian slaves to their receiving them as gifts. Presumably before he called for forced conversion, Sisebut issued a complete prohibition on any Jews owning Christians, and he outlawed Jews hiring or being the patrons of Christians. According to Sisebut, "the orthodox faith will be greatly exalted when the execrable perfidy of the Jews shall no longer have power over Christians."[71]

Whatever the differences in their claims for holy authority, the bishops at Toledo III, Reccared, and Sisebut were all supremely concerned with defining authority in their kingdom as exclusively Catholic. In a society in which the obedience of subordinates was increasingly dependent upon a shared acknowledgment of a tie between authority and divine sanctions, a group of public dissenters like the Jews presented a double problem. First, they could not be expected to honor the divine sanctions leaders attached to oaths, laws,

---

70. Tol. III, c. 13. Rodríguez, 31.

71. *LV,* 12.2.14: "In hos enim ortodoxa gloriatur fidei regula, cum nullam in christinis habuerit potestatem Ebreorum execranda perfidia," 420. When Toledo IV sought to deal with the confusion caused by forced conversion, it too concentrated on the issue of Jewish power over Christians. Among other anti-Jewish measures the council prohibited Jews or their descendants from holding public office, removed children from Jewish parents, and once again called for the separation of Christian wives from Jewish husbands and the freeing of Christian slaves from Jewish owners. See chap. 5, n. 37.

and ecclesiastic punishments like penance and excommunication. Second, by wielding authority outside of the networks explained and sanctioned by orthodox Christianity, Jews could call on Christian subordinates to obey, and thus to recognize the existence of, alternative sources and sanctions for social power. Punishments, oaths, or ceremonies of friendship or obeisance involving Jews would not be Christian ones. More dangerously, if administered by Jews, they might be explicitly Jewish. In such a case Christians might become fully ensnared in the Jewish "perfidy." Sisebut addressed the possibility by decreeing that any Jew who involved a Christian in performing Jewish rites would be executed.[72]

By Sisebut's reign years of coexistence had led to strong social, economic, and political ties between Jews and Christians. Jews not only had become the spouses, patrons, employers, and owners of Christians, but they had also bribed (and, in Sisebut's eyes, sullied) Christian monarchs in order to continue to do so.[73] Sisebut's laws also show that Christians of many ranks perpetrated various frauds in order to shelter Jews from legislated proscriptions. The practice was widespread enough to demand a careful series of prohibitions and penalties. One must assume that these measures did not succeed in extracting Christians from networks of power and obligation that included Jews, for, in his efforts to end the "fatal control of Jews over Christians," Sisebut turned to forced conversion.

Sisebut's successor Swinthila was more tolerant. He did not enforce anti-Jewish laws and seems to have encouraged the return of the Jews who had gone into exile in order to avoid conversion.[74] This period of toleration, the return of exiled Jews, and the ineffectiveness of forced conversion apparently led forced converts to reestablish their relations with non-baptized Jews and to take up some Jewish customs once again. At the same time, forced converts continued to participate in Christian society: holding public offices, giving testimony in Christian courts, baptizing their children, marrying Christians, owning Christian slaves, and giving and receiving gifts and favors from Christian clerics and laypeople.[75] By 633, when the Fourth Council of Toledo attempted to reinstate strict control over the Jewish population, in the eyes of Christian leaders these activities were widespread enough to pose a threat to Christian society.

Now, however, the situation had become much more complex than it had

---

72. *LV,* 12.2,14, 422.

73. *LV,* 12. 2.13, 418.

74. Bachrach, "A Reassessment," 20.

75. These activities among forced converts were all addressed by canons 57–66 at Toledo IV. Of course, these canons may not be accurate reflections of the current situation; they may only represent Christian leaders' suspicions. See chap. 5, n. 37.

been before Sisebut's forced conversions. Although Christian leaders in the past may have considered non-baptized Jews undesirable, untrustworthy, and a threat to the orderly exercise of Christian power, they were at least readily identifiable as infidels and thus theoretically excludable. Their alternative systems of power were not an immediate threat, as long as Christians could be kept out of their "deadly dominion." Baptized Jews, on the other hand, were not immediately identifiable as bona fide infidels. But they were obvious targets for suspicion, especially in the eyes of Christians who denied the efficacy of forced conversion. Indeed, they were more to be distrusted than the newly converted Arians had been, for their former coreligionists were still around, openly practicing their customary way of life. Sisebut's misguided policy had created a whole new threat to the social acceptance of orthodox Christian authority. As Christians, baptized Jews had to be kept separate from the potentially polluting force of Jews and their authorities and customs. As Christians of questionable fidelity, however, they could not be trusted to accept fully Christian holy authority and its divine sanctions. For Christian leaders seeking to ensure obedience and establish kingdom-wide Christian consensus, Sisebut had created a judicial quagmire.[76] Baptized Jews had to be identified and restricted on an ongoing basis. Their oaths, Christian *mores,* and obedience to divine sanctions could not be assumed to be genuine, and, consequently, their power over Christians either had to be supervised carefully or eliminated.

---

76. Converted Jews could disrupt established community relations and confuse identities even when they were not forced into Christianity. Some of the complications arising out of the conversion of the Jews are illustrated in a letter written by Aurasius, the bishop of Toledo, probably early in Sisebut's reign. *EW,* 20, 48, is a letter of excommunication addressed to the Gothic count of Toledo, a man named Froga. According to a scholion of questioned authenticity (49), at the request of the leader of the local synagogue Froga had arranged the public beating of a group of newly baptized Jewish converts as they left their church for the first time. This document does not make clear the circumstances under which these Jews had been baptized. Whether or not these are the actual circumstances behind Aurasius' letter, we can assume that Froga's actions in support of the Jews is testimony to the importance of the Jewish community in Toledo. Aurasius' condemnation of Froga emphasized the public nature of his action and its repercussions on both the Catholic and the Jewish communities: "you not only scourged the Church of God but by openly attacking us you have also humiliated it and encouraged the synagogue . . . and you made us the object of contempt in front of the elders, and the whole palace, the Catholic people, and the assembly of the Hebrews" (eclesiam Dei non solum uerberasti, sed etiam impugnando coram nos humiliasti et synagogam erexisti . . . et presentibus senioribus, cuncto palatio, catholico populo uel cetu Hebreorum nos despectui tradens). The differentiation, as well as the competition, between both communities was supremely important; those who crossed or blurred the line—in this case both Froga and the Jewish converts—caused confusion, humiliation, and public contention for both communities. On this letter, see also Thompson, *Goths,* 167.

A Miscarriage of Conciliar Justice

Sisebut's efforts at Christian governance were not the only ones to cause confusion and contention in the kingdom during the decade before 633. Isidore's untrammeled confidence in provincial conciliar governance supported by clerical education also ran aground. Isidore's model for conciliar procedure did not inspire other provincial episcopates to follow his example. There is evidence of only one council held between 619 and Toledo IV in 633:[77] the Third Council of Seville, held under Isidore's leadership in around 624.[78] More important, at that one council conciliar procedure was grievously abused by conspiring clerics, causing a miscarriage of justice that reverberated through the Iberian episcopate for the next fourteen years. The implications of this episode were so serious that Isidore—or clerics in Seville working under his supervision—later attempted to cover it up by excluding the records of the council from the first recension of the *Hispana*.[79]

Seville III heard a case against the bishop of Ecija, Martianus. Accused of a series of crimes, Martianus had already been the subject of a judicial investigation within his own diocese. The council in Seville condemned him for speaking against the current Visigothic king, Swinthila, for consulting a diviner about the king's life, for having illicit relations with one female slave, and for keeping another as a valet. The council stripped Martianus of his rank and gave his see to his accuser, Aventius. The decision against Martianus was not unanimous.[80] The votes against him, however, must have included

---

77. As usual, an absence of records does not necessarily signify a lack of councils, particularly in this instance, since the records of Seville III do not survive. Still, the fact that the records of Toledo IV specifically discuss the failure of bishops to hold councils, it can be assumed that this period did not see much conciliar activity. See chap. 5, n. 95.

78. Seville III is discussed in a document known as the *Exemplar iudicii inter Martianum et Aventium Episcopos*, ed. Felix Dahn, in *Die Könige der Germanen* 6 (Leipzig, 1885). For an English narrative, see Thompson, *Goths,* 287–89.

79. See Martínez Díez, *Estudio,* 318–21. If Isidore were seeking to remove this judicial miscarriage from the corpus of Visigothic canonical tradition, he was quite successful; the later two recensions of the *Hispana* also excluded Seville III, and its records have not been preserved anywhere. Séjourné (*Le dernier père,* 29) suggests that one anti-Jewish canon found in the *Juliana* recension of the *Hispana* in fact came from Seville III. Martínez Díez (320–21) points out that the records of Seville III were already hard to come by in 638. The *Exemplar,* C.1, refers to the fact that none of the Baetican bishops who had taken part in Seville III and were still alive in 638 knew where the records were. The investigators at Toledo VI were able to get their hands on a copy presented by, according to Martínez Díez, "alguien interesado en la causa." Martínez Díez suggests that this was the avenue by which the one stray canon eventually found its way into the *Hispana*. The *Exemplar* itself survived only among a number of fragmentary documents not associated with the *Hispana*. See Dahn, *Die Könige,* 613.

80. *Exemplar,* C.1, 616.

Isidore's.[81] The fact that Aventius had concocted a complicated conspiracy to frame Martianus did not come fully to light until 638, after Isidore's death. In that year a panel of bishops at the Sixth Council of Toledo heard Martianus' appeal, investigated Aventius' false accusations, restored the wronged man to his see, and published their findings in a document known as the *Exemplar judicii inter Martianum et Aventium Episcopos.*[82] They determined that Aventius had forced clerical clients to give false testimony,[83] that he had presented a witness under the qualifying age of fourteen, that he had had two illiterate women sign statements,[84] and that he had presented another female witness whose testimony was inconsistent and given under torture because she was a slave.[85] The investigating bishops declared that they were unable to find proof of Aventius' accusations in any of the documents from the original case, which they said very clearly revealed "extremely vile and spiteful procedures."[86] Despite this characterization of the previous investigations, the bishops in 638 were careful to exonerate the men who had condemned Martianus at Seville III: they had acted "neither by craft nor corrupted judgment."[87] Rather, they had been duped by the deceit of the witnesses.

Seville III met approximately five years after Seville II. Given the extensive list of witnesses and documents discussed in the *Exemplar judicii,* the council in 624 probably followed, if not elaborated, the legalistic model created in 619. Martianus' case must have begun to call that model into question at an early point. The scandal surrounding the case would have begun to leak out from the time the investigation began in Ecija, where Aventius' accusations were first made and where many of the witnesses were originally examined.[88] The case was then brought before Isidore's provincial council. Despite inconsistencies in testimony and other procedures that were later deemed "extremely vile and spiteful," and despite disagreement among the bishops present, the council ousted one bishop and allowed the elevation of another who had sought the

---

81. Thompson, *Goths,* 287.

82. See n. 78 of this chapter.

83. *Exemplar,* C.3 and F.5, 616 and 618.

84. *Exemplar,* D.3, 617.

85. *Exemplar,* F.3, 618. Seville III apparently followed secular practice in this instance. The *LRV, Pauli sententiae* 5.18.3, provided that slaves could only give evidence if they were tortured. This law code was promulgated in 506 by the Visigothic king, Alaric II, for use in the Roman courts of his kingdom; it was drawn from the late Roman *Codex Theodosianus* and, as in this case, other Roman sources. Alaric's code, also known as the *Breviary,* was used in Hispano-Roman courts until 654, when it was nullified by the promulgation of the *LV,* a territorial code used by both Hispano-Romans and Visigoths. For a modern discussion on the legal status of slaves in seventh-century Spain, see P. D. King, *Law and Society in the Visigothic Kingdom* (Cambridge, 1972), 159–80.

86. *Exemplar,* F.4: "inquisitiones vilissimas et malivolas," 618.

87. *Exemplar,* G.6: "non astu neque deprevando judicium," 619.

88. *Exemplar,* F.2, 618.

office by subverting divine justice. While the details of the conspiracy were not known at the time, Martianus' conviction must have incited further public comment and contention. The ousted man cannot have been without supporters. Divided opinions are obvious in the lack of unanimity among the bishops at Seville III. Without continuing support, Martianus would have had great difficulty mounting the appeal he apparently brought before Isidore and Toledo IV in 633.[89]

Isidore had good reason to try to hush up the affair. Rumors of a miscarriage of justice at the council in Seville would have profound local implications for the authority of the individual bishops at the council. Moreover, they could throw the authority of their collective judgment into question. Such a failure at a church council was not simply a matter of procedural error; it also implied either that the Holy Spirit could be manipulated into offering an incorrect judgment or that the personal holy authority of the gathered prelates had been somehow inauthentic, thereby preventing the Holy Spirit's attendance. In either case a public acknowledgment of the full scope of the debacle would have undermined not only Isidore's own authority and that of his coprovincial bishops but also the divine authorization of church councils in general. A group of presumably educated clerics in a diocese to which Isidore had personal ties (his brother Fulgentius had been bishop of Ecija as recently as 619)[90] were not prevented from conspiring against conciliar authority even when it was fully clothed in Roman legal culture and the precedents of the past. Who then could be expected to obey the decisions of future councils or, for that matter, the entire body of previous canonical legislation?

The episode also laid bare the tension between collective episcopal authority and local networks of loyalty and personal obligation. Many of Aventius' false witnesses had been bound to him by oaths of personal obligation. Others had been personally intimidated by threats and various demands from their superiors.[91] Clearly, for these witnesses Aventius' local power had outweighed the more distant collective authority of the provincial bishops. At the same time, the misuse of that distant authority had resulted in an incorrect decision imposed upon a local community, probably exacerbating an already fractious situation. Finally, through his manipulation of collective episcopal authority, the local ambitions of this corrupt office seeker had compromised

---

89. The case is not explicitly mentioned in the records of Toledo IV. According to the *Exemplar*, B.2, 616, Martianus first appealed his case "in praecedenti universali concilio." Dahn (*Die Könige*, 624) identified this council as the Fifth Council of Toledo, held in 636; however, Séjourné (*Le dernier père*, 196) and Thompson (*Goths*, 287–88) convincingly argue that it must have been Toledo IV.

90. Cazier, *Isidore de Séville*, 32. Fulgentius signed the acts of Seville II.

91. See, e.g., *Exemplar*, C.3, the deacon Eulalius; D.2, Ricchesvindus; F.5, Trasoarius, Stafanus, Adeodatus, and Hospitalis, 616, 617, and 618.

the local authority of each of the province's bishops. It would not be surprising if a growing consciousness of the danger to their own position made bishops hesitant to participate in provincial councils. Whatever the reason, Martianus had to wait until 633 to make his appeal, because no provincial councils met in Baetica between Seville III and Toledo IV.[92]

Isidore's unguarded faith in clerical education and conciliar authority, like Sisebut's confident foray into forced conversion, had resulted in a judicial quagmire of far-reaching proportions. It too would present the council in 633 with important conceptual and practical dilemmas. If Toledo IV acknowledged the miscarriage of justice in Martianus' case, it would implicate the divine authorization of the Baetican episcopate as a whole and consequently its own status as a holy tribunal. In order to continue to develop conciliar justice as a means of ongoing clerical discipline and education, to maintain the individual authority of the clerics who participated in councils, and thus to gain acceptance for these tribunals as a source of holy authority among all the Christians of the kingdom, Martianus' case had to be dealt with quickly and quietly and with as little community disturbance as possible. It is not surprising, therefore, that the actions taken at Toledo IV in response to Martianus' appeal look rather cursory. The hearing there was cut short because of "lack of time,"[93] despite the fact that the same council's fourth canon decreed that no church council should disperse until all its business had been decided "carefully and with tranquillity."[94] Moreover, Toledo IV's settlement of the matter was equivocal: Aventius was allowed to remain in the disputed see, laying the basis for Martianus' second appeal, in 638.[95]

Dynamic Tensions and Continuing Contradictions

After the bleak years under Witteric the resurgence of Visigothic royal power and the conscious regeneration of literate culture stimulated in

---

92. *Exemplar,* C.1, 616, mentions Martianus' inability to appeal.

93. *Exemplar,* B.2: "angustia temporis," 616.

94. Tol. IV, c. 4: "sollicite atque tranquille." Vives, 190. The fact that Martianus and Aventius do not appear in Toledo IV's records indicates another failure by the bishops there to abide by their own rules, perhaps in an effort to stifle the issue: canon 4 also prescribes that councils were not to be adjourned unless "everything has been decided in such a way that whatever has been determined by common deliberation has been signed by the hand of every single bishop" (fuerint cuncta determinata, ita ut quaecumque deliberatione conmuni finiuntur episcoporum singulorum manibus scribantur). Vives, 190. If this rule had been observed in Martianus' appeal in 633, even if the case had not been included in the official records of Toledo IV, there would have been a documentary record of some kind available to the bishops deliberating in 638. There is no indication in the *Exemplar* that they had access to any such documents.

95. *Exemplar,* B.2, states that Martianus was "heard in part and was restored only to his rank, but not his place" (ex parte fuerat auditus, et gradui tantum, et non loco restitutus), 616.

Isidore and Sisebut a level of confidence that rivaled the optimism surrounding Toledo III. Yet much as the rhetoric of harmony and consensus in 589 had masked fundamental disagreements among that council's participants, the shared appeal to the authority of literate culture that legitimized the ideals and practices of these two leaders obscured the differences between them. As in 589, those differences arose partly out of a divergence between the interests of a king attempting to centralize and sanctify his own royal power and the interests of bishops attempting to establish the holy authority of episcopal consensus and conciliar justice while sheltering themselves and their communities from central interference. And, as was the experience of the kingdom's leaders in the 590s, the ideals met formidable social stumbling blocks in practice. In the 620s consensus on the transcendent holy authority and divine sanctions supporting royal and conciliar justice and legislation still did not exist, even among clerics. Other systems of authority, loyalty, and sanctions—customs and relationships that varied between and within different communities—continued to command local peoples' allegiance and obedience.

Yet, while many of the forces in contention and the issues over which they met had remained the same, the situation was by no means a static one, either ideologically or practically. There were tensions between contending ideals of holy authority and the differing practices meant to realize them. The contradictions between those practices and the dynamics of local communities stimulated further development in Iberian ideals and practices of Christian governance and kingdom-wide consensus. Sisebut's forced conversion of the Jews, for instance, resulted in a number of problems associated with lapsed converts. Church leaders like Isidore might reject forced conversion on the basis of ancient Christian teachings, but that did not mean that they could allow baptized Christians to renounce the power of the baptismal rite or threaten Christian consensus. Once baptized, former Jews had to be forced to remain Christians; they needed to be carefully supervised so that they would neither harm other Christians nor be exposed to the polluting force of non-baptized Jews. Eventually, Sisebut's ideals and practices, Isidore's condemnation of them, and the problems they created generated a new round of ideals and practices regarding the place of Jews and baptized Jews within a society governed by Christian consensus.

Similarly, Isidore's procedures for conciliar dispute settlement resulted in a miscarriage of justice and an ecclesiastic scandal. Yet, while Isidore and other bishops might come to share Sisebut's caution about the potential for conciliar abuse, that did not mean that they relinquished claims for the holy authority and divine sanctions of councils and canonical legislation. The scandal surrounding Martianus' case, as well as the potential for any future scandals, had to be addressed in a way that did not undermine those claims nor the position of the individuals who made them. Isidore's ideal conciliar procedures, his attempt to implement them, and the problems they faced generated new ideals and practices concerning the overarching authority of Christian consensus and conciliar justice. In 633 these newly configured ideals and practices were first articulated at yet another church council, Toledo IV.

CHAPTER FIVE

Exclusive Christian Consensus and the Institutionalization of Difference

In 589 the bishops at Toledo III had received their king's participation with exultant acclamations. Reccared took a central role throughout the council: his call for the assembly, his opening speech, the presentation of his *tomus,* his closing statements, and his edict of confirmation were inscribed into canon in ringing words of triumphant royal authority. In 633 such was not the case for Sisenand (631–36), the king who convened Toledo IV. His presence at the assembly, unlike Reccared's Constantinian majesty, was abject. Upon his entrance he prostrated himself before the bishops and "with tears and groans sought God's intervention for himself."[1]

The bishops at Toledo IV did recognize Sisenand as a "most religious king,"[2] devoted to God and "full of care not only in human affairs but also in divine matters."[3] Before his ritual submission the king apparently made something of a grand entrance, surrounded by his "most magnificent and noble" retainers.[4] Following his tearful plea for help, however, his instructions to the assembly were limited:

> He addressed the synod with a religious discourse so that we [the bishops], mindful of the decrees of the fathers, should zealously conserve the ecclesiastic law among ourselves, and correct those things that, through negligence, have begun to be practiced against ecclesiastic custom.[5]

---

1. Tol. IV, preamble: "primum coram sacerdotibus Dei humo prostratus cum lacrymis et gemitibus pro se interveniendum Deo postulavit." Vives, 186.

2. Tol. IV, preamble: "religiosissimi." Vives, 186.

3. Tol. IV, preamble: "non solum in rebus humanis sed etiam in causis divinis sollicitus." Vives, 186.

4. Tol. IV, preamble: "cum magnificentissimis et nobilissimis viris ingressus." Vives, 186.

5. Tol. IV, preamble: "deinde religiosa prosequutione synodum exhortatus est ut paternorum decretorum memores ad conservanda in nobis iura ecclesiastica studium praeferemus, et illa corrigere quae dum per neglegentiam in usum venerunt contra ecclesiasticos mores." Vives, 186.

Only four of the council's seventy-five canons are described as being instigated by the king.[6] Although the council's closing statement acknowledged his assent to the *acta* as a whole, no other canons mentioned the king's active participation or expressed desires. This is not to say that Toledo IV ignored Sisenand. The royal office was the central concern of canon 75, which repeatedly described its measures against perjury and usurpation as having been taken "on behalf of the strength of the kings and the stability of the nation of the Goths."[7] Indeed, one of the primary purposes of this council was to sanction Sisenand's leadership. Two years before, he had seized the throne from the legitimate king, Swinthila. Sisenand's pleas to the bishops, his limited role in the council and in its legislation, and much of the bishops' rhetoric on kings in general can be attributed to the shadow of political scandal that his usurpation had cast upon the Visigothic kingship.

The fall in royal stature from the heights claimed by Sisebut less than twenty years before had not occurred with the death of that literate king in 621, despite an apparently problematic succession. Rumors had circulated about the cause of Sisebut's death.[8] His successor, his young son Reccared II, ruled only for a few days before "his own death intervened."[9] Yet the potential for disaster involved in such a sequence of events was not realized. The kingship passed apparently uneventfully—or, as Isidore put it, "by divine grace"—to one of Sisebut's generals, Swinthila.[10]

Swinthila had already won victories against the Byzantines during Sisebut's campaigns. As king, "he waged war and obtained the remaining cities that the Roman army held in Spain, and, with amazing fortune, triumphed even more gloriously than had the other kings."[11] Swinthila also drove the Basques out of Tarraconensis and back into the mountains, where he forced them to build a city for the Goths "by their own taxes and labor" and to

---

6. Tol. IV, c. 59, 65, 66, and 47. Vives, 211, 213, 214, and 208. The first three were anti-Jewish canons; the last exempted all clerics from taxation.

7. Tol. IV, c. 75: "pro robore nostrorum regum et stabilitate gentis Gothorum." Vives, 217.

8. See chap. 4, n. 69.

9. *HG*, 61: "princeps paucorum dierum morte interueniente habetur." 274. Wolf, 107.

10. *HG*, 62: "Suinthila gratia diuina regni suscepit sceptra." 274. Wolf, 107. It is possible that Isidore's uncritical acceptance of what seems to have been a usurpation by Swinthila can be attributed to what Roger Collins, "Julian of Toledo and the Royal Succession in Late Seventh-Century Spain," in *Early Medieval Kingship,* ed. P. H. Sawyer and Ian N. Wood (Leeds, 1977) 47, calls a "somewhat *laissez-faire* attitude in Isidore's thinking," which involved a recognition of prevailing early-seventh-century royal politics: "usurpation was only usurpation so long as it was unsuccessful." On the other hand, while Isidore and Toledo IV also accepted the usurper Sisenand as a legitimate king, it would be an overstatement to categorize the council's response as "laissez-faire."

11. *HG*, 62: "urbes residuas, quas in Spaniis Romana manus agebat, proelio conserto obtinuit auctamque triumphi gloriam prae ceteris regibus," 276. Wolf, 107.

promise "to be obedient to [his] rule and dominion and to carry out whatever they were ordered to do."[12] In the *Historia Gothorum* Isidore also praised Swinthila's numerous nonmilitary royal virtues, which included faith, industry, and a "vigorous concern for government."[13] Isidore emphasized the king's generosity to the poor: Swinthila "was not only the ruler of the people but was also worthy to be called the father of the poor."[14] The *Historia* also celebrated Swinthila's son Riccimir, who had become a partner on the throne by the time Isidore wrote the work.

As with Witteric's usurpation against Reccared's son Liuva, this move toward establishing a hereditary succession may have sparked Sisenand's rebellion in 631.[15] Yet Riccimir, although young when Isidore wrote the *Historia Gothorum,* had been coruler for at least six years at the time of the revolt. It seems likely that, unlike earlier episodes of usurpation, in this instance the inexperience and youth of the heir were not major contributors to the dissatisfaction with the ruling family. Instead, Swinthila's treatment of the Visigothic nobility appears to have been the catalyst for his downfall, which was further precipitated by a Frankish invasion. According to the *Chronicle* of Fredegar, Swinthila had been "very harsh to his followers and was hated by all the magnates of his kingdom."[16] These men eventually advised one of their own, Sisenand, to bribe the Frankish king Dagobert to send an army to Spain to overthrow the king. According to Fredegar, "as soon as it was known in Spain that the Franks were on the march in support of Sisenand, the entire Gothic army submitted to him,"[17] proclaiming him king in Saragossa in the company of the Frankish army, whose leaders headed home "laden with gifts."[18] Apparently, however, the Visigothic nobles' support of Sisenand was not unconditional. They seem to have exerted some power over Sisenand's prerogatives as king, at least insofar as the Gothic treasury was concerned. The bribe Sisenand had promised Dagobert consisted of a 500-pound golden dish that the Roman patrician Aetius had given the Visigothic king Thoris-

---

12. *HG,* 63: "Ologicus ciuitatem Gothorum stipendiis suis et laboribus conderent, pollicentes eius regno dicionique parere et quicquid imperaretur efficere," 276. Wolf, 108.

13. *HG,* 64: "in regendo cura praecipua," 278. Wolf, 108.

14. *HG,* 64: "non solum princeps popularum, sed etiam pater pauperum uocari sit dignus," 278. Wolf, 108.

15. See chap. 1, n. 16; and chap. 4, n. 9. On Swinthila's reign and deposition, see E. A. Thompson, *The Goths in Spain,* (Oxford, 1969), 171–72.

16. Fredegar, *Chronicle,* 4.73: "cum essit Sintila nimium in suis inimicus et cum omnibus regni suae primatibus odium incurrerit." Ed. and trans. J. M. Wallace-Hadrill, *The Fourth Book of the Chronicle of Fredegar* (London, 1960), 61.

17. Fredegar, 4.73: "Cumque in Espania deuolgatum fuisset exercitum Francorum auxiliandum Sisenando adgredere, omnis Gotorum exercitus se dicione Sisenando subaegit." Wallace-Hadrill, 62.

18. Fredegar, 4.73: "munerebus onorati." Wallace-Hadrill, 62.

mund after he helped defeat the Huns in 451. After Sisenand handed the dish over to the Frankish ambassadors, the nobles retrieved it "by force and would not allow it to be taken away,"[19] forcing Sisenand to make a cash payment to Dagobert instead.

While the noble Goths apparently disliked Swinthila, the attitude of church leaders is more difficult to gauge. Isidore's praise is obviously hyperbolic, but the enthusiasm generated by Swinthila's expulsion of the Byzantines permeates the work and must reflect a generally positive atmosphere surrounding the kingship during the mid-620s. Whatever their attitudes during Swinthila's time on the throne, however, the Iberian bishops came out strongly against the man once he had been deposed. Canon 75 contains a rather cryptic explanation for his fall: fearful of his own crimes, it says, Swinthila had himself renounced the throne. After thus whitewashing Sisenand's usurpation, the canon went on to order all Swinthila's possessions seized because the criminal king had amassed them through "exactions from the poor."[20] The gathering also condemned and banished the erstwhile "father of the poor," along with his wife, children, and brother.

It had taken Sisenand two years to orchestrate the gathering meant to strengthen his feeble grasp on the throne. He had attempted to assemble the episcopate in 632 but was forced to postpone the council until the end of 633.[21] This delay may have been due to a new rebellion in the south.[22] In any case, one can assume that noble dissatisfaction with Swinthila, the resulting rebellion and Frankish invasion, and the post-usurpation turmoil had destabilized Visigothic leadership for a number of years prior to Toledo IV, despite Swinthila's previous military successes and territorial consolidation. These factors, combined with the long-standing episcopal ambivalence concerning the religious role of kings, led the bishops in 633 to use their council as a public platform for exhorting the Visigothic monarchy. Sisenand's pleas for help arose from the crisis at hand, but the council records' careful description of his ceremonial submission also expressed the episcopate's eagerness to publicize and apply the lessons learned and the analyses developed since the failure of the alliance of 589. In a seeming reversal of the roles taken by king and bishops at Toledo III, the Iberian episcopate at Toledo IV put forth an ambitious vision of a centrally ordained and maintained *mos canonicus,* in contrast to their king's hesitant handling of his fragile royal power.

Isidore of Seville, still the most influential bishop in the kingdom, now led

19. Fredegar, 4.73: "a Gotis per vim tolletur, nec eum exinde excobere permiserunt." Wallace-Hadrill, 62.

20. Tol. IV, c. 75: "miserorum sumtibus hauserant." Vives, 221.

21. Thompson, *Goths,* 175.

22. Thompson, *Goths,* 175–77.

his episcopal colleagues in instituting a carefully defined program for conciliar governance and Christian consensus. Toledo IV recognized the dangers that had arisen in earlier years because of Sisebut's religious coercion and because of Isidore's reliance on incomplete clerical education and consensus. Identifying the overall threat to the kingdom in these and numerous other sources of local scandal and religious diversity, the bishops issued detailed rules designed to institutionalize a complex program for absolute uniformity. By ensuring clerical education and by criminalizing liturgical diversity along with many other infractions, the council sought to establish uniform clerical leadership as the means to impose the long-sought kingdom-wide consensus that would render the decisions of provincial councils enforceable. These councils were now envisioned as the forum for community dispute settlements of all kinds, including conflicts between laypeople. The program for consensus centered on conciliar justice was meant to ensure the Christian ordering and consequent political survival of the entire kingdom. Any individual or community that deviated from the carefully prescribed parameters of this consensus would be identified and thus excluded from the kingdom's Christian community.

Political Perjury and Divine Judgment

Despite the ambitious vision they convey, the canons of Toledo IV are permeated with a rhetoric of fear. They contain little evidence of the optimism of Toledo III or the confidence of Isidore's Seville II. In their references to Roman legal principles some of the canons do reflect continuity with Isidore's model of 619.[23] Yet one finds in these records a language and attitude much more reminiscent of the harsh and embattled claims for authority made at Narbonne in 589. Now, however, the Iberian episcopate spoke with the breadth and gravity befitting a general council of "all the bishops of Gaul and Spain,"[24] united to defend a kingdom that had so recently defeated and expelled the armies of the Roman Empire. The fear at work in this gathering was not merely for the integrity and independence of a province's clergy but for the survival and salvation of the entire kingdom.

The most obvious source of fear was the immediate political turmoil. Yet, while the consequences of royal instability and factional maneuvering were clearly momentous, the bishops saw the political threat posed by disloyalty as a symptom of more serious problems among the subjects of their obviously unreliable kings. They took the opportunity provided by the council to issue a

---

23. See, e.g., Tol. IV, c. 34, 46, and 71. Vives, 204–5, 207–8, and 215. See also P. D. King, *Law and Society in the Visigothic Kingdom,* (Cambridge, 1972), 10 n. 8.

24. Tol. IV, preamble: "Spaniae atque Galliae sacerdotes." Vives, 186.

host of rules aimed primarily at clerics. As a group, these canons betray an overriding concern with scandal, contention, and schism among all the communities of the kingdom. Combined with the more explicit language of canon 75, they reveal the bishops' analysis of past mistakes and the consequent fear for the future that inspired their careful delineation of centrally regulated Christian consensus.

Unabashedly grounded in the exigencies of an embattled kingship and kingdom, canon 75 was a lengthy disquisition on royal responsibility and political fidelity.[25] It was also a ringing reminder of the earthly authority of divine judgment, particularly as it would be exercised against those who violated oaths. Paradoxically, although the canon was meant to endorse the position of Sisenand, a usurper, it focused on the perfidy of people who conspired against their kings. It opened with an exhortation on the political consequences of perjury. Attributing political infidelity to a lack of fear in the face of God's judgment, the bishops linked false oaths of loyalty to the kingdom's chances for survival:

> the wrath of the heavens has overturned many kingdoms of the earth in such a way that because of the impiety of their faith and of their *mores,* some have been destroyed by others. Thus it is fitting that we beware the fate of this kind of people, lest we be struck by a similar precipitous plague and be punished by such cruel penalties.[26]

Perjury against the king was a communal sin, characteristic of certain "peoples." Not only did it risk the wrath of the heavens, but it also interfered with foreign relations:

> What hope will there be for such people when they struggle against their enemies? What faith is to be believed in future peace with other peoples? What pact is not to be violated? What agreement sworn to enemies will endure when they do not even keep the faith sworn to their kings?[27]

---

25. On the political ideas behind canon 75, see Jose Orlandis and Domingo Ramos-Lissón, *Historia de los concilios de la España romana y visigoda,* (Pamplona, 1986), 292–96; and Enrique Gallego Blanco, "Canon LXXV of the Fourth Council of Toledo," *Classical Folia* 32 (1978).

26. Tol. IV, c. 75: "Inde est quod multa regna terrarum coelestis iracundia ita permutavit, ut per inpietatem fidei et morum alterum ab altero solveretur: unde et nos cavere oportet casum huiusmodi gentium, ne similiter plaga feriamur praecipiti et poena puniamur crudeli." Vives, 218

27. Tol. IV, c. 75: "Quae igitur spes talibus populis contra hostes laborantibus erit? quae fides ultra cum aliis gentibus in pace credenda? quod foedus non violandum? quae in hostibus iurata sponsio permenebit, quando nec ipsis propriis regibus iuratam fidem conservant?" Vives, 217.

As a group characteristic, infidelity was a matter of *mores,* it was a state of mind, and it was a set of actions that had disastrous consequences for kingdoms.

When it came to the means for ensuring that their own kingdom did not suffer the fate of others, the bishops began by again discussing the problem in group terms, offering a positive program for the communal avoidance of divine judgment. The subjects of the Visigothic kings should, first and foremost, "preserve religious observance and fear towards God."[28] They should remove from their characters impiety, infidelity, "deceitful treachery," the "sin of perjury," and "heinous undertakings of conspiracy."[29] No one should incite sedition or raise rebellions; kings should be allowed to die in peace. New kings should be chosen by "leading men" of the Goths consulting together with the bishops.[30] This would allow the entire kingdom to avoid being torn apart "through violence and ambition."[31]

In outlining the details of royal election procedures, the bishops turned their attention from Catholic consensus and fidelity as a community characteristic to kings as individuals and the problems with successions and legitimacy that had brought so much disruption since the days of Witteric, and even before. Locating immediate legitimacy in the election procedure, the canon also admonished present and future kings on their rights and duties as rulers chosen by God. It anathematized kings who failed to rule with justice and equity, including the recently ousted Swinthila. Isidore and his colleagues clearly believed that their kings owed a debt to Christ and to their subjects for their positions of power and were required to repay that debt by ruling with moderation and humility. This meant revering the law; avoiding pride, domination, and contempt; and, most specifically, refraining from unilaterally imposing sentences in capital cases. Following this program, according to the bishops, would create a situation wherein "the kings may rejoice in the peoples, and the peoples in the kings, and God in both."[32] In other words, by ruling well, good kings would encourage their subjects to keep their promised faith and thereby please God.

In the later seventh century church leaders gave increasing weight to rituals surrounding individual coronations and royal military leadership as they continued to struggle with political instability. Royal unction in the "ceremonial center" of the kingdom, Toledo, as well as complex liturgies for the kings'

---

28. Tol. IV, c. 75: "servemus erga Deum religionis cultum atque timorem." Vives, 218.

29. Tol. IV, c. 75: "infidelitatis subtilitas impia, non subdola mentis perfidia, non periurii nefas, coniurationum nefanda molimina." Vives, 218.

30. Tol. IV, c. 75: "primatus totius gentis." Vives, 218.

31. Tol. IV, c. 75: "per vim atque ambitum oriatur." Vives, 218.

32. Tol. IV, c. 75: "et reges in populis, et populi in regibus, et Deus in utrisque laetetur." Vives, 220.

military expeditions became centerpieces in new practices meant to ensure the legitimacy of successions.[33] In 633, however, the weight of responsibility for stable kingship rested on the other side of the monarch-subject balance. The glue that would keep canon 75's rejoicing construct together was the subjects' duty to refrain from perjury, to preserve religious observances and their fear of God, and thus to "retain the concord of unity."[34]

Finally, the canon recorded a thrice-repeated anathema unanimously called down against individuals who attempted usurpations—successfully or not. The anathema condemned these traitors to future damnation at the final judgment and, for the present, made them "strangers to the Catholic church of Christ, which they have profaned with perjury."[35] The impiety of *mores,* the infidelity of the mind and of acts that afflicted and destroyed other peoples and kingdoms, were to be excised from the subjects of the kingdom by imposing common religious observances, by demanding a faithful state of mind and mode of behavior from the entire community of Christians, and by expelling those individuals who profaned the church and the community with perjury.

This canon differs starkly from the others issued by the council. Yet, despite its unique tone, content, ceremony, legal nature, and announced purpose, canon 75 cannot be separated from the rest of the program put forth at Toledo IV. Its very presence in the records and the crisis it reflects politicize the council's entire agenda, despite the ecclesiastic focus of the majority of its other enactments. Conversely, the program for uniformity in the ecclesiastic canons emphasizes canon 75's demand for religiously based unanimity in support of the kingship. Toledo IV sought to establish a unified Christian community obedient to the authority of divine judgment. Canon 75 focused that obedience on the Visigothic kings, but it also expressed the bishops' insistence on the necessity of establishing and maintaining a Christian consensus on the inviolability of oaths taken in the name of God. Those oaths were not only essential to the stability of the kingship and to conducting foreign affairs. They were also a fundamental element in the administration of justice, especially in church councils. Marking those who committed the sacrilege of perjury as strangers to the "whole community of Christians"[36] would help ensure the grace and favor of God, the survival of the kingdom, and the holy authority of conciliar consensus.

---

33. Collins, "Julian of Toledo," 46–48. See concl., n. 17.

34. Tol. IV, c. 75: "unitatis concordia a nobis retinetur." Vives, 218.

35. Tol. IV, c. 75: "ab ecclesia Christi catholica quam periurio profanaverit efficiatur extraneus." Vives, 219.

36. Tol. IV, c. 75: "omni conmunione christianorum alienus." Vives, 219.

Baptized Jews and the Inclination to "Vice"

Perjurers were not the only group of infidels the bishops deemed it necessary to identify and exclude. In their view Sisebut's ill-fated effort to establish consensus by force had created another threat to Christian unity in the kingdom. By 633 baptized Jews constituted a community of people who were officially marked as Christians but were feared as particularly dangerous religious dissenters. Toledo IV addressed this problem in ten canons aimed at Jews and baptized Jews, the first of which opened with a condemnation of Sisebut's policy.[37] The council ruled that "from now on force should bring no one to believing . . . for unwilling ones will not be saved, only the willing; thus the appearance of justice may remain unbroken."[38] Not only was forced conversion inadequate for the salvation of the "unwilling," but it caused the "appearance" of injustice. If baptized Jews had been made Christians unjustly, they might gain sympathy and tolerance from other Christians for any failures in their performance as good Christians. Despite their theological criticisms of forced conversion, in the bishops' view its most dangerous consequence was the creation of a new group of religious dissenters who could threaten Christian consensus by the apparent injustice of their Christian identity. The canons identified apostatizing Jewish converts as the source of numerous social difficulties, especially in their potential role as agents for scandal and confusion in the delineation of religious identity. In condemning forced baptism, the bishops not only in fact ratified Sisebut's conversions but also set up new procedures for identifying and controlling both Jews and Jewish converts.

The canon condemning forced conversion was intended to reaffirm the indelible nature of Christian baptism and the identity it established. Since forced converts had been made "participants in the blood and body of the Lord," they should now "be forced to keep the faith which they took up by violence or necessity, lest they blaspheme the divine name, and consider the

---

37. These canons are central to analyses of the motivations behind the persecution of Jews in the Visigothic kingdom. See bibliography in chap. 4, n. 29. Isidore's position has been examined repeatedly. Some argue that his stand against forced baptism made him a moderating force against the increasingly repressive anti-Jewish tendencies of church and monarchy. See, e.g., A. Lukyn Williams, *Adversos Judeos: A Bird's Eye View of Christian Apologiae until the Renaissance* (New York, 1935), 217; and Laureano Castán Lacoma, "San Isidoro de Sevilla, Apologista AntiJudaico," in *Isidoriana,* ed. Manuel C. Díaz y Díaz (Léon, 1963). Others contend that Toledo IV's fierce measures place him squarely in the camp of the persecutors. See, e.g., Bernhard Blumenkranz, "Les auteurs chrétiens latins du moyen âge sur les juifs et la judaïsme," *Revue des Études Juives,* n.s. 2 (1951–52): 7; and Paul Séjourné, *Le dernier pére de l'Église. Saint Isidore de Séville* (Paris, 1936), 31.

38. Tol. IV, c. 57: "nemini deinceps ad credendum vim inferre . . . non enim tales inviti salvati sunt sed volentes, ut integra sit forma iustitiae." Vives, 210.

faith they have taken as vile and contemptible."[39] When a forced convert lapsed, their rejection of Christianity was a vilification of the faith, despite the possible injustice of their original baptism. Blasphemy among the converts could be construed in either the fact or the suspicion that they performed Jewish rituals. According to the council, it was "known" that many forced converts practiced "Jewish rites," and they were "believed even to employ the abominable circumcision."[40] Bishops were assigned to "correct" these blasphemers.[41] To prevent any further such damage to the Christian identity of converts, the council prohibited fraternization between converted and unconverted Jews. The bishops sentenced baptized Jews involved in such a crime to an unnamed penalty imposed by Christians; the unconverted Jews with whom they had associated were condemned to public beatings.[42]

Apparently, Sisebut's ill-advised policy had created serious suspicions—at least among the bishops at the council—that converted Jews were by nature untrustworthy. Generally, all converted Jews were "inclined to vice," hence the necessity to keep them from the temptation to lapse through association with nonconverts.[43] Furthermore, any convert known to have "transgressed against the Christian faith" was a threat to the judicial system.[44] If they did not fear the divine judgment against blasphemers, they could not be depended on to honor oaths and therefore could never be trusted to give testimony in legal cases, even if they insisted that they were Christians.[45] Jews and their descendants (a group that must have included all converted Jews) were prohibited from holding public offices, because they might use them to "do injuries to Christians."[46] The bishops apparently envisioned the eventual incorporation of all Jews into the kingdom's God-fearing Christian consensus through the removal of the children of both apostatizing and unconverted Jews from their parents. These children were to be sent to live in monasteries or with Christian families so that they would "advance as much in *mores* as in faith."[47] The

---

39. Tol. IV, c. 57: "quia iam constat eos sacramentis divinis adsociatos . . . oportet ut fidem etiam vi vel necessitate susceperunt tenere cogantur, ne nomen Domini blasphemetur, et fidem quam susceperunt vilis ac contemtibilis habeatur." Vives, 211.

40. Tol. IV, c. 59: "nunc blasphemantes in Christo non solum iudaicos ritus perpetrasse noscuntur, sed etiam abominandas circumcisiones exercere praesumserunt." Vives, 211

41. Tol. IV, c. 59: "huiusmodi transgressores pontificali auctoritate correcti." Vives, 212.

42. Tol. IV, c. 62. Vives, 212.

43. Tol. IV, c. 62: "ad vitia proni sunt." Vives, 212.

44. Tol. IV, c. 64: "in Christi fidem praevaricati sunt." Vives, 213.

45. Tol. IV, c. 64. Vives, 213.

46. Tol. IV, c. 65: "christinis iniuriam faciunt." Vives, 213.

47. Tol. IV, c. 60, Vives, 212. The exact meaning of this canon is debated. Thompson (*Goths*, 178; following Solomon Katz, *The Jews in the Visigothic and Frankish Kingdoms of Spain and Gaul* [Cambridge, 1937], 50), argues that the canon must have applied only to the baptized children of apostatizing Jews, since "it is difficult to believe that so drastic a measure was passed at this date." Ramon Hernández, ("El Problema de los judios on los PP. Visigo-

bishops seem to have believed that being raised by Christians would endow these children with Christian identities, or *mores,* that were strong enough to counteract the Jewish inclination to "vice" that had caused so much confusion after Sisebut's misguided action.

The anti-Jewish canons stand out from the other canons enacted in 633 in a number of ways. Aside from canon 75, they include the only canons that invoke secular authorities in their procedural prescriptions and in their measures for punishment.[48] Aside from a canon calling for freedom from taxation for all clerics,[49] they include the only canons that mention the king as ordering their promulgation.[50] Finally, again with the exception of canon 75, they include the only canons specifically concerned with members of the lay population. Still, these canons were part and parcel of Toledo IV's efforts to identify and eliminate the practices, individuals, and communities whose diversity could provide the cohesive and differentiated identities that might stir up community scandal and contention. Jews, converted Jews, and apostatizing Jews were dangerous because they could confuse and confound the delineations of orthodox Christian identity and power and thereby undermine the consensus on holy authority that was to support that power. One of the primary goals of these canons was to reassert the barrier between Christian and Jewish social

---

dos," *Patrología Toledano-Visigoda* 27, Semana Española de Teología [Madrid, 1970], 108–9) argues along the same lines, while Bernhard Blumenkranz, (*Juifs et Chrétiens dans le monde occidental* [Paris, 1960], 111) and Orlandis (*Historia de los concilios,* 291) take the canon at its word. The canon states: "The sons or daughters of the Jews, lest they spontaneously be involved in the error of their parents, we decree are to be separated from the society of their parents; alloted either to monasteries, or Christian men or women who fear God, so that through their conversation they will become aquainted with the cult of the faith, and placed among better people, they may advance as much in *mores* as in faith." (Iudaeorum filios vel filias, ne parentum ultra involvantur errore, ab eorum consortio separari decernimus deputatos aut monasteriis aut christianis viris ac mulieribus Deum timentibus, ut sub eorum conversatione cultum fidei discant atque in melius instituti tam in moribus quam in fide proficiant.) Since the bishops at Toledo IV so clearly identified apostatizing Jews when they referred particularly to them in other canons, and, given the severity of the anti-Jewish canons as a whole, I do not find it difficult to believe that so drastic a measure was taken against both apostatizing and unconverted Jews in 633.

48. Tol. IV, c. 62 prescribed "public beatings" (publicis caedibus) for Jews found associating with converted Jews. Vives, 212. C. 65 called for "judges of the provinces" (iudices provinciarum) to work with priests to enforce the prohibition against public office holding, and invoked "public beatings" for Jews who "deceptively attained the office" (is qui subrepserit publicis caedibus). Vives, 213.

49. Tol. IV, c. 47, Vives, 208.

50. Tol. IV, c. 65, prohibiting Jews and their descendants from holding public office, was issued "with the most excellent lord and king Sisenand commanding" (Praecipiente domno atque excellentissimo Sisenando rege). Vives, 213. Canon 59 repeated a decree already issued by Sisenand. Vives, 212. Canon 66 was in accord with "the decree of the most glorious prince" (Ex decreto gloriosissimi principis . . .). Vives, 214. This, however, may refer to Sisebut's prohibition on Jews owning Christian slaves. See chap. 4, n. 8.

networks and to place the suspect Christian Jews in a carefully supervised category apart from both.

The council placed the responsibility for maintaining these barriers on clerics and their congregations. In the case of barring Jews and their descendants from public office, the king's judges were ordered to join clerics in protecting Christians from Jewish power, but judges who failed in this duty were to be punished by excommunication and thus were subject to clerical supervision.[51] Local clerics were called upon to punish converts who practiced Jewish rituals and to warn and separate Jews married to Christians.[52] The Christian community was given the task of punishing converts who associated with unbaptized Jews,[53] and "Christian men or women" joined with monasteries in fulfilling the vital responsibility for instilling Jewish children with Christian *mores*.[54] Yet the council recognized that not all Christians would automatically accept the duty of patrolling the boundaries between themselves, Jews, and baptized Jews. Many clerics and laypeople had already "fostered faithlessness by their patronage" of Jews.[55] The council therefore sought to plug this possible leak in their perfect consensus by identifying as "a stranger from the Catholic church and the kingdom of God" any Christian—"bishop, or cleric, or lay person"—who gave "aid or gifts or favors to those against the Christian faith."[56]

The Scandal of Liturgical Diversity

Identifying and isolating political perjurers, baptized Jews, and the Christians who "fostered faithlessness through patronage" was a relatively straightforward matter. These canons stand out from the rest partly because they are so direct in explaining the threats they address and the reasoning behind their measures. They do not, however, constitute the core of the bishops' analysis of past mistakes or current dangers. Toledo IV's primary concern was with preventing the "scandal" of religious dissension in established Christian congregations. Their concept of scandal included a nexus of meanings, the most explicitly articulated of which was the traditional Christian meaning of the

---

51. Tol. IV, c. 65. Vives, 213.

52. Tol. IV, c. 59 and c. 63. Vives, 212–13.

53. Tol. IV, c. 62. Vives, 212.

54. Tol. IV, c. 60. Vives, 212.

55. Tol. IV, c. 58: "perfidiam eorum patrocinio suo foveant." Vives, 211.

56. Tol. IV, c. 58: "episcopus sive clericus vel secularis illis contra fidem christianam suffragium vel munere vel favore praestiterit . . . ab ecclesia catholica et regno Dei efficiatur extraneus." Vives, 211.

Latin word *scandalum:*[57] a stumbling block to the faith, or the occasion failure of belief. Yet the dangers of scandal also encompassed contempt ... the church or its clerics, accusations of heresy, widespread popular errors, or the inspiration for actual schism. Thus, scandal could grow from being a stumbling block for an individual's faith to the occasion for contention among and between communities of the faithful, and so to a threat to the whole kingdom.

The bishops tied the scandal of religious dissension most explicitly to liturgical diversity. In their second canon they called for establishing a unanimity of prayer and practices throughout the kingdom. They based this demand on the canonical precedent directing that one province must follow one set of religious observances.[58] Despite this claim for canonical precedent, however, the call for liturgical unification was quite out of keeping with the diversity prevalent in the regional Christianities of the era, which was perfectly acceptable to luminaries like Gregory the Great.[59] The bishops at Toledo IV were quite aware of this. Their canon calling for uniformity in the baptismal rite quoted a letter from Gregory written to Leander of Seville in the 590s in which the pope had said: "the diverse custom of the holy church in no way harms the one faith."[60] The bishops in 633, however, saw danger in this liberal

---

57. The word appears four times in the records of Tol. IV: c. 2, 6, 22, and 41. Vives, 188, 192, 201, and 207.

58. Séjourné (*Le dernier pére,* 137–44) attributes to Isidore the idea that liturgical unity was necessary in order to avoid the appearance of schism. Séjourné cites two sixth-century councils as the only precedents for this principle that could have been known in 633: the Council of Gerona in 517, and Braga I in 563, both of which called for liturgical unity within their respective provinces, Tarraconensis and Galicia. While the bishops in 633 were consciously building on these precedents, according to Séjourné, Toledo IV replaced the idea of unity within one province with that of kingdom-wide unity—a move that he sees as revealing a "tendance nationaliste." Orlandis, *Historia de los concilios,* 268–69, amplifies the "national" interpretation of the principle of liturgical unity: "era la afirmación de la inseparable unidad religiosa y política, que durante largos siglos habría de constituir el principio cardinal de la nacionalidad española." On the other hand, Peter Brown (*The Rise of Western Christendom: Triumph and Diversity,* A.D. 200–1000 [Oxford, 1996], 220–21) attributes the urge for liturgical unity to an effort to create a self-sustaining regional version of universal Christianity in the kingdom, or, as he calls it, a "micro-Christendom." Whether or not the development reveals incipient nationality in the Visigothic kingdom, the development is an important one and, as Professor Sabine MacCormack has pointed out to me, somewhat out of line with prevailing late antique conceptions of the transcendency of the universal church over ethnic or political boundaries. On the power of the principle of transcendent universalism in fourth- and fifth-century North Africa, see Peter Brown, "Religious Dissent in the Later Roman Empire: The Case of North Africa," *Religion and Society in the Age of St. Augustine* (London, 1972).

59. See his *Responsiones* to Augustine recorded in Bede, *Historia Ecclesiastica gentis Anglorum, Bede Ecclesiastical History of the English People,* ed. and trans. B. Colgrave and RAB Mynors (Oxford, 1969), 1.27.

60. Tol. IV, c. 6: "in una fide nicil officit sanctae ecclesiae consuetudo diversa." Vives, 191.

attitude. Uniformity in "ecclesiastic custom" was necessary, they said, "lest our diversity should seem to show to the ignorant or the carnal the error of schism, and the variation in the churches should be a scandal for many."[61]

Canon 2 specifically linked religious uniformity to political identity: "let the ecclesiastic customs no longer be diverse among us, who are joined by one faith and one kingdom."[62] The bishops' program for ritual uniformity, however, did not directly attribute the danger of liturgical diversity to political considerations or to Sisenand's embattled position. Rather, diversity caused the more general and widespread threat of scandal and schism. In the effort to end such scandal, the council issued a detailed listing of punishable ritual errors. Canons 5 through 18 were devoted to minute details of Christian ritual and were aimed at uniform practice.

In the canon calling for uniform baptisms, the bishops were quite clear about how this scandal might threaten Christian communities:

> Because in Spain, in the sacrament of baptism some bishops make a triple immersion and some make only one, some people consider this to be a schism and the unity of the faith seems to be rent, for when the parts act in a diverse and almost contrary way, some contend that others have not been baptized.[63]

The canon ordered all bishops to use the single immersion. The triple immersion, the rite practiced in Rome, had been specifically recommended by Pope Vigilius to the Galician church in 537 or 538. It had also been the Arians' traditional form of baptism. At Toledo IV the bishops used Gregory I's endorsement of diversity to explain their own divergence from Roman practice. The canon went on to quote Gregory's further advice to Leander that the kingdom's churches should follow the single immersion, "lest when [the heretics] count the immersions they divide the divinity, and when they do as they were accustomed, they glory that they have conquered your custom."[64] Apparently, following the Visigoths' conversion to Catholicism, diverse baptismal practices had made it possible for individuals and entire communities to be charged

---

61. Tol. IV, c. 2: "ne qualibet nostra diversitas apud ignotos seu carnales schismatis errorem videatur ostendere, et multis existat in scandalum varietas ecclesiarum." Vives, 188.

62. Tol. IV, c. 2: "nec diversa sit ultra in nobis ecclesiastica consuetudo qui una fide continemur et regno." Vives, 188.

63. Tol. IV, c. 6: "De babtismi autem sacramento propter quod in Spaniis quidam sacerdotes trinam, quidam simplam mersionem faciunt, a nonnullis schisma esse conspiciunt et unitas fidei scindi videtur; nam dum partes diverso et quasi contrario modo agunt, alii alios non babtizatos esse contendunt." Vives, 191.

64. Tol. IV., c. 6: "ne dum mersiones numerant divinitatem dividant, dumque quo faciebant faciunt, morem vestrum se vicisse glorientur." Vives, 192. See Orlandis, *Historia de los concilios*, 269–84.

with inauthentic Christianity. In the bishops' analysis ritual diversity thus had led to religious dissension among individuals and between local churches; because unity appeared to be rent, consensus had indeed been destroyed.

A number of other canons indicate additional ways that the scandal of liturgical diversity might have played out in daily life. For instance, communities in areas with distinctive geographical or political identities could be further differentiated by local divergent practices. Some canons implied that Narbonensis and Galicia were particular problem areas.[65] These two provinces at times had been the homes of overtly dissenting communities. Narbonensis had been the seat of numerous rebellions and invasions, and Galicia had been an independent kingdom under Sueve kings until 586 as well as the traditional home of Priscillianism, a heresy dating from the fourth century. By incorporating these areas into a kingdom-wide uniformity of ritual, Toledo IV sought to overcome their histories of separation by eliminating any basis for defining regionally distinctive religious identities. Such an identity would be dangerous in two ways: it could be asserted by the inhabitants of the provinces in seeking to avoid the constraints of a kingdom-wide Christian consensus, or it could be used by people from other areas as the basis for excluding them from that construct. In either case Toledo IV considered the potential for regionally based religious contention a threat to its program for the kingdom's survival.

The bishops in Toledo were not only concerned with incorrect practices setting apart entire provinces. In their experience the isolation of a single parish could enable ignorance to engender variation, causing the divine sacraments to be offended and also, one can assume, allowing that community to enter into, if not the reality, the appearance of schism. Canon 26 was particularly direct in tying variation to isolation. The council ordered bishops to give each new parochial priest a "ritual manual" at their ordination, "so that they may go to their churches instructed, lest through ignorance they offend the divine sacraments."[66] The canon also ordered that the priests, whenever they came into the city for processions or councils, were to report to their bishops

---

65. Tol. IV, c. 9; Vives, 194, singled out the churches of Gaul (i.e., Narbonensis) for not blessing the lanterns and wax during Easter rituals. Canon 41 outlawed a style of tonsure peculiar to Galician clerics, for it had been used by "the heretics in Spain" and was a "scandal to the church" (ritus . . . in Spanias haereticorum . . . ecclesiae scandalum). Vives, 206–7. Tol. IV, c. 13; Vives, 196–97, and canon 6 also seem to refer to Galician practices. Canon 13 accepted and promoted the singing of nonscriptural hymns, which had been specifically prohibited by Braga I, canon 12, held during the period of Galician independence under the Suevi. The triple immersion baptism outlawed by Tol. IV, c. 6, had been Galician practice. See n. 63 of this chapter. Orlandis (*Historia de los Concilios,* 269–73) suggests that Tol. IV, c. 12, 14, and 18, also were directed against Galician practices.

66. Tol. IV, c. 26: "libellum officiale a sacerdote suo accipiant, ut ad ecclesias sibi deputatas instructi succedant, ne per ignorantiam etiam in ipsis divinis sacramentis offendant." Vives, 202.

"as to how they celebrate their masses, and how they baptize."[67] The liturgical education and supervision of clerics, whether in an entire province or a single rural parish, was essential to maintaining agreement throughout the kingdom on how to identify the authentic Christian practices, communities, and individuals joined in the absolute Christian consensus that would prevent scandal and contention and so ensure divine favor.

Clerical Impurity and Conciliar Justice

The canons on liturgical diversity show that Isidore's efforts at clerical education in the past twenty years had not born lasting fruit. Clerics at all levels disagreed on correct practices. In response, the council established centrally defined mechanisms for achieving clerical consensus on these most basic aspects of Christian community life and identity.[68] Yet it would be difficult for a priest, or even a bishop, to change a community's traditional Christian rituals unilaterally—particularly one so fundamental as baptism—solely on the basis of a distant authority's demand. In gaining community acceptance for such a change, it is likely that a cleric's personal holy authority would be at least as important, if not more so, as the decision of a council. Therefore, in order to ensure the authenticity of each community's Christian consensus, individual clerics had to be accepted by their congregations as bona fide representatives of divine authority. Local clerics could not afford to be marked by any blemish on their personal reputations.

There was no guarantee, moreover, that individual clerics would themselves accept the authority of mechanisms for uniformity instituted from the upper reaches of the church's hierarchy. A cleric whose personal authority was weak might not be willing to risk the resistance an attempt at ritual change might provoke from a community or from powerful factions within a community. Furthermore, clerics who did wield considerable local authority were not necessarily immune from the personal local loyalties, ambitions, or obligations that for years had militated against the development of provincial or kingdom-wide clerical consensus. In order for centralized ecclesiastic mandates to be implemented in local communities, it was necessary not only to educate the clerics of Iberia but also to supervise them carefully, ensuring their obedience to the standards set by the highest sources of divine authority: Holy Scripture, canonical tradition, and the present and future decisions of church councils.

---

67. Tol. IV, c. 26: "qualiter susceptum officium celebrant, vel babtizant." Vives, 202.

68. The council also issued a rule designed to achieve episcopal consensus on the date of Easter each year through a sequence of consultations by letter. Tol. IV, c. 5. Vives, 191.

By the council's own admission, clerical ignorance, impurity, and corruption reached from the parochial churches to the episcopate. In addition to a number of canons calling on bishops to supervise the lives of their diocesan clergy closely,[69] the council issued rules against such failures as episcopal illiteracy;[70] communication between bishops and foreign enemies;[71] marriages between clerics and prostitutes;[72] and clerics consulting diviners,[73] participating in armed rebellion,[74] or destroying sepulchers.[75] Clerical impurity and indiscipline not only threatened the establishment of uniformity, but, if such failures occurred within the episcopate, they could undermine the entire system of supervision and discipline, including the conciliar judicial process.[76]

Isidore and his colleagues had good reason to be particularly sensitive to the problem of clerical corruption and its consequences. Martianus of Ecija, ousted from his episcopal office at Seville III, had brought his appeal before the bishops gathered in 633. While the council's records do not contain any explicit mention of the case, some of its canons dealing with the dangers of clerical indiscipline appear to be tied to the miscarriage of conciliar justice at Seville III. That incident, and Martianus' appeal at Toledo IV brought into sharp focus the threat posed to consensus and to conciliar authority by the scandals of impurity and corruption among clerics. The repercussions from Martianus' case had gone far beyond the local configurations of power and reputation from which it originated. The power struggle that had riven the consensus on Martianus' authority in Ecija had eventually cast its shadow on the holy authority of Seville III and on the episcopate of Baetica.

Toledo IV reinstated Martianus to the episcopacy, but it allowed Aventius, Martianus' false accuser, to retain his ill-gotten see, thus leaving Martianus a bishop without a diocese.[77] Paradoxically, the bishops at Toledo IV seem to have held Martianus primarily responsible for the scandal his case had created. It is not difficult to see Martianus' situation behind canon 22, which accused "certain bishops" of creating "more than a little scandal when they have been charged with excess rather than maintaining a reputation for a vir-

---

69. See, e.g., Tol. IV, c. 26, 27, 36, 44. Vives, 202, 205, 207.

70. Tol. IV, c. 19. Vives, 199.

71. Tol. IV, c. 30. Vives, 203.

72. Tol. IV, c. 43. Vives, 207.

73. Tol. IV, c. 29. Vives, 203.

74. Tol. IV, c. 45. Vives, 207.

75. Tol. IV, c. 46. Vives, 207.

76. On clerical purity as an aspect of ecclesiastic and social reform in a later medieval context, see Amy G. Remensnyder, "Pollution, Purity, and Peace: An Aspect of Social Reform between the Late Tenth Century and 1076," in *The Peace of God: Social Violence and Religious Response in France around the Year 1000*, ed. Thomas Head and Richard Landes (Ithaca, 1992).

77. *Exemplar*, B.2, 614.

tuous life."[78] In order to prevent any future "suspicion of evil or the actual deed"[79] as well as the opportunity for secular gossip, the canon called on bishops to make sure their conclaves included witnesses who would testify to their purity, something apparently lacking in Martianus' defense. The council extended the responsibility for preventing gossip to providing live-in witnesses of purity for elderly priests confined to their cells and for groups of adolescent clerics. Martianus had not adequately protected himself from the treacherous networks of local power and so had undermined his own authority. If communities were aware that bishops could protect themselves and their lower clergy with the "testimony of persons of good life,"[80] ambitious men like Aventius would not be able to marshal the witnesses and gossip needed to unseat them and, in doing so, to unravel the fabric of clerical consensus.

While the council viewed Martianus as culpable for the scandal his case had aroused, Aventius' maneuvering also provided them with an illustration of the dangers of an impure and undisciplined clergy. If bishops who neglected to provide witnesses to their own reputation could cause debilitating scandal, bishops who had reached the office through avenues of personal power or by concealing past crimes or defects could do inestimable damage. Aventius' shady pursuit of Martianus' see may have been the inspiration behind canon 19, which railed against a "pernicious custom" disturbing the entire church:

> some seek the episcopacy through illegal canvassing [per ambitum], others get the office by offering bribes, and some implicated in crimes or dedicated to military life unworthily come to the honor of the highest holy order.[81]

The canon sought to clear future bishops of any possible suspicions by rendering a list—drawn from the "rules of the canons"[82]—of all those who henceforth should not be promoted to the episcopate:

> those who have been detected in some crime, . . . those who are stained by the mark of infamy, those who have lapsed into heresy, those who are known to be baptized or rebaptized in heresy, those who have amputated themselves or are known to have something

---

78. Tol. IV, c. 22: "quidam hucusque sacerdotum non modicum scandalum creaverunt, dum in accusatione luxuriae, non bonae famae existunt." Vives, 201.

79. Tol. IV, c. 22: "omnis nefanda suspicio aut casus." Vives, 201.

80. Tol. IV, c. 22: "testimonium probabilium personarum." Vives, 201.

81. Tol. IV, c. 19: "alii per ambitum sacerdotia appetunt, alii oblatis muneribus pontificatum adsummunt, nonnulli etiam sceleribus inplicati vel seculari militiae dediti indigni ad honorem sumi ac sacri ordinis pervenerunt." Vives, 199.

82. Tol. IV, c. 19: "ex regulis canonum." Vives, 199.

missing either by a natural defect of the members or by mutilation
. . . those who have concubines for fornication, those who are subjected to a servile condition, those who are of low birth, those who are
neophytes or laymen, those who are given to the secular militia, those
who are obligated to the *curia*, those who are ignorant of letters, those
who have not yet reached 30 years, those who have not come up
through the ecclesiastic ranks, those who seek honor by illegal can-
vassing, those who strive to obtain honor with gifts, those who have
been chosen for the office by their predecessors.[83]

Since kings regularly interfered in episcopal elections during the seventh century, the canon may represent an implicit criticism of the royal appointees.[84]
The canon's procedure for election is rather vaguely delineated, however, and
does not specifically rule out royal participation.[85] It seems more likely that the
exhaustive rendition of possible defects represents Isidore's careful research on
canonical precedents more than it does the presence of each of these impurities
among the Iberian episcopate in 633.[86]

Still, while it is impossible to know whether there were bishops around
who had castrated themselves in order to avoid sin, the canon's language does
indicate that Aventius was not the only bishop who had reached his office *per*

83. Tol. IV, c. 19: "Qui in aliquo crimine detecti sunt, qui infamiae nota adspersi sunt
. . . qui in haeresim lapsi sunt, qui in haeresi baptizati aut rebabtizati esse noscuntur, qui
semetipsos absciderunt, aut naturali defectu membrorum aut decisione aliquid minus habere
noscuntur, . . . qui concubinas ad fornicationes habuerunt, qui servili conditioni obnoxii sunt,
qui ignoti sunt, qui neofyti vel laici sunt, qui seculari militiae dediti sunt, qui curiae nexibus
obligati sunt, qui inscii litterarum sunt, qui nondum ad XXX annos pervenerunt, qui per
gradus ecclesiasticos non accesserunt, qui ambitu honorem quaerunt, qui muneribus honorem
obtinere moliuntur, qui a decessoribus in sacerdotio eliguntur." Vives, 199. In addition to the
rapid elevation in status involved in these promotions, incentives for illegally seeking the episcopal office included control over the ever-growing estates of the church. On the church's mas-
sive landholdings and the roles of bishops as landholders during the Visigothic period, see
Abilio Barbero and Marcelo Vigil, *La formación del feudalismo en la Península Ibérica*
(Barcelona, 1978), 53–96.
84. On the appointment of bishops in the seventh century, see Thompson, *Goths*, 296–98.
85. Tol. IV, c. 19 directed that "in the future no one shall be a bishop who is not a cleric,
or has not been chosen by the people of his own city, or whom the authority of the metropolitan or the assent of the provincial bishops has not selected" (sed nec ille deinceps sacerdos erit,
quem nec clerus, nec populus propriae civitatis elegit, vel auctoritas metropolitani vel provin-
cialium sacerdotum assensio exquisivit). Once the candidate had been presented and "examined" and his life and teaching found to acceptable, he was to be consecrated "according to the
synodal and decretal rules . . . with the will of all the clerics and citizens" (examinatus . . .
secundum synodalia vel decretalia constituta cum omnium clericorum vel civium volumtate).
Vives, 199. Whether this procedure would disallow the casting of lots outlined at the Council
of Barcelona in 599 is not clear. See chap. 3, n. 92.
86. On the dangers of assuming that the comprehensive coverage contained in Visigothic
laws and canons can be used as literal reflections of the contemporary society, see Collins,
"Julian of Toledo," 33–34.

ambitum and that episcopal impurity was widespread enough to constitute a threat to the church's authority. The canon explicitly exempted bishops currently in office from being removed for past crimes or inadequacies, for, although such action "certainly would have been fitting," it would have "stirred up a great disturbance of the church" to do so.[87] Instead, the bishops looked to the future in their effort to ensure episcopal purity and consensus. Henceforth, episcopal candidates were to be carefully investigated and examined prior to consecration to assure that they were free from the numerous sins listed and that their "life and learning" were "acceptable."[88] The results of this examination would be made public at the new bishop's consecration, the procedure for which was also spelled out in detail. In the future any person who attempted to gain, or succeeded in gaining, the rank of bishop "against the above-named prohibitions of the canons" would lose his office, "along with those who had ordained him."[89] Thus, the bishops countered the possibility of future scandals centered on bishops and their ambitions by bolstering the preventive power of canonical precedent with new procedures that carried the threat of public scrutiny, much as they did in their call for "witnesses of life." A careful examination before his consecration might have uncovered Aventius' excessive ambition and penchant for perjury and thus prevented the resulting scandal. While Isidore and the other Baetican bishops escaped the consequences of having ordained an "unworthy" candidate, the canon also provided for more careful inquiries with its threat of expulsion against "those who ordained" such men in the future.[90]

Thus, unlike Seville II, Toledo IV explicitly recognized that church councils were not immune from judicial abuses and took measures to protect conciliar integrity that may have been inspired by Martianus' case. In addition to the provisions for ensuring witnesses to refute false accusations, canon 28 outlined a ceremony for reinstating clerics who had been "unjustly ejected from their rank" and found innocent at "a second synod."[91] Canons 68 and 74 pro-

---

87. Tol. IV, c. 19: "de quorum scilicet casu atque remotione oportuerat quidem statuendum, sed ne perturbatio quamplurima ecclesiae oriretur." Vives, 199.

88. Tol. IV, c. 19: "probabilis vita atque doctrina." Vives, 199.

89. Tol. IV, c. 19: "contra praedicta vetita canonum . . . cum ordinatoribus suis." Vives, 200.

90. In 546 the Council of Lérida issued a similar measure against unworthy ordinations. Canon 12 (*La colección,* 305) provided that those who had to that point ordained clerics "without discretion" (indiscrete) would be pardoned but reiterated previous canons' provisions that in the future those who performed such ordinations would henceforth be prevented from ordaining anyone, and those they ordained inappropriately would lose their positions. Toledo IV thus followed the precedent of this canon in excusing past offenders but increased the punishment to be applied in the future.

91. Tol. IV, c. 28: "a gradu suo iniuste deiectus in secunda synodo innocens repperiatur." Vives, 202. See Thompson, *Goths,* 287 n. 6.

hibited freed church slaves from testifying against their former owners, an action that may have been taken in response to some of the witnesses Aventius had called.[92] Oddly, however, the council took no measures against those who made false accusations or suborned witnesses, that is, Aventius' crimes. Isidore and his colleagues were more concerned with the scandal and gossip associated with the appearance of impurity. Ultimately, they held Martianus, and others like him, responsible for maintaining their own reputations and thus the community consensus supporting their authority.

The apparent refusal to prosecute past crimes or correct prior mistakes, like the focus on scandal, is characteristic of Toledo IV. Most obviously, canon 75's resounding condemnation of perjury was accompanied by an assurance that it "would condemn none of us by present or eternal judgment."[93] While canon 19 acknowledged that prior episcopal appointments had disturbed the whole order of the church, it explicitly disallowed the removal of any inappropriate prelates from their present offices.[94] Martianus' case cannot be seen as the sole inspiration for this attitude or for the complex problems addressed and the actions taken at Toledo IV. It does, however, illuminate more general problems confronting the Iberian episcopate in 633. Faced with an unstable central authority, local religious variation, and the petty power struggles of small, traditionally independent communities, the bishops could not assert their authority and consensus by punishing past crimes or correcting their own judicial mistakes. This would have risked further disturbances and factionalization. Instead, they sought to prevent future scandals by demanding that all ecclesiastic communities provide the education, supervision, proper elections, witnesses of purity, episcopal candidates, investigatory procedures, and spotless reputations necessary to maintain their congregation's consensus on the holy authority of their clerics. Discipline and community consensus would in turn make possible the orderly settlement of disputes and the local enforcement of the decisions of church councils, both general and provincial.

The Conciliar Remedy: New Ceremonies and Jurisdictions

In the Toledan view from 633 scandal had arisen from a legion of sources: the violation of religious oaths, ritual diversity, apostasy among forced converts, unworthy bishops, an undisciplined and ignorant clergy, and the corruption of ecclesiastic justice. Such errors could become the basis of contention between

---

92. Tol. IV, c. 68 and 74. Vives, 214 and 216. See chap. 4, n. 91.

93. Tol. IV, c. 75: "condemnet nullum ex nobis praesenti atque aeterno iudicio." Vives, 220.

94. See n. 87 of this chapter.

individuals. Even more disastrously, contention between individuals could create cohesion among groups of people identified by their common undesirable practices, their shared loyalty or subjection to unworthy clerics, their common complaints against kings, clerics, or the church, or suspicions about the authenticity of their Catholic faith. In addressing these problems, the bishops focused on misuses or failures in legal, ceremonial, and educational procedures. These included such practices as forced baptism, false oaths, not providing witnesses to the purity of clerical life, not maintaining supervision over parochial priests, not investigating the worthiness of episcopal candidates, and so on. In the bishops' hindsight, the failure to follow correct, clearly defined and mutually understood procedures along with failures in clerical education had made possible the continued and scandalous existence of individuals and communities that threatened the faith, the church, and the power of its leaders. Their program for uniform practices, doctrine, and clerical discipline was designed to make possible the identification and elimination of those seeds of scandal. The procedure for implementing the program was to be the regular convocation of properly orchestrated church councils.

According to the council's third canon, "nothing hinders the *mores* of discipline within the church of Christ more than the negligence of bishops, who, despising the canons, fail to call synods for amending ecclesiastic *mores*."[95] Toledo III had made a similar claim about decay and the absence of councils in 589. In 633, however, the bishops could no longer blame this failure on an Arian monarchy. Decay in *mores* had occurred in direct contravention of the call for yearly provincial councils issued in Toledo III's canon 18. Toledo IV responded to the preceding negligence among Iberian bishops by creating an elaborate set of instructions that focused not simply on the need for conciliar continuity but also on the need for a centrally established and meticulously defined ceremonial and legal procedure. Thus, the bishops in 633 leveled retrospective criticism not only at the "negligence" of the episcopate but also at the procedures followed in earlier councils—including, presumably, the provincial councils of the immediate post-589 period and the ill-fated Seville III.

Reiterating the call made in 589, canon 3 ordered provincial councils to be held yearly. Unlike the directions of canon 18, however, this canon clearly distinguished between general and provincial councils.[96] General councils were to

---

95. Tol. IV, c. 3: "Nulla pene res disciplinae mores ab ecclesia Christi depulit quam sacerdotum neglegentiam, qui contemtis canonibus ad corrigendos ecclesiasticos mores synodum facere neglegunt." Vives, 188.

96. On the significance of this distinction, especially in regards to the "institutionalization" of general councils, see José Orlandis, *La Iglesia en la España visigótica y medieval* (Pamplona, 1976), 83–85.

be called concerning "matters of the faith . . . or any other concern which is common to the whole church."[97] Provincial councils were to deal with everything else. Canon 4 described in detail correct conciliar ceremony.[98] After appropriately gathering, seating themselves, praying together and hearing previous canons on conciliar ritual, the bishops were to begin business. The metropolitan would first invite the bishops present to raise "any complaint that goes against the canons."[99] After the episcopal cases had been heard, any lower clerics or laymen waiting outside who thought "the council should be called on for whatever affair"[100] could present their case to the archdeacon of the metropolitan church, who in turn would present it to the council, which would then grant entry to the waiting litigant. Each case was to be fully addressed before another was taken up, and no one was to adjourn or leave the council until all cases had been resolved and all decisions signed by all the bishops.

These directions provided the basic conciliar pedagogy that had been lacking in the canons of preceding councils. Future council participants would know the correct procedures, people, and jurisdictions involved in provincial and general councils. Moreover, the meticulous description of every aspect of conciliar ceremony in canon 4 also conveyed fundamental principles of conciliar authority. By enacting their ceremonies regularly and correctly, future council goers would establish a cycle of self-authorization that could support the divine authority—and thus the enforcement—of their decisions. In the orchestration of these rituals the physical ordering of the councils was particularly important. Canon 4 gave detailed instructions on the entrance and seating of the bishops, priests, deacons, and laypeople. It prescribed the position of the doorkeepers and the "appropriate" door beside which they were to be placed[101] and provided instructions on the opening and shutting of that door. These various configurations of people and places reflected differing principles. The gathering of the bishops outside the church prior to entrance was a "coming together" of equals in harmony and consensus.[102] On the other hand, the entrance and seating of, first, bishops by seniority, second, priests, and,

---

97. Tol. IV, c. 3: "fidei causa . . . aut quaelibet alia ecclesiae conmunis." Vives, 189.

98. This canon laid the basis for the later seventh-century development of the Visigothic *ordo de celebrando concilio.* For a description of the genesis, development, and diffusion of these ceremonial rules, see Charles Munier, "L'*ordo de celebrando concilio* wisigothique," *Revue des Sciences Religieuses* 37 (1963). For early medieval depictions of conciliar ceremony and commentary on their relationship to the Visigothic *ordo,* see Roger Reynolds, "Rites and Signs of Conciliar Decisions in the Early Middle Ages," *Settimane* 33, no. 1 (Spoleto, 1987).

99. Tol. IV, c. 4: "quamquumque querellam quae contra canones agit." Vives, 190.

100. Tol. IV, c. 4: "concilium pro qualibet re crediderit adpellandum." Vives, 190.

101. Tol. IV, c. 4: "unam ianuam per quam sacerdotes ingredi oportet ostiarii stent." Vives, 189.

102. Tol. IV, c. 4: "convenientes omnes episcopi pariter." Vives, 189.

finally, the standing deacons, laypeople, and notaries reflected the hierarchy deemed necessary for maintaining discipline.[103]

In addition to the attention given the positioning of the councils and their participants in space and time, the canon provided for the deliberate positioning of the decisions of each council within conciliar tradition. Canon 4 described in detail the entrance and role of the "codex of the canons." This was the pivotal moment when the assembly turned from ritual submission to God to exercising its own authority. According to the canon, after praying together, the assembly would rise as one, and,

> when all are sitting together in their places in silence, a deacon, clothed in the alb, shall bring forth into the middle of the assembly the codex of the canons and shall read aloud the entries on holding councils. When the canons have been read, the metropolitan bishop shall address the council, saying, "Behold, most holy bishops, the sentences on celebrating councils have been recited from the canons of previous fathers; therefore if any action troubles any of you, put it forth before your brothers."[104]

The reading of previous conciliar actions not only verified the correct ritual fulfillment of the council's responsibilities toward tradition and God, but it authorized in advance the deliberations and decisions to come. The presentation of the codex, the embodiment of tradition's authority, enacted a material continuity that opened the pages of that authority to receive the wisdom of the

---

103. Much of the stage-managing instructions in canon 4 can be interpreted as a give-and-take between the physical representation of equality before God and rigid hierarchy in the maintenance of discipline. For instance, following the mass prostration in prayer, at the direction of a deacon, everyone was to arise together and retake their hierarchical position. The wording of the canon calls attention to both the commonality of the actions and the hierarchy of the assembly: "all [participants] shall immediately rise, and with all fear of the Lord and discipline the bishops as well as the priests shall sit, and thus with all sitting together in their places in silence" (confestim omnes surgunt, et cum omni timore Dei et disciplina tam episcopi quam presbyteres sedeant, sique omnibus in suis locis in silentio consedentibus). Vives, 190.

On the relationship between "sacred topography" and religious hierarchy and social ordering in late antiquity, see Sabine MacCormack, "Loca Sancta: The Organization of Sacred Topography in Late Antiquity," in *The Blessings of Pilgrimage*, ed. Robert Ousterhout (Urbana, 1990). On the principles and disputes involved in ceremonial expressions of rank in the tenth century, see Heinrich Fichtenau, *Living in the Tenth Century. Mentalities and Social Orders*, trans. Patrick Geary (Chicago, 1991), 3–29, especially the section entitled "Seating Arrangements at Religious Assemblies," 18–20.

104. Tol. IV, c. 4: "sicque omnibus in suis locis in silentio consedentibus diaconus alba indutus codicem canonum in medio proferens capitula de conciliis agendis pronuntiet, finitisque titulis metropolitanus episcopus concilium adloquatur decens: Ecce, sanctissimi sacerdotes, recitatae sunt ex canonibus priscorum patrum sententiae de concilio celebrando; si qua igitur quem piam vestrum actio conmovet, coram suis fratribus proponat." Vives, 190.

present gathering. Once the remaining instructions had been correctly followed—the completion of each case in turn, the acceptance of cases in order from lesser clergy and laypeople, the enforced attendance till the closing of the agenda, and the absence of "tumult"—the signatures of the prelates would verify the presence of God and figuratively close the pages once again. This would ensure that the actions of the moment would be embraced by the written perpetuity of canonical legitimacy.[105]

Toledo IV's meticulous definition of conciliar ceremony, participants, and jurisdictions indicates an overarching desire for centralized regulation of local conciliar practice, a distinct departure from the fluidity of previous interpretations of conciliar authority. Centralization as a general principle had also been on the agenda at Toledo III, most obviously in Reccared's speeches. Although the principle was recorded and apparently accepted in 589, however, outside the directions concerning the oversight of royal fiscal agents, the practical meaning of centralization—either royal or ecclesiastic—was ill defined. Unlike Reccared, the bishops at Toledo III had been hesitant to wield central authority in the face of the complex dynamics of local communities. The lack of definition in 589 had allowed the variety in local conciliar practice evident in the provincial councils of the following forty years. During those years tensions between the authority of episcopal consensus and local clerics, difficulties in gaining collaboration between local clerics and secular officials, episcopal resistence to royal interference, and the "negligence of the bishops in holding synods" had continued to obstruct the development of central authority over conciliar practice. Now, in 633, the Iberian episcopate sought to explicitly define, regulate, and thus control the actions and role of provincial councils—and of their individual participants—in local communities.

Despite canon 4's ritual emphasis on correct hierarchy, however, Toledo

---

105. The pivotal position assumed by written tradition in canon 4's prescribed presentation and reading of previous canons, and in its call for the presence of record-keeping notaries, is also apparent in most conciliar records of this era; references to the "decisions of previous fathers," presumably known through *codices canonum,* functioned as a formulaic opening for multitudes of canons on a wide variety of subjects. For early medieval depictions of lecterns, notaries, and codices as central props in conciliar gatherings, see the scene depicted in the Utrecht Psalter, Bibl. der Rijksuniv. 32, f. 90v. This illustration shows a *corona* of seated persons, in the middle of which are two lecterns holding open codices, two groups of scribes with inkpots and rolls, a standing individual holding and pointing to a parchment scroll, as well as another figure who appears to be being helped into his stole, or the *alba* worn by the deacon who was to read the canons on the celebration of councils. See Reynolds, "Rites and Signs," fig. 17, with description on 222–23. According to Reynolds, it is widely believed, but not certain, that the scene represents a conciliar gathering—despite the fact that the illustration appears in a psalter. The Utrecht Psalter was written about 820 and thus does not represent a contemporary source; however, as Reynolds points out, many of the details depicted do reflect elements prescribed in canon 4 and in later versions of the Visigothic *ordo de celebrando concilio.*

IV did not promote kingdom-wide ecclesiastic obedience to a preeminent prelate or diocese. In 633 the definition of ecclesiastical centralization remained fluid in the sense that the bishops envisioned central control as resting in the collective conciliar authority of the kingdom's episcopate, rather than in the bishop of a primatial see. While this general council, like the one in 589, was held in the royal city of Toledo, the location was linked to the king's agenda; the presiding bishop was the most prestigious prelate in the kingdom, Isidore.[106] Like the development of individual royal rituals, the primacy of the Toledan see emerged through the course of the seventh century, culminating in the granting of extraordinary powers to Julian of Toledo (and subsequent Toledan bishops) in 681.[107] While some historians trace the beginning of this process to a council purportedly held under the royal direction of Gundemar in 610,[108] it is clear that in 633 the church's center of intellectual authority lay in Seville.

With the backing of this authority, Isidore and his colleagues assumed the efficacy of their collective central control and so significantly expanded the role of provincial councils in the ordering of local community life. Simply in terms of the number of clerical cases directed to provincial councils, the breadth of competence and activity envisioned for these tribunals was significantly increased from earlier interpretations. Some of the canons against liturgical diversity carried the penalty of excommunication or loss of rank for erring or dissenting clerics.[109] Given the rule issued at Seville II calling for conciliar hearings when a cleric was to be deposed, one can assume that the forum intended for invoking these punishments was the provincial council. Additional cases were directed to provincial councils by the canons against clerical impurity. Many of the punishments for these also would have involved conciliar hearings.[110] The responsibilities now assigned to provincial councils also included the oversight of some episcopal elections as well as various details of diocesan financial arrangements, landholdings, and slaves.[111]

Isidore and his colleagues also changed the emphasis on the supervision of secular fiscal agents that had been the core of Toledo III's vision of the community role of bishops in councils.[112] Explicitly and with careful ceremonial

106. See José María Lacarra, "La Iglesia visigoda en el siglo VII y sus relaciones con Roma," *Settimane* 7, no. 1 (Spoleto, 1959), 376–77.

107. See Tol. XII, c. 6. Vives, 393–94; and concl., n. 22.

108. See chap. 4, n. 13.

109. E.g., Tol. IV, c. 15 provided for the excommunication of clerics who said "Glory to the Father" instead of "Glory and Honor to the Father" at the end of psalms; Tol. IV, c. 12 did the same for singing *laudes* before preaching rather than after. Vives, 196–98.

110. See, e.g., Toledo IV, c. 30, c. 32, c. 41, and c. 51. Vives, 203, 204, 206, and 208.

111. Tol. IV, c. 19, c. 33, c. 34, and c. 68. Vives, 199–200, 204, 205, and 214.

112. Tol. III, c. 18. See chap. 2, n. 95.

definition, canon 3 opened provincial councils to any layperson with a case against "bishops, judges, or powerful men, or against anyone else."[113] Secular offenders were to be compelled to attend by an agent of the king, the "royal executor,"[114] who was also responsible for returning to the rightful owners anything found to have been "wrongly seized."[115] Apparently, by expanding provincial conciliar jurisdiction, the bishops felt they had made day-to-day collaboration between "priests and judges" unnecessary. There is only one canon in the records that called for judges and priests to work together in policing the lay population—canon 65, which prohibited Jews and their descendants from holding public office.[116] Indeed, aside from the duties of the "royal executor," Toledo IV seems conscientiously to have avoided explicit mention of secular authorities imposing punishments; even the anti-Jewish canons that called for public beatings did not name the parties responsible for inflicting them.[117] Canon 43 reiterated the call made in 590 at Seville I for the removal of serving girls from clerics[118] but removed the responsibility for doing so from the judges designated by the previous council and placed it upon bishops instead.[119]

Perhaps learning from the difficulties with defining and enforcing local collaboration in the 590s, Isidore and his colleagues appear to have believed that the measures they took to ensure religious uniformity, clerical fidelity, and thus conciliar authority would also serve to prevent procedural abuse and enforce decisions in any Christian community—without councils and bishops becoming mired in the conflicting loyalties and networks of power associated with secular "judges."[120] By ensuring religious uniformity among the diverse communities of the kingdom and by making legally actionable any deviation

113. Tol. IV, c. 3: "causas adversus episcopos aut iudices vel potentes aut contra quoslibet alios." Vives, 189.

114. Tol. IV, c. 3: "regii executoris." Vives, 189. On the significance of this figure, see Cazier, *Isidore de Séville,* 232; and Orlandis, *La Iglesia,* 180. For local parallels to the royal executor in secular courts, see Thompson, *Goths,* 142.

115. Tol. IV, c. 3: "prave usurpata." Vives, 189.

116. See n. 46 of this chapter. Tol. IV did address the participation of bishops as judges in secular courts, a practice that was apparently widespread. Canon 31 (Vives, 203) limited the king's capacity for making these appointments to cases that did not involve capital punishment.

117. See n. 48 of this chapter.

118. See Seville I, c. 3. Vives, 153; and chap. 3, n. 32.

119. Tol. IV, c. 43. Vives, 207.

120. The "royal executor" (see n. 114) was obviously envisioned as further aiding in the enforcement of conciliar decisions against powerful laypeople. It is unclear what the position of such an official would have been within a local community or the nature of the actual power he might have wielded, other than his title and prescribed association with the bishops' collective authority. On the complex relationship between local dispute settlement and central secular authorities in early medieval Europe, see Chris Wickham et al., "Conclusion," in *The Settlement of Disputes in Early Medieval Europe,* ed. W. Davies and P. Fouracre (Cambridge, 1986), 228–40.

from the *mores* of church discipline, Toledo IV sought to use provincial councils to establish the social and religious consensus necessary for obedience to the authority of provincial conciliar dispute settlements, a consensus that had evidently been missing in the initial settlement of Martianus' case.

The Unanimous Voice of Christian Leadership

The subject communities of the Visigothic kingdom were at variance with one another in numerous areas of life. According to the testimony of Toledo IV, conflicts between people and communities often were manifested in accusations of religious deviance and in factions formed around local clerical leaders. The council responded to this situation by strictly defining the practices and appearances of genuine Christians. In the interests of combating contention between communities, Toledo IV imposed procedures for the identification, accusation, and punishment of those perceived as different. Thus, they provided the basis for making legally actionable the accusations of inauthentic Christian identity that were themselves seen as one reason that religious diversity was dangerous. Toledo IV attempted to create the religious uniformity thought to constitute consensus. In fact, however, the council institutionalized difference through the creation and enforcement of new legal avenues for religious contention.

Despite such contradictions, in 633 the Christian leaders of Iberia spoke with a unanimity that betrays no trace of the dialogue evident in the sources for the preceding forty-four years. The development of this unified voice does not signify that the dynamic tensions between differing ideals, governmental practices, and social circumstances had evaporated. The unanimity of this council probably arose largely as a response to the political instability that surrounded it. But it was also an expression of a shared ideological framework that since 589 had made Christian leadership and conciliar authority not only contingent upon but also necessary for the realization of an exclusive kingdom-wide Christian consensus. This framework had been reshaped over the years, as doctrinal differences between Goths and Hispano-Romans faded, as Visigothic kings suffered defeats and then achieved military ascendency, and as cultural regeneration made imaginable widespread clerical education and discipline as well as royal cultural leadership. Yet the fundamental structure of that framework—its basic premises, ideals, and reliance on traditional authority—had remained constant.

In response to the immediate crisis and the failures of the recent past, Isidore and his colleagues at the council built upon this basic framework. Their complex array of rules and procedures was designed to support a specific definition of the language, location, and exercise of holy authority in their kingdom and thus to overcome the paradox of conciliar judicial authority. Armed with the language and authority of Christian education and ancient precedents, carefully regulated church councils would create and maintain the universal acceptance of divine sanctions against any and all forms of dissent. In turn, absolute Christian consensus would constitute the consistent coercive power of enforcement that previously had been lacking in conciliar justice because of the unreliability of Visigothic royal authority and the various conflicting dynamics of local power structures. Episcopal consensus, conciliar ceremony, and the presence of the Holy Spirit were thus envisioned as the means to their own end; they were meant to be the central elements in establishing and maintaining the very unity that would ensure the enforcement of their own decisions. The circular nature of this program for gaining and maintaining God's favor left no room for the expression of difference or dialogue. Consequently, Toledo IV brought rigidity and permanence to the construction of ideal consensus in the Visigothic kingdom. At the same time, it left unresolved the contradictions that since 589 had militated against the realization of ideal consensus. Episcopal agreement still faced the interests of individual bishops. The centralizing aspirations of kings continued to confront the independent power of local leaders. And the immutable authority of conciliar precedent remained foreign to much of the daily experience of Iberian community life.

Conclusion

Throughout the rest of the seventh century Iberian leaders followed Toledo IV's principle that their kingdom's survival depended upon absolute Christian consensus among their subject communities. Until at least 694 general councils and secular legislation issued demands for consensus with mounting urgency. Councils and kings repeatedly called for mass oaths of allegiance[1] and king-dom-wide days of prayer for the expiation of sins.[2] Increasingly harsh measures against Jews and other perceived dissenters from Christian consensus—including heretics, idolaters, homosexuals, attempted suicides, and political criminals—were apparently meant to ensure the integrity of this kingdom-wide unanimity before God.[3] At the same time, the unanimous voice of Catholic leadership, speaking in the language of conciliar consensus, espoused ever higher levels of collaboration between *regnum* and *sacerdotium*.[4] After 633 general councils met more regularly, particularly at times of political crisis. While the general councils should not be interpreted as representative assemblies in any modern, or even medieval, sense,[5] the gathered bishops can

---

1. See, e.g., Tol. X, c. 2.Vives, 310. *LV*, 2.1.7, and *LV*, 2.5.19, 52 and 118–20.

2. See, e.g., Tol. V (636), c. 1; Tol. VI (638), c. 2; Tol. XVII (694), c. 6. Vives, 226–27, 236, and 532.

3. See, e.g., Tol. VI, c. 3 (against Jews); Tol. XII, c. 9 (against Jews); Tol. XVI, c. 1 (against Jews), c. 2 (against idolators), c. 3 (against "sodomites"), c. 4 (against suicides), c. 10 (against political criminals); Tol. XVII, c. 8 (against Jews). Vives, 236, 396–97, 407–501, 509–12, and 534–36. See also *LV*, 12.2–3 (numerous previous and new laws against heretics and, primarily, Jews, collected and promulgated by Recceswinth in 654, Erwig [680–687] in 681, and Egica [687–702] c. 693), 410–56.

4. For instance, a call for absolute religious uniformity issued at Toledo VI also served as a forceful statement of common accord among the kingdom's leaders. According to canon 3, the bishops acted "in harmony of heart and mouth" with the king (Chintila, 636–39) and with "consent from the deliberation of his *optimates* and illustrious men" (consonam cum eo corde et ore promulgamus Deo placituram sententiam, simul etiam cum suorum obtimatum inlustri-umque virorum consensu ex deliberatione). Vives, 236.

5. According to G. Martínez Díez ("Los concilios de Toledo," *Anales Toledanos* 3 [Toledo, 1971], 120) such a characterization was popular in the nineteenth century. See also Aloysius Ziegler, *Church and State in Visigothic Spain* (Washington, D.C., 1930), 36, quoting François Guizot, *Histoire de la civilisation en France* (Brussels, 1835), I, 326: "The Councils of Toledo were the national assemblies of the Spanish monarchy."

be seen as giving symbolic representation to the Christian consensus among all subjects deemed necessary for divine favor and political survival.

As general councils met more frequently, efforts to ensure uniform conciliar practice and to expand the scope of conciliar jurisdictions also continued. The second two recensions of the *Hispana* were compiled in 681 and 694,[6] and the fully developed *ordo de celebrando concilii*, based on Toledo IV's canon 4, is traditionally dated to 675.[7] By 694 conciliar jurisdictions included a wide array of very specific political crimes[8] as well as the protection of the royal family[9] and the ratification of political actions taken by the king, such as tax amnesties,[10] reversals of previous kings' decisions,[11] and the expulsion of freedmen from palatine offices.[12] For their part lawmaking kings during this period, like Reccared during the 590s, availed themselves of conciliar consensus to legitimate territorial legislation but now on a sweeping scale. In 654 Recceswinth promulgated a new, extensive law code designed to apply to all Visigothic subjects, Goth and Roman.[13] Apparently with the editorial help of Isidore's most famous student, Braulio of Saragossa,[14] Recceswinth made broad claims not only for his own position as head to the Visigothic body politic but also for the efficacy, jurisdiction, and divine inspiration of his lawmaking and kingship.[15] Recceswinth asked that the Iberian episcopate ratify

---

6. See intro., n. 51.

7. See chap. 5, n. 98.

8. The councils of the 680s and 690s were frequently concerned with political issues arising from rebellions. For instance, Tol. XVI (693), c. 9, specifically condemned Sisebert, the bishop of Toledo, who had led a conspiracy against the current king, Egica (687–702), and sentenced him to excommunication, dispossession, and exile. Vives, 507–9. Tol. XVI, c. 10, barred the sons of oath-breaking rebels from holding palatine offices and from suing for the return of their families' goods. Vives, 509–12.

9. See, e.g., Tol. XIII (683), c. 4; Tol. XVI, c. 8; and Tol. XVII (694), c. 7. Vives, 419–21, 505–7, and 533–34.

10. Tol. XIII, c. 3. Vives, 419.

11. Tol. XIII, c. 1. Vives, 415–16.

12. Tol. XIII, c. 6. Vives, 422–23.

13. P. D. King, *Law and Society in the Visigothic Kingdom* (Cambridge, 1972), 18–19, argues that Recceswinth's code was in fact merely a reedition of a code published by Chindaswinth. I follow the traditional view, which attributes the actual promulgation as an organized code to Recceswinth. See chap. 2, n. 70.

14. On Braulio's role in the promulgation of the code, see Charles H. Lynch, *Saint Braulio, Bishop of Saragossa (631–51): His Life and Writings* (Washington, D.C., 1938), 136–40. Braulio's participation is assumed from the content of a series of letters between he and the king prior to the bishop's death in 651. See Braulio of Saragossa, *Epistulae*, 38–41, in *Epistolario de S. Braulio de Zaragoza*, ed. José Madoz, (Madrid, 1941); English translation by Claude Barlow, in *Iberian Fathers*, vol. 2: *Braulio of Saragossa, Fructuosus of Braga*, The Fathers of the Church Series, vol. 63 (Washington, D.C., 1969).

15. See, e.g., *LV*, 1.2.2; 1.2.3; 1.2.5; and 1.2.6, 41–42. Some of these royal laws also renewed the call for judicial collaboration between local bishops and secular judges. See, e.g., *LV*, 2.1.24, 72–75.

his code at the Eighth Council of Toledo, as did another legislating king, Erwig (680–87), at the Twelfth Council of Toledo in 681.[16]

These lawmakers' claims for centralized royal power were bolstered by the development of a "royal liturgy."[17] Julian of Toledo, a prolific author and bishop of Toledo from 680 to 690, is particularly associated with renewed efforts at developing and publicizing principles of legitimate succession, including the ritual of royal unction.[18] The initial date of this ceremony's introduction is unknown, but its first recorded use is found in the description of the accession of Wamba (672–80) that Julian presented in a work known as the *Historia Wambae*.[19] By associating unction and legitimacy specifically with the city of Toledo, Julian also contributed to the lengthy process by which that city came to be recognized as not only the royal seat but also the ecclesiastic center of the kingdom.[20] Isidore and the bishops at Toledo IV had attached the notion of ecclesiastic centralization to the collective power of the kingdom's episcopate.[21] In 681 Julian and the bishops at Toledo XII enacted a canon that located preeminent power in the see of Toledo, the bishop of which would henceforth have the power to approve new bishops in "whatever province" of the kingdom.[22]

Thus, in the decades following Toledo IV the unified voice of *regnum* and

---

16. On apparent differences between Toledo VIII and Recceswinth over the content of his code, see E. A. Thompson, *The Goths in Spain* (Oxford, 1969), 202–4.

17. Roger Collins, "Julian of Toledo and the Royal Succession in Late Seventh-Century Spain," in *Early Medieval Kingship*, ed. P. H. Sawyer and Ian N. Wood (Leeds, 1977), 46. These included ceremonies for the departure and return of kings' military expeditions. *Liber Ordinum, Le liber ordinum en usage dans l'Église wisigothique et mozarabe d'Espagne*, ed. Marius Férotin, *Monumenta Ecclesiae Liturgica*, vol. 5 (Paris, 1904), 149–55.

18. Collins, "Julian of Toledo," 48. On Visigothic problems with royal succession, see chap. 1, n. 16; chap. 4, n. 9.

19. Julian of Toledo, *Historia Wambae Regis*, 2–4, ed. Wilhelm Levison, Corpus Christianorum, Series Latina, 115 (Turnhout, 1976), 219. The previous king, Recceswinth, had died outside of Toledo. Wamba was elected at his funeral but subsequently insisted on having the official coronation back in Toledo, apparently in order to quell any rumors that he had usurped the throne. It was during this ceremony that he was annointed by the bishop of Toledo, Quiricius. See Collins, "Julian of Toledo," 45–46. More generally on early medieval royal unction, see Janet Nelson, "Inauguration Rituals," *Early Medieval Kingship*. Julian's writings were extensive, and his participation in the four Toledan councils of the 680s has been widely celebrated. His *Life* was written by his successor Felix, in the 690s: *S. Juliani Toletani Episcopi Vita seu Elogium, PL*, 95, 445–52. On his life and works, see José Madoz, "San Julián de Toledo," *Estudios Eclesiásticos* 26 (1952). On his controversial role in Wamba's deposition and subsequent political events, see Frances X. Murphy, "Julian of Toledo and the Fall of the Visigothic Kingdom in Spain," *Speculum* 27 (1952). On his role in various religious controversies, see Frances X. Murphy, "Julian of Toledo and the Condemnation of Monothelitism in Spain," *Melanges de Joseph de Ghellinck*, vol. 1: *Antiquité* (Gembloux, 1951). On his works and their diffusion in the Medieval period, see Jocelyn N. Hillgarth, "St. Julian of Toledo in the Middle Ages," *Journal of the Warburg and Cortauld Institutes* 21 (1958).

20. See chap. 3, n. 105; and chap. 5, n. 107.

21. See chap. 5, n. 106.

22. Tol. XII, c. 6: "in quibuslibet provinciis." Vives, 394. The canon also recognized the king's power to select the episcopal candidates. See Thompson, *Goths*, 277.

sacerdotium, in its territorial lawmaking and centralized political claims, its broadening jurisdiction for conciliar legislation, and its harsh program for exclusive Christian consensus, began—at least on paper—to fulfill Reccared's vision of a centrally defined, kingdom-wide *mos canonicus* governing every aspect of "the ravings of human *mores*" throughout the kingdom.[23] These legislative demonstrations of unanimous leadership, the mass prayers and oaths designed to signify popular consensus, and the expanding use of procedures meant to identify and exclude deviants indicate the continuing development and attempted implementation of a governing ideology whose trajectory was delineated by the program of Toledo IV in 633. They do not, however, represent the successful establishment of Christian consensus in the kingdom's local communities.

The story of the elaboration of Visigothic visions of coercive consensus in the latter seventh century is as complex as the story of that vision's initial development. At first glance the measures against perceived deviants taken during this period seem more in keeping with the attitudes of church leaders in the later twelfth and thirteenth centuries than with those of leaders in other early medieval kingdoms.[24] Yet seventh-century Iberian Christian leaders, unlike their later medieval counterparts, failed to put their measures into practice. This failure was rooted in the ongoing tension between their own demands for uniformity and the local diversity that was common to the entire early medieval West. Indeed, the unusual levels of legalistic rigidity and repressive policy-making reached in the kingdom's final decades—most notably the attempted enslavement of the entire Jewish population in 694[25]—in many ways arose out of the typically early medieval contradiction between ideal and practical consensus with which this book has been concerned.

It is my hope that, by analyzing the genesis of the Visigothic interpretation of Christian consensus, this study has established the necessary context for understanding developments in the later kingdom as well as the influence of Visigothic visions on other areas and eras in western Europe. This book will conclude, therefore, with a preliminary gesture toward future analyses by briefly looking at various social obstacles that confronted Toledo IV's program for coercive consensus in the later seventh century.

Episcopal Dissensus

There is little datable, specific evidence for the reception of Toledo IV's program in local communities. This lack of evidence arises partly from the fact

---

23. See chap. 2, n. 49.

24. On parallel ideas in the later medieval period, see Robert I. Moore, *Formation of a Persecuting Society* (Oxford, 1987). On the general lack of such attitudes in the early medieval period, see 11–13 and 27–29.

25. Tol. XVII, c. 8. See n. 91 of this chapter.

that the core feature of that program, the yearly convocation of provincial councils, did not become established practice. The records of only five provincial councils survive from the period between 633 and 711.[26] While there may have been councils during these years for which records do not survive, there are indications that the Iberian episcopate generally did not heed repeated calls for yearly councils. The earliest such call in the kingdom, Toledo III's canon 18, had also directed each council to close by designating the time and place of the next year's council. Of the five provincial councils recorded after 633, only one, the Ninth Council of Toledo, held in 655, appears to have observed this rule; the call for the next year's meeting appears in the council's records, and a council did, in fact, meet in 656: the Tenth Council of Toledo, a general council. The failure of most provincial councils to record instructions for the next year's meeting may reflect the knowledge of an ongoing irregularity in provincial council convocation, on the part of either the councils' participants or the editors of the *Hispana*. It is certain that the episcopate of Cartaginiensis (Toledo's province) did not meet between 656 and 675, for the Eleventh Council of Toledo, a provincial council in 675, bemoaned the absence of any councils since 656 and once again called for yearly councils.[27] The metropolitans in this province, at least, obviously had knowledge of the rules for holding yearly councils and keeping signed records; Toledo was the see from which the two later-seventh-century recensions of the *Hispana* came, and it was also the source of the fully developed *ordo de celebrando concilii*. Yet after Toledo XI there are records for only one more provincial council held in Cartaginiensis. It is unlikely that this well-informed provincial episcopate would fail to record, and include in the *Hispana*, its own meetings. If the metropolitan bishops of Toledo, the inheritors of the Isidorian tradition, did not convene their provincial episcopates with any semblance of regularity, there is little reason to believe that metropolitans in less central provinces would have done so.

The extant records do contain some hints about continuing problems with conciliar justice on the local level. One such problem was the cooperation of kings. Four of the five provincial councils during the period were called at the behest of the current king,[28] and their language seems to indicate that royal permission was viewed as a necessity for convocation. One of these councils, held in Mérida in 666, called for bishops to attend yearly councils. At the same

26. Tol. IX (655), Tol. XI (675), and Tol. XIV (684), although included in the *Hispana's* numbered sequence of general Toledan councils were provincial in terms of their attendance and agendas. The other two provincial councils during this period were Mérida (666) and Braga III (675). Saragossa II (691), although held outside Toledo, appears to have been a general council. See José Orlandis and Domingo Ramos-Lissón, *Historia de los concilios de la España romana y visigoda* (Pamplona, 1986), 469.

27. Tol. XI, c. 15. Vives, 366.

28. Mérida, Toledo XI, Braga III, and Toledo XIV.

time, however, the council acknowledged that the metropolitan could not assign the time or place for councils "outside the royal will."[29] Toledo XI repeatedly expressed gratitude to the king at the time, Wamba, who with "fervent solicitude" had made it possible for "the renewed light of councils" to shine once again after the eighteen years that "the divine word" had been banished from the province under the previous king, Recceswinth.[30] Obviously, an unwilling king could pose a formidable obstacle to regular councils.

There is also evidence that provincial bishops themselves resisted attending councils.[31] In fact, the acknowledged necessity of royal involvement in councils may reflect episcopal unwillingness to gather unless compelled by a royal order. Two of the five provincial councils included sentences of excommunication for bishops who failed to attend councils;[32] one of them also provided for excommunicating the entire provincial episcopate if a year passed in which no council met.[33] It would seem that many bishops during this period had good reason to avoid tribunals of their peers. If the canons of these councils are any indication, Toledo IV's provisions for episcopal probity and orderly conciliar procedures were ineffectual. Apparently, bishops were involved in all sorts of heinous activity.

For instance, one council issued a canon providing for the punishment of bishops who "defiled" the wives, daughters, and nephews of the kingdom's magnates or killed or maimed palatine officials.[34] Another ruled against bishops who substituted milk for wine at communion, ate and drank out of holy vessels, and lived unsupervised with women.[35] The "haughtiness" of some bishops in Galicia seems to have reached the point that at processions for martyrs they draped the relics around their own necks and had themselves carried through the streets on litters "as if they themselves were the arc of the relics."[36] Bishops were fathering children,[37] beating their underlings as if they were "bandits,"[38] accepting bribes for ordination,[39] charging money for bap-

---

29. Mérida, c. 7: "non extra regiam . . . volumtatem." Vives, 330. Tol. XI, c. 15 also mentions that "princely power" (principis potestate) could impede the celebration of a council. Vives, 367.

30. Tol. XI, preamble: "cuius fervidae sollicitudinis voto et lux conciliorum renovata resplenduit"; "sermo divinus." Vives, 344–45.

31. On attendance at councils throughout the seventh century, see Thompson, *Goths,* 284–87.

32. Mérida, c. 7 and Tol. XI, c. 15. Vives, 330, 366.

33. Tol. XI, c. 15. Vives, 366.

34. Tol. XI, c. 5: "faedaverit." Vives, 359.

35. Braga III, c. 1, 2, and 4. Vives, 372–75.

36. Braga III, c. 5: "praesumtio . . . quasi ipsi sint reliquiarum arca." Vives, 376.

37. Tol. IX, c. 10. Vives, 303.

38. Braga III, c. 6: "personae latrocinantium." Vives, 377.

39. Braga III, c. 7 and Tol. XI, c. 8. Vives, 377, 361.

tismal chrism,[40] stealing goods donated to their churches,[41] allowing monasteries and parochial churches to fall into ruin,[42] and plundering the estates of fellow bishops after they had died.[43] Bishops involved in such activities would be unlikely to put themselves voluntarily before the judgment of the Holy Spirit. Nor would such proud and autocratic bishops be likely to contribute willingly to a collective source of authority that might conflict with their own interests.

Toledo IV had taught that corruption among bishops threatened the administration of ecclesiastic justice. Bishops who undermined their own holy authority through the "suspicion of evil or the actual deed"[44] could besmirch the authority of the episcopal consensus in which they took part. Furthermore, councils themselves had to proceed in an orderly, harmonious way in order to convey the principle of common accord among the bishops present. It appears from the later evidence that not only were many bishops involved in widespread "actual deeds" of evil, but the power struggles and infighting between them made it difficult to achieve harmony and justice at church councils.

The bishops who finally heard Martianus' appeal in full and returned him to his see in 638 recognized the continuing dangers of the abuse of conciliar procedure by power seekers like Aventius. Their decision to reinstate Martianus to his see began by acknowledging the fact that

> wicked men often shatter the lives of the innocent through dishonesty when, under the guise of justice, they diabolically stain local churches with iniquitous slander. Since envy always emulates virtue, such men use false criminal accusations to harm those whom they cannot ruin through overt actions.[45]

These bishops also seem to have recognized the danger of punishing such wicked men once their diabolical plots came to light. In punishing Aventius, they equivocated in much the same way that the bishops at Toledo IV had in dealing with Martianus. Although they removed Aventius from his see, they declined to strip him of his rank, sentencing him instead to penitence while

---

40. Mérida, c. 9 and Tol. XI, c. 8. Vives, 332, 361.
41. Tol. IX, c. 1. Vives, 354–55.
42. Tol. IX, c. 2. Vives, 355–56.
43. Tol. IX, c. 9. Vives, 302.
44. See chap. 5, n. 79.
45. *Exemplar*, A.1: "saepe improbitatibus malorum quatitur vita innocentium, et interserit se sub colore justitiae iniquitas fallaciae quum diabolicis infligitur macula in ecclesiis, quoniam semper aemula virtutibus invidia illum vulnerat mendacio criminis, quem nequit perimere opere actionis," 615.

threatening anyone protesting their decision with excommunication and
tion from clerical office.

Apparently, the contradictions involved in assuring individual clerical
probity and community consensus while avoiding the scandal arising from
punishing offenders already in office could neither be covered up nor legislated
away. Moreover, Toledo IV had created numerous new crimes for which clerics could be deposed. The council's criminalization of deviations in liturgy and
clerical *mores* provided abundant opportunities for accusations, whether false
or genuine. It is difficult to imagine what might have happened in provincial
councils if all these infractions had in fact become the subjects of conciliar
adjudication. Ambitious men like Aventius probably would have found such
opportunities irresistible, making it particularly dangerous to provide them
with official avenues for pursuing local episcopal power.

Episcopal harmony was further compromised by personal enmity between
bishops. According to Toledo XI, "certain bishops" in the province had
"boiled over in such a great discord of obstinacy" that "Christ, the sun of justice, had set in their hearts":[46] they refused to resolve quarrels and reconcile
with episcopal brothers.[47] The same council eloquently described what might
happen when such obstreperous feuders gathered in councils. In its first canon
Toledo XI acted against the "tumult" that would compromise the justice of
conciliar decisions. Councils, the bishops said, "should not be rattled by any
indiscrete voices, nor disturbed by any tumult, nor moved by any vain stories
or laughter, and what is worse, no tumultuous voices should pour forth in
obstinate controversies."[48] Justice would be lost if such activities disrupted "the
silence of the tribunal."[49] Therefore, the bishops themselves, or anyone bringing a case before them, should speak in a "very gentle" manner, "so that they
do not disturb the hearers with contentious voices nor weaken the vigor of the
judges with tumult."[50] Anyone who violated this order was to be thrown out of
the council "with all dishonor and confusion" and excommunicated for three
days.[51] Apparently, a provincial church council could be a volatile event.

---

46. Tol. XI, c. 4; "quorundam sacerdotum personae in tantum obstinationis effervuisse
discordiam . . . in quorum cordibus iam sol iustitiae Christus occubuit." Vives, 357.

47. These grudge holders were to be excommunicated until they reconciled with their
enemy and were sentenced to penitence for double the time that they had "served discord"
(servierunt discordiae). Vives, 358.

48. Tol. XI, c. 1: "nullis debent aut indiscretis vocibus praestrepi aut quibuslibet tumulti-
bus proturbari, nullis etiam vanis fabulis vel risibus agi, et quod deterius obstinatis concerta-
tionibus tumultuosas voces effundere." Vives, 354–55.

49. Tol. XI, c. 1: "silentia iudicii." Vives, 355.

50. Tol. XI, c. 1: "mitissima . . . ut nec contentiosis vocibus audientiam turbent, nec iudi-
cantium vigorem de tumultu enervent." Vives, 355.

51. Tol. XI, c. 1: "cum omnis confusiones dedecore abstractus." Vives, 355.

According to the canons of Toledo XI, some bishops intentionally avoided the pitfalls and conflicts of interest involved in relying on the authority of episcopal consensus to settle disputes in their communities. Instead, they inappropriately decided cases on their own authority. The council issued a canon that condemned the "excess of dishonest emotion" displayed by these men and chastised them for undermining the authority of the very tribunals they ought to support.[52] Rushing to judgment could turn a bishop into "a nursery for strife and plunder" because he might render harmful and corrupt decisions.[53] The council accused any prelate who had done so with illegal behavior, sentenced him to penitence, and ordered him to make restitution "according to the laws of the most excellent prince" for any damage he had inflicted.[54] Bishops also might assert their individual judicial authority by inflicting "judgments of blood" for capital crimes that members of their own households committed.[55] Both Toledo XI and the council in Mérida enacted canons against this form of episcopal rage.[56] Bishops also used their office to make judgments by secretly imposing harsh penitential discipline. Bemoaning the use of "severity," "threats," and "power" against those who should be corrected by "benevolence," "love," and "exhortation," Toledo XI prohibited such secret judgments and called for bishops to use either public discipline or witnesses when imposing penitence.[57]

Toledo IV's careful prescriptions for ensuring the reputations of bishops and the power of their collective will had not resolved the contradictions between conciliar authority and the local interests of individual prelates. In order for church councils to establish and maintain the holy authority that would make their decisions enforceable, local communities had to accept their individual bishops as suitable conduits for divine judgment as it passed from the Holy Spirit through the provincial council and into their own lives. It would not be surprising if communities questioned the presence of the Holy Spirit at these gatherings of contentious, ambitious, morally suspect, and noisy bishops. Nor would it be surprising if local bishops, faced with the compro-

---

52. Tol. XI, c. 5: "excessibus motionum." Vives, 358.

53. Tol. XI, c. 5: "seminarium litis atque rapinae." Vives, 358.

54. Tol. XI, c. 5: "iuxta leges excellentissimi principis sarciant." Vives, 359. This sentence applied as long as such restitution came out of the bishop's own property and not his church's.

55. Tol. XI, c. 6: "iudicium sanguinis." Vives, 360.

56. Mérida, c. 15. Vives, 335–36.

57. Tol. XI, c. 7: "plus erga corrigendos agere debeat benivolentia quam severitas, plus cohortatio quam conmotio, plus caritas quam potestas." Vives, 360. The problems attributed here to private penance constitute a mirror image of those addressed in 589 by Tol. III, c. 11, which prohibited laypeople's abuse of private penance as a means to commit sins with impunity, demanding reconciliation repeatedly. See chap. 3, n. 54.

mised holy authority of councils, were more concerned with their personal power and local relationships than with enforcing the directives of distant authorities, whether conciliar or otherwise.

Local Scandals

Without a practical consensus on the divine authority of conciliar decisions, there was little hope for establishing systems of day-to-day cooperation between clerical and secular authorities. The dynamics of local communities themselves remained fraught with sources of dissension. While assertions of ruling unanimity were repeated through these years, collaboration seems to have remained as elusive as it had been in the decade after Toledo III. In addition to undermining conciliar authority through individual judgments, local bishops apparently were also transgressing the jurisdictions of secular authorities by their involvement in capital cases. The council in Mérida not only chastised bishops who inflicted capital punishment on household members but also ordered bishops to turn such cases over to the "judge of the city."[58] Toledo XI also called upon secular authorities to deal with church slaves and clerics who, accused of capital crimes, had been inappropriately judged by their bishops.[59]

Most disastrously, clerical and secular authorities were not cooperating in maintaining fidelity and mutual defense among the subjects of the kings. In 673 the current monarch, Wamba, promulgated a law designed to abolish an evil custom: his subjects' inopportune habit of draft evasion.[60] According to the king, the inhabitants of the kingdom's border provinces tended to disappear whenever a foreign enemy invaded. Without exemption for rank or ecclesiastic office, Wamba imposed harsh punishments on all subjects who did not provide mutual defense in the face of foreign invasion. The language of this law indicates that Wamba shared the by now traditional assumption that unanimous concord among his subjects would ensure the stability of the kingdom. His assertion of this principle was aimed primarily at those who failed to defend against invasions. His law also applied, however, to the more amorphous crime of "scandal." It demanded that individual subjects come to the aid of any target of an "arising scandal" as soon as the crime became known

---

58. Mérida, c. 15: "iudice civitatis." Vives, 335.

59. Tol. XI, c. 5. Vives, 359–60. Clerics who murdered or maimed palatine officials, nobles, or women and children were condemned to suffer either secular provisions for retaliation or be made slaves to those they had injured.

60. *LV*, 9.2.8, 370–73.

in that citizen's particular locality,[61] whether it was announced by a cleric, an agent of the secular government, or anyone else. Anyone who failed to respond would suffer exile and the loss of their property, whether they were bishops, lower clerics, palatine officials, or persons of any other rank.

For Wamba, like the bishops at Toledo IV, scandal arose in specific localities[62] but provided a seed bed for infidelity that could threaten the entire kingdom. Wamba's vision of defense against scandal centered around collaboration among local leaders: bishops, priests, dukes, counts, etc.,[63] who would ensure the "speedy allegiance" of each subject in the neighborhood.[64] Indeed, this community-based response was so important that subjects who were physically incapable of coming to the rescue were ordered to render any other power or influence available in the aid of their local bishops or clerics and "on behalf of the royal dignity, the interests of their fellow citizens, and of their country."[65] The law's universality in application was mirrored in its language of consensus, which built to a closing exhortation that described legally enforced common accord as a central element in the kingdom's stability. The king had promulgated the law so that its "severe censure" might abolish "the vice that has evilly come down from past times to our own, . . . and unanimous concord may establish the peace of the people, and the defense of the fatherland."[66]

While clerics and secular leaders could not be depended on to cooperate in encouraging unanimous defense and suppressing scandal without the threat of drastic penalties, neither could they be relied on to refrain from joining together in rebellion. Wamba, for instance, had good reason to fear locally based scandal and infidelity. Shortly after his accession in 672, the king faced a violent and widespread rebellion in Narbonensis, which involved some of the highest palatine officials and military leaders as well as a number of bishops.

According to Julian of Toledo's *Historia Wambae,* Wamba was chosen as king in a sudden, divinely inspired consensus among all those present at the funeral of the previous king, Recceswinth, in 672.[67] When the rebellion in Narbonensis erupted almost immediately, Wamba sent a general by the name of

61. *LV,* 9.2.8: "exortum scandalum," 373.

62. *LV,* 9.2.8: "in vicinis locis," 372.

63. *LV,* 9.2.8: "sacerdotes, clerici, duces, comites, thiufadi, vicarii," 372.

64. *LV,* 9.2.8: "citata devotione," 373.

65. *LV,* 9.2.8: "pro utilitate regie potestatis, gentis et patrie fideliter laborantium dirigebunt," 373.

66. *LV,* 9.2.8.: "ut vitium, quod ex preteritis temporibus male usque hactenus inoleverat, et severe legis huius censura redarguat, et concors adque unanimis adsensio quietem plebium et patrie defensionem adquirat," 373.

67. *Historia Wambae,* 2–4, 219.

Paul against the "perfidious" Gauls.[68] This *dux* quickly turned against the king and took over the leadership of the rebellion. He then had himself crowned and anointed in Narbonne as what he called "the eastern king," opposed to Wamba, whom he addressed in a threatening letter as "the southern king."[69] Wamba gathered a new army and set off, according to Julian, accompanied by a guard of angels flying above. Needless to say, Julian's king was completely victorious. Paul and his fellow rebels were put on trial before the king, the elders of the palace, the palatine officials, and the whole army.[70]

In this instance bishops and secular leaders in Narbonensis had collaborated to the point of swearing oaths of loyalty to a usurper. According to Julian, they had sworn to "fight against our glorious lord King Wamba and [to] contend in his overthrow to the point of shedding blood."[71] At the rebels' trial these oaths, along with the oaths that the rebels had originally sworn (and signed) to Wamba at the time of his coronation, were brought before the prisoners, who were utterly confounded by the evidence of their own perfidy. Having broken faith with God by breaking their sacred oaths, the rebels had gone against one of the most fundamental principles of governance in their kingdom. They were convicted by a reading of the sentence of anathema against such perjurers from Toledo IV's canon 75, along with a reading of Chindaswinth's anti-treason law, which had been the cause of so much debate at Toledo VIII.[72] This combination of ecclesiastic and secular law made the outcome of the trial obvious to the gathered officials:

> Instructed by the precept of this sacred canon it was not to be doubted further by us that we should fear those men according to the sentence of this law and to punish with severe judgment in body and in temporal things those whom the fathers already had damned in spirit by perpetual anathema with so terrible a judgment.[73]

---

68. *Historia Wambae,* 5: "Galliarum terra, altrix perfidiae," 221. Julian devoted numerous pages of invective against the people of the Gallic province in his *Insultatio Vilis Storici in Tyrannidem Galliae,* ed. Wilhelm Levison, Corpus Christianorum, Series Latina 115:1 (Turnhout, 1976).

69. Preserved as the "Epistola Pauli perfidi, qui tyrannice rebellionem in Gallias fecit Wambani principis magni." Levison, 217.

70. This procedure is described in a document known as the *Iudicium in tyrannorum perfidia promulgatum,* ed. Wilhelm Levison, in Corpus Christianorum, Series Latina 115:1 (Turnhout, 1976).

71. *Iudicium* 6: "contra gloriosum domnum nostrom Wambanem regem pugnarent atque in deiectionem eius vel periculum usque ad effusionen sanguinis dimicarent," 254.

72. See intro., n. 1.

73. *Iudicium,* 7: "Cuius sacri canonis praeceptione instructi, non ultra nobis est dubitandum, ut illos paueamus iuxta legis huius sententiam et in corpore et in rebus temporali puniri censura, quos iam patres illi perpetuo anathemate tam terribili iudicio damnauerunt in anima," 255.

The officials then left the question of sentencing to Wamba, with the proviso that all of the rebels' worldly possessions should be given to the king, so that "his power would remain undoubted, and so that the name of the seditious should disappear entirely from the land and future ages should avoid imitating their mournful memory."[74]

Despite the invocation of Toledo IV and despite Wamba's draft law, which was probably promulgated after Paul's rebellion, this was not to happen. No matter how many times Wamba, or other kings, reiterated the concepts put forth in 633, the fact remained that those concepts had been developed in a conscious effort to deny the conditions that made them futile and illusory. Local leaders continued to respond to loyalties and relationships of power that worked against the repeated invocations of consensus, divine sanctions, and centralized control.[75] Diversity, difference, and dissension, like the "mournful memory" and imitation of sedition, never did disappear from the Visigothic kingdom.

Royal Mercy and Divine Judgment

In 654 the bishops and nobles at Toledo VIII had received the decision of the Holy Spirit on a fundamental contradiction in their legal and political system between the divine sanctions of oaths and the peacemaking powers of royal mercy. This contradiction had been inscribed into ecclesiastic law by Toledo IV's canon 75, which had sought to support political stability by calling upon the subjects of the Visigothic kings to honor oaths. Chindaswinth had responded to the continuing failure to honor divine sanctions against oath breakers by insisting on the death penalty against rebels.[76] In doing so, he contravened Toledo IV's explicit instructions that kings should exhibit mercy by refraining from such sentences.[77] Recceswinth and the bishops at Toledo VIII had sought to reestablish elite consensus by resolving the contradiction and making mercy possible. Their compromise ultimately proved as inadequate as Toledo IV's formula, as did Wamba's law calling for collaboration and mutual defense nineteen years later.

Apparently, Wamba's law sent local judicial procedures into turmoil. As a result of violating the law's call for mutual defense against invasion and

---

74. *Iudicium* 7: "potestas illi indubitata permaneat, ut seditiosorum nomen funditus a terra dispereat et lugubrem eorum memoriam . . . sequutura saecula imitari refugiant," 255.

75. For a discussion of the economic problems, social conflicts, and political developments during this period, see Luis A. García Moreno, *El fin del reino Visigodo de Toledo* (Madrid, 1975), 103–212.

76. See intro., n. 1.

77. See chap. 5, n. 32.

internal scandal, numerous nobles had lost their status and thus their right
testify. In 681 Toledo XII returned the rights of noble rank to these men.[78]
Wamba's insistence that individual culpability for local contention and a
shared responsibility for mutual defense would create the consensus necessary
for political survival had caused widespread disruption in local relationships
of power. It may also have contributed to the new round of political turmoil
that cost Wamba his throne.

Wamba was deposed in 680. A group of disgruntled nobles may have conspired in an innovative deployment of divine authority to achieve his removal.
In so doing, they apparently received if not actual support at least legitimation
from the highest levels of church leadership. Although the presence of a conspiracy is not certain, the sequence of events offers room for suspicion. The
king fell ill and lapsed into unconsciousness. His retainers summoned Julian,
whom Wamba had appointed bishop of Toledo only months before.[79] The
bishop placed the unconscious king under penance, as was the practice with
dying Christians at the time. Wamba was tonsured and dressed in a habit,
making him ineligible to serve any longer as king. When the king awoke and
in fact did not die, he was convinced by those around him to sign documents
that testified to his acceptance of penance and selected one of the nobles present, Erwig, to be consecrated as his successor. The penitent king then retired
to a monastery.

These events were recorded in detail at Toledo XII, which Erwig called
only three months after his coronation.[80] There the new king brought forth the
documents Wamba had signed, and the bishops described their contents in the
text of their first canon. Once the written evidence had been recorded and
approved, the canon went on to proclaim that "before all time, in the hidden
judgments of God," Erwig had been "predestined to rule" and should now "be
considered consecrated by the common decisions of all the bishops."[81] They
went on to absolve the population from their oaths of allegiance to Wamba and
called for "a grateful and obliging obedience" toward Erwig, whom Wamba
and God had chosen and "whom the love of the whole people [had] sought
out."[82] The canon closed by imposing "the sentence of anathema" on anyone
who from then on might plot against or injure the new king.[83]

---

78. Tol. XII, c. 7. Vives, 393–94.

79. Madoz, "San Julián," 41.

80. Tol. XII, c. 1. Vives, 386–87. See also Murphy, "Julian of Toledo and the Fall," 2.

81. Tol. XII, c. 1: "qui ante tempora in occultis Dei iudiciis praescitus est regnaturus,
nunc manifesto in tempore generaliter omnium sacerdotum habeatur definitionibus consecra-
tus." Vives, 387.

82. Tol. XII, c. 1: "quem et divinum iudicium in regno praeelegit et decessor princeps suc-
cessurum sibi instituit, et quod superest quem totius populi amabilitas exquisivit." Vives, 387.

83. Tol. XII, c. 1: "anathematis sententia." Vives, 387.

The careful recording of the written evidence, as well as the repeated assertion of Erwig's divine election, suggest that this unorthodox succession was considered suspect by contemporaries. Ninth-century Spanish sources state that Erwig poisoned Wamba.[84] Whether this is so, or merely represents a continuing legend based in suspicions at the time,[85] there were precedents in secular law for waiving the canonical prohibition on tonsured monarchs.[86] Erwig and the bishops at Toledo XII chose not to exercise the flexibility of canonical tradition in this manner. Rather, the bishops enacted a second canon aimed specifically against those who had received the tonsure while unconscious and who then

> [made] vain pretexts and execrable arguments as to how they might remove from themselves the venerable sign of the tonsure and throw away the habit of religion, most impudently asserting that they are therefore held by no rule of ecclesiastic discipline under oath because they neither themselves requested penitence nor consciously received it.[87]

Receiving penitence while unconscious, according to the canon, was no different than the baptism of infants, who received "the sacrament of baptism without being able to ask for it by any sense and with no capacity for discernment."[88] The bishops made it clear that they were not enacting the canon in order to "let loose bishops so they may dare to travel all over freely giving the gift of penitence to those not seeking it," but, on the other hand, they did intend that the canon should "bind those who in whatever way have received penitence so that they may not return again to the military girdle."[89]

Wamba had been the subject of joyous consensus and episcopal approval

---

84. They are the *Epitome Ovietense*, MGH, *Chronica Minora* 2, 370–75; and the *Chronique d'Alphonse III*, in *Chroniques Asturiennes (fin IXe siècle)*, ed. Yves Bonnaz, (Paris, 1987). The two chronicles are discussed by Murphy, "Julian of Toledo and the Fall," who rejects the poisoning story and thus any culpability on Julian's part. Other scholars are not so generous as far as Erwig is concerned. See, e.g., Thompson, *Goths*, 230 n. 1.

85. Murphy, "Julian of Toledo and the Fall," 19.

86. A law of Chindaswinth's from the 640s, *LV*, 3.5.3, 161–63, allowed an exemption from the bonds of penitence to any persons who took them up without knowing what they were doing. On this episode, see Ziegler, *Church and State*, 114–18, and n. 70, in which he gives a list of conciliar precedents for the prohibition on Wamba's return to the throne.

87. Tol. XII, c. 2: "agunt cautionibus vanis et oppositionibus execrandis qualiter a se tonsurae venerabile signum expellant atque habitum religionis abiciant, inpudentissime adserente ideo se nullis regulis ecclesiasticae disciplinae sub hoc voto teneri, quia poenitentiam nec ipsi petierint nec sentientes acceperint." Vives, 388.

88. Tol. XII, c. 2: "babtismi accipiat sacramentum, nullo sensu, nulla etiam discretionis industria id adpetere possunt." Vives, 388.

89. Tol. XII, c. 2: "nec enim ista instituentes sacerdotes quosque ut passim et licenter donum poenitentiae non petentibus audeant prorogare, absolvimus, sed hos qui qualibet sorte poenitentiam susceperint ne ulterius ad militare cinculum redeant religamus." Vives, 388.

only eight years before. He had enjoyed the favor of God and his angels in his war with Paul. In punishing the rebels, he had utilized, in conjunction with the power of secular law, Toledo IV's demands for uniform sworn obedience. He had called forth that council's ideology in his own lawmaking against the seed beds of scandal. Now, in 681, he suffered the consequences of the practical contradictions underlying such abstract governmental tools as consensus, oaths of allegiance, and conciliar authority. The unified voice of Christian leadership absolved the population of its responsibility for consensual support of one king and called upon its own unanimity, expressed through the divinely sanctioned power of conciliar consensus and tradition, to legitimize another.

The Failure of Christian Consensus

These continuing but ineffective manipulations of mechanisms for elite consensus provide perhaps the most dramatic evidence for the failure of Toledo IV's program. Efforts by Toledo IV, by Chindaswinth, by Toledo VIII, and by Wamba to invoke the divine authority of Christian consensus as the means to enforce loyalty among nobles and bishops ultimately contributed to disunity and political instability. The failure of Christian elites to accept the divine sanctions supporting oaths and church councils does not necessarily reflect the absence of such a consensus in local communities. Still, these leaders' repeated demands for public displays of unanimous obedience illustrate a continuing absence of practical Catholic consensus among the ordinary subjects in the kingdom as well.

For instance, beginning in 637, the Jews of Toledo (and presumably other cities in the kingdom) were forced to make public oaths (*placiti*) swearing to their renunciation of Judaism. These were rendered into formulas and in 654 and 681 were inserted into the Visigothic legal code.[90] The lengthy series of anti-Jewish measures taken by kings and councils after Toledo IV reached hysterical proportions during the 680s and 690s, culminating in the call for enslaving the Jews in 694, which was predicated on rumors of an international Jewish conspiracy against Christians in general and against the Visigothic throne in particular.[91] Similarly, the mass loyalty oaths first mentioned in Toledo IV's

---

90. The text of the *placitum* of 637 can be found in Felix Dahn, *Die Könige der Germanen*, vol. 6 (Leipzig, 1885), 650–53; it is translated in James Parkes, *The Conflict of the Church and the Synagogue: A Study in the Origins of Antisemitism* (London, 1934), 394–97. The formulas of 654 and 681 appear in the law code as *LV*, 12.2.17 and 12.3.14–15, 425–26, and 442–46. The futility of these oaths is again testified to by the fact that the formula of 654 begins with an admission that the oaths sworn in 637 had been systematically violated.

91. Tol. XVII, *tomus* and c. 8. Vives, 522–24 and 534–36. For analyses of this council's anti-Jewish acts, see Soloman Katz, *The Jews in the Visigothic and Frankish Kingdoms of Spain and Gaul* (Cambridge, 1937), 20–21 and 116–17; Thompson, *Goths*, 247–48; Orlandis, *Historia de los concilios*, 497–99 and 502–5.

canon 75 were apparently demanded on an ongoing basis at least until 694, when Toledo XVII bewailed the fact that the "habit of erring has greatly extended, as has the transgression of oath-taking."[92] A tendency to ignore the divine sanctions of oaths was apparently not limited to the kingdom's nobility; in response to the "habit of erring," the bishops called for all the kingdom's subjects to participate in mass prayers on a monthly, rather than yearly basis,

> through all the provinces of Spain and Gaul, on behalf of the condition of the church of God, the safety of our prince, the salvation of the people, the indulgence of all sins and the expulsion of the devil from the hearts of all the faithful.[93]

The futility of these oaths and prayers is obvious. Not only did ordinary people join in rebellions until 711, but Jewish communities continued in Iberia long after the fall of the Visigoths. The repetition of secular and conciliar laws demanding obedience and conformity indicates an ongoing failure in the mechanisms of enforcement. It is clear that Toledo IV's centralized directions for liturgical uniformity, clerical purity, and provincial councils had not established a lasting Christian consensus on the divine sanctions against oath breaking, infidelity, and inauthentic Christian identity.

Modern scholars have sought the causes of the fall of the Visigothic kingdom in a multitude of social, political, economic, and cultural factors, such as noble factionalism, regional disunity, economic crisis, moral decay, ideological stagnation, the actions of individual kings and councils, and a general tendency toward self-destruction.[94] It is not the purpose of this study to contribute a new and ultimately unprovable theory of causation to this debate. Rather, this book has been intended as a contribution to an understanding of the interweaving of ancient ideals, Christian authority, and local diversity in the conflictual and contradictory communities of the early medieval West. In the Visigothic kingdom Christian leaders failed to maintain an ongoing practical consensus among themselves on the location of divine authority and the mechanisms of divine judgment. Despite their own struggles and manipulations, however, in 633, at the Fourth Council of Toledo, they did achieve

---

92. Tol. XVII, c. 6: "multa inolevit oberrandi consuetudo et iusiurandi transgressio." Vives, 532.

93. Tol. XVII, c. 6: "decernimus ut deinceps per totum annum in cunctis duodecim mensibus per universas Spaniae et Galliarum provincias pro statu ecclesiae Dei, pro incolomitate principis nostri atque salvatione populi et indulgentia totius peccati et a cunctorum fidelium cordibus expulsione diaboli." Vives, 532.

94. For a discussion of various explanations offered by historians from 754 to 1972, see García Moreno, *El fin del reino*, 19–45. See also Roger Collins, *The Arab Conquest of Spain* (Oxford, 1989), 6–22.

agreement on the rhetorical and ceremonial framework for their visions of ideal consensus. During the remaining years of the kingdom this framework enabled them to continue to institute practices designed to enforce loyalty, obedience, and Christian consensus from the subject communities they sought to control. The rigidity of their visions, the notion that consensus could be both coerced and coercive, and the absence of workable mechanisms for translating ideal into practical consensus may have made it impossible for local leaders and their communities to develop and maintain other avenues for maintaining social and political cohesion. This, in turn, may have contributed to the inability of those leaders to maintain their control in 711. What is certain is that the leaders of the Visigothic kingdom never found their way out of the paradoxical nature of conciliar authority nor found an avenue for the exercise of divine judgment that would adequately command the obedience of their subjects.

The compiled records of the Visigothic church councils were widely and enthusiastically received in western Europe in the centuries following the fall of the Visigothic monarchy.[95] So too were the works of the leading lights of the Isidorian Renaissance, especially, of course, Isidore himself.[96] The circumstances of dissension and diversity in Iberia were also replicated in most of western Europe during this period. Toledo IV's analysis of scandal and contention, as well as its program for coercive consensus, must have had important, and possibly adaptable, meanings for ruling parties in many areas of late antique and early medieval Europe. The process through which that analysis and program were developed over the years from 589 to 633—the interplay between culture, ideals, practices, and communities—illuminates not only the continuing life of the Visigothic vision in Iberia during the latter seventh century but also the construction of other early medieval versions of Christian consensus.

---

95. According to Martínez Díez, "Nota sobre la colección 'Hispana'," in Vives, xiii, the *Hispana* experienced a wide diffusion and influence outside Spain from the end of the eighth century: "Las dos colecciones principales de la reforma carolingia, la Hispana y la Hadriana, por necesidad y uso práctico se fundieron en una sola, . . . la principal colección canónica de la primera mitad del siglo IX y cuyo influjo en la Iglesia perdurará hasta la reforma gregoriana." The Gallic form of the *Hispana* was used by "los grandes falsificadores" of the ninth century (most notably the compiler of the Pseudoisidorian Decretals) who "continueron la Hispana transcribiéndose y divulgándose por todo el Sacro Imperio Romano Germánico."

96. On the diffusion of Isidore's works throughout western Europe during the following centuries, see the bibliography in Jocelyn N. Hillgarth, "The Position of Isidorian Studies: A Critical Review of the Literature, 1936–1975," *Studi Medievali*, ser. 3, 24 (Spoleto, 1983), reprinted in *Visigothic Spain, Byzantium and the Irish* (London, 1985), 883–96; Hillgarth, "Isidorian Studies, 1976–1985," *Studi Medievali*, ser. 3, 31, no. 2 (Spoleto, 1990), 963–73; and Jacques Fontaine, "Mozarabie hispanique et monde carolingien; les échanges culturels entre la France et l'Espagne du VIIe au Xe siècle," *Anuario de Estudios Medievales* 13 (1983).

References

Primary Sources

Bede. *Historia Ecclesiastica gentis Anglorum.* Edited and translated by B. Colgrave and R. A. B. Mynors. *Bede: Ecclesiastical History of the English People.* Oxford, 1969.

Braulio of Saragossa. *Epistulae.* Edited by José Madoz. *Epistolario de S. Braulio de Zaragoza.* Madrid, 1941. Translated by Claude Barlow. *Iberian Fathers,* vol. 2: *Braulio of Saragossa, Fructuosus of Braga.* The Fathers of the Church Series, vol. 63. Washington, 1969.

Chronicle of Fredegar. Edited and translated by J. M. Wallace-Hadrill. *The Fourth Book of the Chronicle of Fredegar.* London, 1960.

Chronique d'Alphonse III. Edited and translated by Yves Bonnaz. *Chroniques Asturiennes (fin IXe siècle).* Paris, 1987.

Codex Euricianus. Edited by Karl Zeumer. *MGH Leges* I.3–27. Hannover, 1902.

La colección canónica Hispana, vol. 4. Edited by Gonzalo Martínez Díez and Félix Rodríguez. *Monumenta Hispaniae Sacra,* Serie Canónica. Madrid, 1984.

Concilia Galliae A. 314–A. 506. Edited by Charles Munier. Turnhout, 1963.

Concilios hispano-romanos y visigodos. Edited and translated by José Vives. Barcelona, 1963.

Confessio vel professio judaeorum civitatis Toletanae. Edited by Felix Dahn. *Die Könige der Germanen,* B.6. Leipzig, 1885.

Constantius of Lyons. *Vita Germanii.* Edited and translated by René Borius. *Vie de Saint Germain d'Auxerre.* Sources Chrétiennes 112. Paris, 1965.

Epistola Pauli perfidi, Edited by Wilhelm Levison. Corpus Christianorum, Series Latina, 115:1. Turnhout, 1976.

Epistolae Wisigothicae. Edited by Juan Gil. *Miscellanea Wisigothica.* Seville, 1972.

Epitome Ovietense. Edited by Theodor Mommsen. *Auctores Antiquissimi* 11, *Chronica Minora,* vol. 2: *MGH.* Berlin, 1894.

Eusebius of Caesarea. *Historia Ecclesiastica.* Edited by E. Schwartz. Leipzig, 1903. Translated by Geoffrey A. Williamson. *The History of the Church from Christ to Constantine.* Baltimore, 1965.

Exemplar judicii inter Martianum et Aventium Episcopos. Edited by Felix Dahn. *Die Könige der Germanen,* B.6. Leipzig, 1885.

Felix of Toledo. *S. Juliani toletani episcopi vita seu elogium, PL* 95, cols. 445–52.

Gesta Senatus Urbis Romae. Translated by Clyde Pharr. *Theodosian Code and Novels.* New York, 1969.

Gregory I. *Dialogues.* Edited and translated by Adalbert de Vogüé. Sources Chrétiennes 251:2. Paris, 1978. Translated by Odo John Zimmerman. Fathers of the Church Series vol. 39. Washington, 1959.

———. *Epistolae.* Edited by Paulos Ewald and Ludo Hartmann. *Epistolarum* II, *MGH.* Berlin, 1894.

———. *Moralia in Iob.* Edited by Robert Gillet. Paris, 1952.

Gregory of Tours. *Liber in gloria confessorum.* Edited by Bruno Krusch. *Scriptores rerum merovingicarum* I, *MGH.* Hannover, 1885. Translated by Raymond Van Dam. *Gregory of Tours. Glory of the Confessors.* Liverpool, 1988.

———. *Libri Historiarum X.* Edited by Bruno Krusch and Wilhelm Levison. *Scriptores rerum merovingicarum* I, *MGH.* Hannover, 1951. Translated by Lewis Thorpe. *The History of the Franks.* Middlesex, 1974.

———. *Libri de virtutibus Martini.* Edited by Bruno Krusch. *Scriptores rerum merovingicarum* I, *MGH.* Hannover, 1885. Translated by Raymond Van Dam. *Saints and Their Miracles in Late Antique Gaul.* Princeton, 1993.

Ildefonsus of Toledo. *De viribus illustribus. PL* 96, cols. 195–204.

Isidore of Seville. *Chronicon. PL* 83, cols. 1017–58.

———. *De natura rerum.* Edited and translated by Jacques Fontaine. *Isidore de Séville. Traité de la nature suivi de l'épitre en vers du roi Sisebut à Isidore.* Bordeaux, 1960.

———. *De viris illustribus.* Edited by Carmen Codoñer Merino. *El de viris illustribus de Isidoro de Sevilla.* Salamanca, 1964.

———. *Etymologiarum sive originum libri XX.* Edited by William M. Lindsay. Oxford, 1911. Translated by Luis Cortés y Góngora. *Etimologías.* Madrid, 1951.

———. *Historia Gothorum, Wandalorum, Sueborum.* Edited and translated by Cristóbal Rodríguez Alonso. *Las historias de los Godos, Vandalos, y Suevos de Isidoro de Sevilla. Edición critica y traducción.* León, 1975. Translated by Kenneth Wolf. *Conquerors and Chroniclers of Early Medieval Spain.* Liverpool, 1990.

Iudicium in tyrannorum perfidia promulgatum. Edited by Wilhelm Levison. Corpus Christianorum, Series Latina, 115:1. Turnhout, 1976.

John of Biclar. *Chronica.* Edited by Theodor Mommsen. *Auctores Antiquissimi* 11, *Chronica Minora* II, *MGH.* Berlin, 1894. Translated by Kenneth Wolf. *Conquerors and Chroniclers of Early Medieval Spain.* Liverpool, 1990.

Julian of Toledo. *Historia Wambae Regis.* Edited by Wilhelm Levison. Corpus Christianorum, Series Latina, 115:1. Turnhout, 1976.

———. *Insultatio Vilis Storici in Tyrannidem Galliae.* Edited by Wilhelm Levison. Corpus Christianorum, Series Latine, 115:1. Turnhout, 1976.

Justinian. *Institutes.* Translated by Peter Birks and Grant McLeod. *Justinian's Institutes.* Ithaca, 1987.

Leander of Seville. *Homilia de triumpho Ecclesiae ob conversione Gothorum.* Edited and translated by Félix Rodríguez. "El Concilio III de Toledo." *Concilio III de Toledo. XIV Centenario, 589–1989.* Toledo, 1991.

Leges Visigothorum. Edited by Karl Zeumer. Legum Sectio 1, *Legum Nationum Germanicum* 1, *MGH.* Hannover, 1902.

Les canons des conciles Mérovingiens (VIe–VIIe siècles). 2 vols. Edited and translated by Jean Gaudemet and Brigitte Basdevant. Paris, 1989.

Lex Romana Visigothorum. Edited by Gustavus Haenel. Leipzig, 1889.

Liber Ordinum. Edited by Marius Férotin. *Le liber ordinum en usage dans l'Église wisigothique et mozarabe d'Espagne, Monumenta Ecclesiae Liturgica,* vol. 5. Paris, 1904.

Sidonius Apollinaris. *Epistulae*. Edited and translated by W. B. Anderson. *Sidonius, Poems and Letters*. Cambridge, 1965.

Sisebut. *Vita Desiderii*. Edited by Juan Gil. *Miscellanea Wisigothica*. Seville, 1972.

Third Council of Toledo, *acta*. Edited and translated by Félix Rodríguez. "El Concilio III de Toledo." *Concilio III de Toledo. XIV Centenario, 589–1989*. Toledo, 1991.

Vincent of Lérins. *Commonitoria*. Edited by Gerhard Rauschen. Bonn, 1906.

Vita S. Caesarii Arelatensis a discipulis scripta. Edited by Germain Morin. *S. Caesarii Arelatensis opera omnia*, 3. Maredsours, 1942.

Vitas patrum sanctorum emeritensium. Edited and translated by Joseph N. Garvin. Washington, D.C., 1946. Edited by Antonio Maya Sánchez. Corpus Christianorum, Series Latina, 116. Turnhout, 1992. Translated by A. F. Fear. *Lives of the Visigothic Fathers*, 45–105. Liverpool, 1997.

Secondary Sources

Adams, Jeremy duQuesnay. "Ideology and the Requirements of 'Citizenship' in Visigothic Spain: The Case of the *Judaei*." *Societas* 2 (1972): 317–32.

Albert, Bat-Sheva. "De fide catholica contra Judaeos d'Isidore de Séville: La polémique anti-Judaïque dan l'Espagne du VIIe siècle." *Revue des Études Juives* 142 (1982): 289–316.

Bachrach, Bernard. "A Reassessment of Visigothic Jewish Policy, 589–711." *American Historical Review* 78 (1973): 11–34.

Barbero, Abilio, and Marcelo Vigil. *La formación del feudalismo en la Península Ibérica*. Barcelona, 1978.

Basdevant-Gaudemet, Brigitte. "Les évêques, les papes et les princes dans la vie conciliare en France du IVe au XIIe siècle." *Revue Historique de Droit Français et Étranger* 69 (1991): 1–16.

Baynes, Norman H. "Eusebius and the Christian Empire." *Byzantine Studies and Other Essays*. London, 1955.

Beck, Henry G. J. *The Pastoral Care of Souls in South-East France during the Sixth Century*. Rome, 1950.

Blumenkranz, Bernhard. "Les auteurs chrétiens latins du moyen âge sur les juifs et la judaïsme." *Revue des Études Juives*, n.s. 2 (1951–52): 5–61.

———. *Juifs et Chrétiens dans le monde occidental*. Paris, 1960.

Brown, Peter. *The Cult of the Saints: Its Rise and Function in Latin Christianity*. Chicago, 1981.

———. *Power and Persuasion in Late Antiquity*. Madison, Wisc., 1992.

———. "Relics and Social Status in the Age of Gregory of Tours." *Society and the Holy in Late Antiquity*. Berkeley, 1982.

———. "Religious Dissent in the Later Roman Empire. The Case of North Africa." *Religion and Society in the Age of St. Augustine*. London, 1972.

———. *The Rise of Western Christendom: Triumph and Diversity, A.D. 200–1000*. Oxford, 1996.

———. "St. Augustine's Attitude to Religious Coercion." *Religion and Society in the Age of St. Augustine*. London, 1972.

———. "Society and the Supernatural: A Medieval Change." *Society and the Holy in Late Antiquity*. Berkeley, 1982.

Castán Lacoma, Laureano. "San Isidoro de Sevilla, apologista antijudaico." In *Isidoriana,* edited by Manuel C. Díaz y Díaz. León, 1963.

Cazier, Pierre. *Isidore de Séville et la naissance de l'Espagne catholique.* Paris, 1994.

Chadwick, Henry. *Priscillian of Avila: The Occult and the Charismatic in the Early Church.* Oxford, 1976.

Claude, Dietrich. "Der Bestellung der Bischöfe im merowingischen Reiche." *Zeitschrift der Savigny-Stiftung für Rechtsgeschichte, Kanonistiche Abteilung* 49 (1963): 1–75.

Cohen, Jeremy. *The Friars and the Jews.* Ithaca, 1982.

Collins, Roger. *The Arab Conquest of Spain.* Oxford, 1989.

———. "¿Donde estaban los arrianos en el año 589?" *Concilio III de Toledo. XIV Centenario, 589–1989.* Toledo, 1991.

———. *Early Medieval Spain: Unity in Diversity, 400–1000.* 2d ed. New York, 1995.

———. "Julian of Toledo and the Royal Succession in Late Seventh-Century Spain." In *Early Medieval Kingship,* edited by P. H. Sawyer and Ian N. Wood. Leeds, 1977.

———. "Mérida and Toledo." In *Visigothic Spain, New Approaches,* edited by Edward James. New York, 1980.

Cranz, F. E. "Kingdom and Polity in Eusebius of Caesarea." *Harvard Theological Review* 45, no.1 (1952): 47–66.

D'Abadal, Ramon. "Els concilis de Toledo." In *Dels Visigots als Catalans.* Barcelona, 1968.

Dahn, Felix. *Die Berfassung der Westgothen. Das Reich der Sueven in Spanien. Die Könige der Germanen. Das Wesen des ältesten Königthums der germanischen Stämme und seine Geschichte bis sur Auflösung des Karolingischen Reiches.* B. 6. Leipzig, 1885.

Díaz y Díaz, Manuel C. "Los discursos del rey Recaredo: El *Tomus.*" In *Concilio III de Toledo. XIV Centenario, 589–1989.* Toledo, 1991.

———. "La obra literaria de los obispos visigóticos toledanos: supuestos y circumstancias." *La Patrología Toledano-Visigoda* 27. Semana Española de Teología. Madrid, 1970.

d'Ors, Alvaro. "La territorialidad del derecho de los Visigodos." *Settimane* 3. Spoleto, 1955.

Ewig, Eugen. "Résidence et capitale pendant le haut moyen âge." *Revue Historique* (1963): 31–61.

———. "Zum Christlichen Königsgedanken im Frühmittelalter." *Spätantikes und Fränkisches Gallien. Gesammelte Schriften* 1. Munich, 1976.

Fernández Alonso, Justo. *La cura pastoral en la España romanovisigoda.* Rome, 1955.

Ferreiro, Alberto. "The Omission of St. Martin of Braga in John of Biclaro's *Chronica* and the Third Council of Toledo." *Los Visigodos, historia y civilización.* Antiqüedad y Christianismo, 3. Murcia, 1986.

———. *The Visigoths in Gaul and Spain, A.D. 418–711: A Bibliography.* Leiden, 1988.

Fichtenau, Heinrich. *Living in the Tenth Century: Mentalities and Social Orders,* translated by Patrick Geary. Chicago, 1991.

Fontaine, Jacques. "Conversion et culture chez les Wisigoths d'Espagne." *Settimane*

14. Reprinted in *Culture et spiritualité en Espagne du IVe au VIIe siècle*. London, 1986.

―――. "Fins et moyens de l'enseignement ecclésiastique dans l'Espagne Wisigothique." *Settimane*, 19. Reprinted in *Culture et spiritualité en Espagne du IVe au VIIe siècle*. London, 1986.

―――. "La homilía de San Leandro ante el Concilio III de Toledo: temática y forma." *Concilio III de Toledo. XIV Centenario, 589–1989*. Toledo, 1991.

―――. *Isidore de Séville et la culture classique dans l'Espagne wisigothique*. Paris, 1959.

―――. "King Sisebut's *Vita Desiderii* and the Political Function of Visigothic Hagiography." In *Visigothic Spain: New Approaches*, edited by Edward James. Oxford, 1980.

―――. "Mozarabie hispanique et monde carolingien; les échanges culturels entre la France et l'Espagne du VIIe au Xe siècle." *Anuario de Estudios Medievales* 13 (1983): 17–46.

Fransen, Gerard. *Les collections canoniques*. Turnhout, 1973.

Frend, W. H. C. *The Donatist Church*. Oxford, 1952.

Funkenstein, Amos. "Anti-Jewish Propaganda: Pagan, Christian, and Modern." *Jerusalem Quarterly* 19 (1981): 56–72.

Gallego Blanco, Enrique. "Canon LXXV of the Fourth Council of Toledo." *Classical Folia* 32 (1978): 135–40.

García Moreno, Luis A. "La coyuntura política del III Concilio de Toledo. Una historia larga y tortuosa." In *Concilio III de Toledo. XIV Centenario, 589–1989*. Toledo, 1991.

―――. *El fin del reino Visigodo de Toledo*. Madrid, 1975.

―――. *Historia de España Visigoda*. Madrid, 1989.

García Rodríguez, Carmen. *El Culto de los Santos en la España Romana y Visigoda*. Madrid, 1966.

Garvin, Joseph N. Introduction and Commentary. *Vitas patrum sanctorum emeritensium*: Washington, D.C., 1946.

Gaudemet, Jean. *La Bréviaire d'Alaric et les Epitome*. Ius romanum medii aevi I. Milan, 1965.

―――. *L'église dans l'Empire Romain IVe—Ve siècles*. Paris, 1989.

―――. "Regards sur l'histoire du droit canonique antérieurement au Décret de Gratien." *Studia et Documenta Historiae et Iuris* (Rome) 51 (1985): 73–130. Reprinted in *Droit de l'Église et vie sociale au Moyen Âge*. London, 1989.

―――. *Les sources du droit de l'Église en Occident du IIe au VIIe siècle*. Paris, 1985.

Geary, Patrick. *Before France and Germany: The Creation and Transformation of the Merovingian World*. Oxford, 1988.

Gibert, Rafael. "El reino Visigodo y el particularismo Español." *Settimane* 3. Spoleto, 1956.

Goffart, Walter. "Byzantine Policy in the West under Tiberius II and Maurice: The Pretenders Hermenegild and Gundovald (579–585)." *Traditio* 13 (1957): 73–118.

González Blanco, Antonino. "El Decreto de Gundemaro y la historia del siglo VII." *Los Visigodos. Historia y civilización*. Antigüedad y Christianismo 3. Murcia, 1986.

———. "La historia del S.E. peninsula entre los siglos III–VIII d.C. (Fuentes literarias, problemas y sugerencias)." *Del Conventus Cathaginiensis a la Chora de Tudmir. Perspectivas de la Historia de Murcia entre los siglos III–VIII.* Antigüedad y Christianismo 2. Murcia, 1985.

Guizot, François. *Histoire de la civilisation en France.* Brussels, 1835.

Guterman, Simeon. *The Principle of Personality of Law in the Germanic Kingdoms of Western Europe from the Fifth to the Eleventh Century.* New York, 1990.

Hefele, Charles J. *A History of the Councils of the Church.* 4 vols. 1895. Reprinted in New York, 1972.

Hernández, Ramon. "El problema de los judios en los PP. Visigodos." *Patrología Toledano-Visigoda* 27. Semana Española de Teología, 99–120. Madrid, 1970.

Herrin, Judith. *The Formation of Christendom.* Princeton, 1987.

Hillgarth, Jocelyn N. "Coins and Chronicles: Propaganda in Sixth-Century Spain and the Byzantine Background." *Historia* 15 (1966): 483–508. Reprinted in *Visigothic Spain, Byzantium and the Irish.* London, 1985.

———. "El Concilio III de Toledo y Bizancio." *Concilio III de Toledo. XIV Centenario, 589–1989.* Toledo, 1991.

———. "Historiography in Visigothic Spain." *Settimane* 17. Spoleto, 1970. Reprinted in *Visigothic Spain, Byzantium and the Irish.* London, 1985.

———. "Isidorian Studies, 1976–85." *Studi Medievali,* ser. 3, 31, no. 2. Spoleto, 1990.

———. "The Position of Isidorian Studies: A Critical Review of the Literature, 1936–1975." *Studi Medievali,* ser. 3, 24. Spoleto, 1983. Reprinted in *Visigothic Spain, Byzantium and the Irish.* London, 1985.

———. "St. Julian of Toledo in the Middle Ages." *Journal of the Warburg and Courtauld Institutes* 21 (1958): 7–26.

James, Edward. "*Beati Pacifici*: Bishops and the Law in Sixth-Century Gaul." In *Disputes and Settlements: Law and Human Relations in the West,* edited by John Bossy. Cambridge, 1983.

Jones, A. H. M. *The Later Roman Empire, 284–602.* 2 vols. Oxford, 1964.

Katz, Solomon. *The Jews in the Visigothic and Frankish Kingdoms of Spain and Gaul.* Cambridge, 1937.

King, P. D. "King Chindasvind and the First Territorial Law-code of the Visigothic Kingdom." In *Visigothic Spain: New Approaches,* edited by Edward James. Oxford, 1980.

———. *Law and Society in the Visigothic Kingdom.* Cambridge, 1972.

Lacarra, José María. "La Iglesia visigoda en el siglo VII y sus relaciones con Roma." *Settimane* 7, no. 1. Spoleto, 1959.

———. "Panarama de la historia urbana en la Península Ibérica desde el siglo V al X." *Settimane* 6. Spoleto, 1959.

Lamirande, Emilien. *Church, State, and Toleration: An Intriguing Change of Mind in Augustine.* Villanova, 1975.

Levy, Ernst. "Reflections on the First 'Reception' of Roman Law in the Germanic State." *American Historical Review* 48 (1942): 20–29.

———. "Vulgarization of Roman Law in the Early Middle Ages." *Medievalia et Humanistica* 1 (1943): 14–40.

———. *West Roman Vulgar Law: The Law of Property.* Philadelphia, 1951.

Lynch, Charles H. *Saint Braulio, Bishop of Saragossa (631–51): His Life and Writings.* Washington, D.C., 1938.

MacCormack, Sabine. *Art and Ceremony in Late Antiquity.* Berkeley, 1981.

———. "Loca Sancta: The Organization of Sacred Topography in Late Antiquity." In *The Blessings of Pilgrimage,* edited by Robert Ousterhout. Urbana, 1990.

Madoz, José. "San Julián de Toledo." *Estudios Eclesiásticos* 26 (1952): 39–69.

Markus, Robert A. *The End of Ancient Christianity.* Cambridge, 1990.

———. "Gregory the Great and a Papal Missionary Strategy." *The Mission of the Church and the Propagation of the Faith.* Edited by G. J. Cuming, Studies in Church History 6. Cambridge, 1970. Reprinted in *From Augustine to Gregory the Great History and Christianity in Late Antiquity.* London, 1983.

Martínez Díez, Gonzalo. *La colección canónica Hispana,* vol. 1: *Estudio. Monumenta Hispania Sacra,* Serie Canónica. Madrid, 1966.

———. "Los concilios de Toledo." *Anales Toledanos* 3. Toledo, 1971.

———. "Concilios españoles anteriores a Trento." *Repertorio de historia de las ciencias eclesiásticas en España* 5. Salamanca, 1976.

———. "Nota sobre la colección 'Hispana.'" In *Concilios hispano-romanos y visigodos,* edited by José Vives. Barcelona, 1963.

McCormick, Michael. *Eternal Victory: Triumphal Rulership in Late Antiquity, Byzantium and the Early Medieval West.* Cambridge, 1986.

Momigliano, Arnaldo. "The Disadvantages of Monotheism for a Universal State." *On Pagans, Jews, and Christians.* Scranton, Pa., 1987.

———. "The Origins of Ecclesiatical Historiography." *The Classical Foundations of Modern Historiography.* Berkeley, 1990.

Moore, Robert I. *Formation of a Persecuting Society.* Oxford, 1987.

Morrison, Karl. *Tradition and Authority in the Western Church.* Princeton, 1969.

Munier, Charles. "Nouvelles recherches sur l'*Hispana* chronologique." *Revue des Sciences Religieuses* 40 (1966): 400–410.

———. "L'*ordo de celebrando concilio* wisigothique." *Revue des Sciences Religieuses* 37 (1963): 250–71.

Murphy, Frances X. "Julian of Toledo and the Condemnation of Monothelitism in Spain." *Mélanges de Joseph de Ghellinck,* vol. 1: *Antiquité.* Gembloux, Belg., 1951.

———. "Julian of Toledo and the Fall of the Visigothic Kingdom in Spain." *Speculum* 27 (1952): 1–27.

Nelson, Janet. "Inauguration Rituals." In *Early Medieval Kingship,* edited by P. H. Sawyer and Ian N. Wood. Leeds, 1977.

Orlandis, José. *Historia del reino visigodo.* Madrid, 1988.

———. *La Iglesia en la España visigótica y medieval.* Pamplona, 1976.

———. *El poder real y la sucesión al trono en la monarquía visigoda.* Madrid, 1962.

———. "Zaragoza, cuidad conciliar." *Hispania y Zaragoza en la antigüedad tardia. Estudios varios.* Saragossa, 1984.

Orlandis, José, and Domingo Ramos-Lissón. *Historia de los concilios de la España romana y visigoda.* Pamplona, 1986.

Parkes, James W. *The Conflict of the Church and the Synagogue: A Study in the Origins of Antisemitism.* London, 1934.

Pontal, Odette. *Clercs et laïcs au Moyen Âge d'après les statuts synodaux.* Paris, 1990.

———. *Die Synoden im Merowingerreich Konziliengeschichte.* Paderborn, 1986. French version, *Histoire des conciles mérovingiens.* Paris, 1989.

Remensnyder, Amy G. "Pollution, Purity, and Peace: An Aspect of Social Reform between the Late Tenth Century and 1076." In *The Peace of God: Social Violence and Religious Response in France around the Year 1000*, edited by Thomas Head and Richard Landes. Ithaca, 1992.

Reydellet, Marc. *La royauté dans la littérature latine, de Sidoine Apollinaire à Isidore de Séville*. Rome, 1981.

———. "La conception du souverain chez Isidore de Séville." In *Isidoriana*, edited by Manuel C. Díaz y Díaz. León, 1961.

Reynolds, Roger. "Rites and Signs of Conciliar Decisions in the Early Middle Ages." *Settimane*. 33, no. 1. Spoleto, 1987.

Rivera Recio, Juan Francisco. "Encumbramiento de la sede toledana durante la dominación visigótica." *Hispania Sacra* 8 (1956): 3–34.

Schwöbel, Heide. *Synode und König im Westgotenreich. Grundlagen und Formen ihrer Beziehung*. Cologne, 1982.

Séjourné, Paul. *Le dernier père de l'Église. Saint Isidore de Séville*. Paris, 1936.

Shils, Edward. *Center and Periphery: Essays in Macrosociology*. Chicago, 1975.

Stach, Walter. "König Sisebut ein Mäzen des isidorischen Zeitalters." *Die Antike 19*, no. 1 (1943): 63–76.

Stocking, Rachel L. "Martianus, Aventius, and Isidore: Provincial Councils in Seventh-Century Spain." *Early Medieval Europe* 6, no. 2 (1997): 169–88.

Thompson, E. A. "The Conversion of the Spanish Suevi to Catholicism." In *Visigothic Spain, New Approaches*, edited by Edward James. Oxford, 1980.

———. *The Goths in Spain*. Oxford, 1969.

———. *Romans and Barbarians: The Decline of the Western Empire*. Madison, Wisc., 1982.

Van Dam, Raymond. *Leadership and Community in Late Antique Gaul*. Berkeley, 1986.

———. *Saints and Their Miracles in Late Antique Gaul*. Princeton, 1993.

Van der Lof, L. J. "Der Mäzen König Sisebutus und sein 'De eclipsi lunae.'" *Revue des Études Augustiniennes*. 18, nos. 1–2 (1972): 148–81.

Wallace-Hadrill, J. M. "The Bloodfeud of the Franks." *The Long-Haired Kings and Other Studies in Frankish History*. Toronto, 1962.

———. *The Frankish Church*. Oxford, 1983.

Wickham, Chris. "Land Disputes and Their Social Framework in Lombard-Carolingian Italy, 700–900." In *The Settlement of Disputes in Early Medieval Europe*, edited by Wendy Davies and Paul Fouracre. Cambridge, 1986.

Wickham, Chris., et al. Conclusion to *The Settlement of Disputes in Early Medieval Europe*, edited by Wendy Davies and Paul Fouracre. Cambridge, 1986.

Williams, A. Lukyn. *Adversos Judaeos: A Bird's Eye View of Christian Apologiae until the Renaissance*. New York, 1935.

Wolf, Kenneth. *Conquerors and Chroniclers of Early Medieval Spain*. Liverpool, 1990.

Wolfram, Herwig. *History of the Goths*. Berkeley, 1988.

Wood, Ian N. "Disputes in Late Fifth- and Sixth-Century Gaul: Some Problems." In *The Settlement of Disputes in Early Medieval Europe*, edited by Wendy Davies and Paul Fouracre. Cambridge, 1986.

———. "The Ecclesiastical Politics of Merovingian Clermont." In *Ideal and Reality in Frankish and Anglo-Saxon Society: Studies Presented to J. M. Wallace-Hadrill*, edited by Patrick Wormald, Donald Bullough, and Roger Collins. Oxford, 1983.

————. "Forgery in Merovingian Hagiography." In *Fälschungen im Mittelalter,* vol. 5: *Fingierte Briefe Frömmigkeit und Fälschung Realienfälschungen.* MGH, Schriften 33. Hannover, 1988.

Wormald, Patrick. "*Lex Scripta* and *Verbum Regis:* Legislation and Germanic Kingship, from Euric to Cnut." In *Early Medieval Kingship,* edited by P. H. Sawyer and Ian N. Wood. Leeds, 1977.

Ziegler, Aloysius K. *Church and State in Visigothic Spain.* Washington, D.C., 1930.

Index

Index to Conciliar *Acta*